THE
ROAD
TO WAR

THE
ROAD
TO WAR

PRESIDENTIAL COMMITMENTS
HONORED AND BETRAYED

MARVIN KALB

BROOKINGS INSTITUTION PRESS
Washington, D.C.

Copyright © 2013
THE BROOKINGS INSTITUTION
1775 Massachusetts Avenue, N.W., Washington, D.C. 20036
www.brookings.edu

Library of Congress Cataloging-in-Publication data is available
ISBN: 978-0-8157-2493-3 (hardcover : alk. paper)
9 8 7 6 5 4 3 2 1

Printed on acid-free paper

Typeset in Minion

Composition by Cynthia Stock
Silver Spring, Maryland

Printed by R. R. Donnelley
Harrisonburg, Virginia

To Estelle Levine,
my little sister,
who in her advancing years
has set an example for us all
of courage, dignity, and class

CONTENTS

ACKNOWLEDGMENTS

THIS BOOK IS one product of my time at the Brookings Institution. It would be foolhardy to list all of my colleagues there who have been so generous with their time, support, and encouragement. They know who I mean. I must, though, name Vassilis Coutifaris, whose technological wizardry always dazzled me, and Melissa Wear, whose grace and intelligence eased my problems with interview transcriptions. I thank them both.

I want also to thank Strobe Talbott and Martin Indyk, who opened the door for me at Brookings and made my time there such a rich and rewarding experience. Brookings is truly an extraordinary place.

At the Brookings Institution Press, a class publisher, I am indebted to Robert Faherty, Chris Kelaher, Melissa McConnell, and Janet Walker for their professional support, and John Felton, who did a superb job of editing.

I am grateful as well to the Washington Institute for Near East Policy, run by Robert Satloff, for its help, especially on U.S.-Israeli relations, and I want also to express my deep gratitude to Michael Freedman, Heather Date, and Lindsay Underwood, my colleagues on the Kalb Report, a program I have done at the National Press Club for the past nineteen years. They were always there at the right time to say the right things.

Finally, no project of mine can ever succeed without the warmth, love, and encouragement of my family: my wife, Mady, who, for the past fifty-five years, has always been at my side, supporting the whole family with goodness, generosity, intelligence, and the sort of love that never dims; my daughters, Deborah and Judith, mothers of my precious grandchildren, Aaron and Eloise, the lights of my life—thanks to all of them for their good cheer, love, and constant support; my sons-in-law, David and Alex, whom I love and admire, both always there when I need help of any kind; David's son, Jeremy, my step-grandson and buddy, who shares with me a love of sports; my brother, Bernard, and his wife, Phyllis, whose passion for Vietnam is contagious; and finally my sister, Estelle, to whom this book is dedicated.

THE
ROAD
TO WAR

INTRODUCTION

OVER THE YEARS, presidential commitments have come in different shapes and sizes, suggesting honor and integrity, strength and determination, the word of a president backed by the military power of the United States. No trifling matter, in diplomatic affairs. And yet . . .

Some commitments, such as America's to the North Atlantic Treaty Organization, have been successful and durable, in part because they have been based on solemn treaties ratified by Congress. Another example is America's commitment to South Korea, also based on a mutual defense treaty, supported by the presence of 28,500 American troops armed with nuclear weapons until December 1991.

South Vietnam represented a very different challenge. It was war by presidential commitment, the United States sliding mindlessly, one administration after another, into a guerrilla war in Indochina, which cost more than 58,000 American lives. Few in Congress or the media questioned the war's provenance or legitimacy, until it was too late.

Finally, in this book, which focuses on American commitments to South Korea, South Vietnam, and Israel, the one to Israel is perhaps the most fascinating. Here we have an unusually close relationship, culturally, religiously, politically in alignment, more or less, yet one without any basis in a formal treaty linking the interests of one nation to the other. It is based primarily on private presidential letters to Israeli prime ministers, rich with American promises and pledges to Israeli security. Over the years many of the promises have been honored, but some were betrayed, leaving feelings of anxiety among Israeli leaders about the ultimate reliability of an American commitment.

No doubt, presidential commitments are seen as serious, almost sacred, promises to act made by a chief executive on behalf of his administration. And other nations may view these commitments as binding nation-to-nation promises that succeeding administrations will honor, too. But there is a problem. Will they?

In 1982, for example, President Ronald Reagan pledged America's "iron-clad commitment to the defense of Israel." The commitment made sense to Reagan at the time, and it has been echoed by one president after another ever since. But does Reagan's pledge have the same resonance now that it did then? Does it mean that if Israel feels it must bomb Iran to stop its nuclear program that America must join in the attack? Much has to do with trust between leaders and countries. Do Israeli leaders trust President Barack Obama as much as they did Bill Clinton and George W. Bush? These are questions that cut to the heart—and viability—of a presidential commitment.

Since World War II, presidents have relied more on commitments, public and private, than they have on declarations of war, even though the U.S. Constitution declares rather unambiguously that Congress has the responsibility to "declare war." Interestingly, only five times in American history has a president asked Congress for a declaration of war: the War of 1812, the Mexican-American War of 1846, the Spanish-American War of 1898, World War I in 1917, and World War II in 1941. During and since the cold war, no president has asked Congress for a declaration of war, although presidents have gotten different degrees of congressional support for wars, both through formal resolutions and through the appropriations process. War declarations now seem so old-fashioned, relics of an earlier era in world affairs, when, by the gentlemanly etiquette of the time, nations felt obliged to inform an enemy of an impending attack, when opposing armies stood on hilltops awaiting dawn's early light for the start of battle. Think no further than Shakespeare's classic rendition of the battle at Agincourt.

Now wars follow a new calculus—they operate in a new technological and strategic environment, forcing presidents to confront not only the possibility of surprise attack but modern challenges, such as cyber warfare. During the cold war, presidents explained their motivation by pointing to communist aggression; now, after 9/11, they point to the dangers of global terrorism in Iraq, Afghanistan, Somalia, and Yemen, and always, with genuine concern, they point to an expanding nuclear threat, which may in a short time be used to justify American military action against Iran if negotiations fail to reach agreement. Even though, since World War II, presidents have ordered American troops into wars all over the world—from Korea to Vietnam, Panama to Grenada, Lebanon to Bosnia, and, more recently, as America's focus has turned to the turbulent Middle East, from Kuwait to Afghanistan, then to Iraq, and then back again to Afghanistan before treading lightly in Libya and Syria—they have not requested a declaration of war, and no one has been storming the White House demanding one.

Only once, in 1973, has Congress acted broadly to reassert its right to a major role in an American decision to go to war. That was when Congress, frustrated by the never-ending war in Vietnam, passed the War Powers Act over President Nixon's strenuous objection. It limited American military action abroad to sixty or ninety days unless specifically extended and approved by Congress. But the legislation had little bite, in large part because Congress never wanted, or never had the political will, to challenge the president on matters of national security. When President Obama in 2011 used military power against the Qaddafi regime in Libya, he did not even notify Congress. A few in Congress mumbled, but did nothing.

The Korean War and the Vietnam War were the bastard children of the cold war, which provided the dramatic backdrop for most confrontations between the United States and the Soviet Union. President Harry Truman was understandably concerned about Soviet dictator Josef Stalin's expanding empire. Truman believed in the domino theory—that the fall of one country to communism would lead almost automatically to the fall of others in the same region.

When the North Koreans, with Stalin's blessing, attacked South Korea in June 1950, Truman felt he had no option but to send American troops to stop them. He did not check with Congress, which later proved to be a serious political problem. He got his authority, he claimed, from the United Nations. In this way, Truman attracted more international support, diplomatic and military. He called the war a "police action" and thought it would end quickly. It lasted for three years, cost more than 54,000 American lives, and finally whimpered to an embarrassing stalemate (reporters called it "die for a tie"), largely because Truman feared the escalation then being pushed by his commanding general, Douglas MacArthur, might lead to a nuclear war with Russia or China or both. An armistice agreement between the two sides was finally negotiated in 1953, leaving Korea, like Germany, a country split in two.

In the embers of this war, Truman and his immediate successor, Dwight D. Eisenhower, figuring that half a loaf or country was better than none, negotiated a mutual defense treaty with South Korea, pledging the United States to rush to South Korea's defense if it were again attacked. As the best bona fides of America's commitment, the United States left tens of thousands of American troops in South Korea, numbering as many as 60,000 at one point, as a kind of trip-wire defense against another possible communist assault. Years later, nuclear weapons were added to the trip-wire defense, and North and South Korea went their separate ways. The North, allied with Russia and China, became an economic basket case, though armed ironically with nuclear weapons and long-range missiles. The South, protected by the United States, became an economic powerhouse—the eighth most productive trading nation on earth.

Over the years, the United States has tried to midwife a live-and-let-live arrangement between the two Koreas but has met with only limited success. Disappointment has almost always followed the effort. Now there is new leadership in both Koreas, modest blips of hope, too—Park Geun-hye in the south, a tough-minded conservative, whose foreign policy has been officially labeled "Trust-Politik," suggesting she is ready to deal with the North under certain conditions; and Kim Jong-un in the north, a young, comparatively dynamic and dedicated communist, who claims he wants to reunify Korea through negotiations. "An important issue in putting an end to the division of the country and achieving its reunification is to remove confrontation between the north and the south," he said shortly after taking power in 2011. "The past records of inter-Korean relations show that confrontation between fellow countrymen leads to nothing but war."[1] Kim's rhetoric has, on occasion, been promising; his actions much less so. He continues to produce long-range rockets, to test nuclear warheads, and, most recently, to threaten the United States with a nuclear attack and to abandon the 1953 armistice agreement.

For the foreseeable future, the U.S. commitment to South Korea remains strong. American diplomats see little prospect of change. They stress, in convincing fashion, that if South Korea were attacked, it would be defended by the United States. But, as always, there are questions. If, for compelling economic reasons, the United States had to pull its troops out of South Korea, would the alliance survive? As strong as it was? And what then would America do to protect its interests in north Asia? Can the United States trust China to play a helpful role in North-South reconciliation talks? What if South Korea chooses to go its own way?

THE OTHER BASTARD child of the cold war was the long, costly struggle in South Vietnam. From Truman to Nixon, one president after another pledged the United States to a course of action that led to a disastrous war and a humiliating defeat. There was no surprise attack on the United States, such as Pearl Harbor, no terrorist strike, such as 9/11, to justify their decisions. The presidents feared the spread of communism—to them, an unacceptable prospect, especially during the cold war.

The American descent into Vietnam started in the late 1940s, when the French were trying to re-impose their colonial rule over Indochina. Truman strongly opposed European colonialism in Asia, but he opposed even more strongly the spread of Soviet totalitarianism in Europe. He struck a hardheaded bargain with his conscience: to secure France's help in Europe, he started to help France in Indochina—at the beginning, with limited military support. With each shipment of aid, though, he and Eisenhower deepened the American involvement in Indochina, until finally, in 1955, the French withdrew, having been defeated at Dien Bien Phu, and the Americans were left to pick up their tattered banner.

In the mid-1950s, the United States justified its Vietnam policy by citing the anti-communist rhetoric of the Southeast Asia Treaty Organization, which tended to satisfy Congress. But in the 1960s, when the United States committed combat troops to the war, Lyndon Johnson felt he needed direct congressional support. With little effort, he persuaded Congress in August 1964 to pass the Gulf of Tonkin resolution, which gave him unlimited authority to fight the communist insurgency in Indochina.

By then, the war had become America's war. More than any other president, Eisenhower, who should have known better, made the key decisions that tied the uncertain future of South Vietnam to the national interests of the United States. In 1954, after the Geneva Convention, he supported the division of Vietnam into two parts: the north controlled by the communists, and the south by a rickety, unpopular monarch. In 1959, in a speech often ignored by scholars, Eisenhower took the next crucial step: He officially linked the national security interests of the United States to the continued existence of an independent, non-communist South Vietnam. The upshot was that when South Vietnam said it needed help, the United States provided it—military aid, money, trainers, and ultimately hundreds of thousands of American troops. Did anyone criticize, or challenge, Eisenhower's judgment on the reputedly central importance of South Vietnam to the United States? No one, as it turned out. Was there any debate in Congress or in the media? No. The questionable policy of linking South Vietnam's future to America's national interest was adopted in unanimous silence.

John F. Kennedy, against his better instincts, sent thousands of military advisers to South Vietnam and, several weeks before his own assassination in 1963, approved an ugly coup against its authoritarian president, Ngo Dinh Diem. Kennedy worried about Diem's ability to hold off the communists.

Johnson, not wanting to be the first president to lose a war, sent hundreds of thousands of *combat* troops, explaining that his decision was the latest in a succession of presidential "commitments" to defend South Vietnam against communist aggression. He based his decisions, he explained, on Eisenhower's commitments. By January 1968 Johnson had sent 548,000 troops to South Vietnam. By war's end in 1975, more than 58,000 of them were killed. And for what? Within twenty years, the United States and a united Vietnam were courting each other in a new defensive alliance against China.

Even when Nixon, changing strategy, began to withdraw American troops from Vietnam, he explained his policy by citing America's commitment to South Vietnam, a commitment that finally expired with the communist conquest in late April 1975. For Nixon, the commitment represented a sacred American promise; to South Vietnam's president, Nguyen Van Thieu, it represented a shameful betrayal.

AS AN EXAMPLE of presidential commitment, Israel's is different from the twin examples of South Korea and South Vietnam. Israel was born in the ashes of the Holocaust, but it has, almost miraculously, flourished as an economic and military powerhouse in a turbulent Middle East. Time and again, Israel has fought for its very survival, and won, increasingly with American diplomatic, economic, and military support. But although the bilateral relationship has been remarkably close, it has never been based on a treaty. It has been based on the word of the president-in-power, conveyed in letters to Israeli prime ministers.

Words have consequence. Spoken by a president, they can often become American policy, with or without congressional approval. When a president "commits" the United States to a controversial course of action, he may be setting the nation on the road to war or on a road to reconciliation. In matters of national security, his powers have become awesome—his word decisive. Who decides when we go to war? The president decides. As former national security adviser Zbigniew Brzezinski told me, it "all depends" on the president. "It's his call." Likewise, it is his decision when and whether, and under what conditions, to support a friendly nation.

A president, such as Barack Obama, for example, pledges that the United States has "an ironclad commitment" to Israel's security—meaning, one would imagine, that if Israel were attacked, the United States would come to Israel's defense. Is there anything more to this commitment than a presidential promise? Obviously, yes. Israel enjoys broad-based support from Congress and the American people. For the most part, both nations share common values and common aims. But the president is the key to determining the flow and texture of this delicate relationship.

A question often asked by political leaders in Israel is whether Obama will live up to his word. Will his commitment be honored or betrayed by him or by a successor? The answer to this question can mean war or peace. Might it not be better for both nations to negotiate a formal defense treaty—and, in this way, try to reduce or even eliminate areas of doubt in their relationship? Those who question the value or relevance of a U.S.-Israeli defense treaty point out that in recent years Obama has tried to organize Israeli-Palestinian peace talks only to fail abysmally because of Palestinian objections to Israeli settlements and Israeli insistence on building such settlements in the name of security. How would a treaty resolve these problems, they ask? Indeed, even the effort to negotiate a defense treaty would likely kick up fresh tumult and anxiety among Arab states, which are apt to see a U.S. treaty with Israel as proof that the United States can no longer be counted on as an impartial negotiator.

Another question: Obama has warned, more than once: "Let there be no doubt—America is determined to prevent Iran from getting nuclear weapons." Though the world has heard this warning, there are still many, especially in the Middle East, who question whether Obama would really use American military power to stop Iran from "getting nuclear weapons," however that phrase might be defined. It is said in Washington and Jerusalem that never before have Israel and the United States been in closer alignment on stopping Iran from developing a nuclear weapon. True, and yet not quite true. In the final analysis, for reasons both political and military, Israel may, on its own, strike Iran. Would it then expect American diplomatic and military support? Obama has strongly implied yes. But, without a mutual defense treaty, there may always be a question about the durability and reliability of a presidential commitment.

As we learned in Vietnam and in the broader Middle East, a presidential commitment could lead to war, based on miscalculation, misjudgment, or mistrust. It could also lead to reconciliation. We live in a world of uncertainty, where even the word of a president is now questioned in wider circles of critical commentary. On domestic policy, Washington often resembles a political circus detached from reason and responsibility. But on foreign policy, when an international crisis erupts and some degree of global leadership is required, the word or commitment of an American president still represents the gold standard, even if the gold does not glitter as once it did.

CHAPTER ONE

TRUMAN'S WAR IN KOREA

"An Iron Curtain has descended over the continent."
—WINSTON CHURCHILL

IT WAS A very unusual war. It started in Europe but soon enveloped the world.

As the United States demobilized and dramatically swung from a war-time to a peace-time economy after World War II, the Soviet Union tightened its military and ideological grip over Eastern Europe, gobbling up first Albania, then Yugoslavia, and then, in short order, from 1945 to 1947, Poland, Romania, Bulgaria, Hungary, and East Germany. In February 1948, the communists seized power in Czechoslovakia, throwing the few optimists left in Washington into a strategic depression. Moscow also pushed for communist takeovers in China, Vietnam, France, and Italy. The one in Vietnam led to a major war in Southeast Asia that would cost more than 58,000 American lives.

Walter Lippmann, then the preeminent Washington columnist, defined the emerging crisis in 1947 in a short book that helped name an era; it was entitled *Cold War*. The United States and the USSR, he wrote, were already engaged in tough, dangerous competition, using proxies, jockeying for advantage, building up their military power—but stopping short of actually going to war. He envisaged a cold war, not a hot one. Striking a similar theme, George Kennan, an old Moscow hand and diplomat, published an article in *Foreign Affairs*, called "The Sources of Soviet Conduct," in which he recommended the "containment" of Soviet expansionism, while later explaining that he did not mean by using military power.

Lippmann and Kennan were actually echoing the somber judgment of Winston Churchill. It was not peace that stood before the world, Churchill prophesied, but the prospect of another war. So soon after the end of a world war, Churchill was already speaking of another one. On March 5, 1946, at

Westminster College in Fulton, Missouri, Britain's legendary wartime prime minister scanned the map of Europe and concluded reluctantly that an "Iron Curtain has descended over the continent," creating a "Soviet sphere" of expanding influence and power.[1] The American president, Harry Truman, who shared the platform with the British leader, also shared his gloomy judgment of world affairs. He saw a world split in two: half free; the other half "bent on the subjugation of others." It was the beginning of the cold war.

When Truman left office in January 1953, he reflected on his presidential tenure: "I have hardly had a day in office that has not been dominated by this all-embracing struggle."

The Man from Missouri

Harry Truman was a humble, machine-made politician from Missouri, who happened to be in the right place at the right time. In 1944, Truman was a Democratic senator, known for his struggle against wartime corruption, and his president, Franklin D. Roosevelt, was facing a slow death and a fast re-election campaign for an unprecedented fourth term in office. The leaders of the Democratic Party were certain Roosevelt would win—the world was still at war—but they wanted to drop Vice President Henry Wallace from the ticket, believing he was too liberal to be president when Roosevelt died, which they expected within months.

Who would replace Wallace? Truman was not a party favorite, but he did have a reputation for probity and integrity; and when a few of the more likely candidates dropped out of the running, Truman got the party's nod. On January 20, 1945, the man from Missouri was sworn in as vice president, and, a few hurried months later, on April 12, 1945, after Roosevelt's death, as president, the only one to serve in that office since 1896 without a college degree.

When he took the oath of office, Truman did not know that he would shortly have to make a number of presidential commitments and decisions that would transform the post-war world. In one of his most consequential decisions, he approved the dropping of atomic bombs on Hiroshima and Nagasaki, effectively ending World War II but at the same time ushering in a new age of atomic power and threat. His reasoning was that he wanted to save the many thousands of American lives that were almost certain to be lost in an invasion of the Japanese homeland. Within a year or two, other challenges crowded his desk.

In early 1947, Soviet leader Josef Stalin moved (or faked a move) toward Azerbaijan, which Truman interpreted as a Soviet effort to control the supply of oil from the Middle East. Truman, influenced by Churchill, decided to act. In March, he announced a military and economic aid package for Greece and Turkey valued at $400 million. It was the birth of a new anti-communist policy, quickly dubbed "The Truman Doctrine." The president said it was to "support free peoples who are resisting attempted subjugation by armed minorities or by outside pressures," meaning communist insurgents and aggressive Soviet maneuvering.[2] And in June, at Harvard, Secretary of State George C. Marshall announced an extraordinary four-year, $13-billion aid package to reconstruct the West European economy. It was called "The Marshall Plan." "Our policy is not directed against any country," the secretary stated, even disingenuously offering the Soviet Union an opportunity to receive some of the aid but with conditions everyone knew in advance Moscow would find unacceptable.[3]

With the Truman Doctrine and the Marshall Plan, the United States, by presidential proclamation and commitment, embarked on a new cold war policy that led to a series of major confrontations between the United States and the Soviet Union. The pattern on policymaking was set early: The president made the big decisions, Congress in effect acquiesced by providing the money. On matters of national security, even when there was an occasional disagreement between the two branches of government, the president's views prevailed.

These early decisions by Truman were examples of the unfolding postwar power of presidential rhetoric, using the bully pulpit of the White House, not only to create policy but to lead the nation toward controversial goals, even toward war—and to do so without serious congressional consultation, without a declaration of war, and sometimes even without a congressional resolution. Not everyone approved of this mushrooming executive power, but, in a period of hair-trigger anxiety, there was no one in the U.S. government whose authority could match the president's. He was the only nationally elected leader. When it came to issues of war and peace, especially during the cold war, he was supreme—at least then.

The world was changing, and not for the better. On June 24, 1948, the Soviet Union blocked rail, water, and highway access into the three western sectors of Berlin, which was located in Soviet-controlled East Germany. The West had a choice: It could reclaim access by smashing its way into Berlin, which might have triggered a new war; it could accept communist domination; or it could begin the unprecedented job of airlifting vital supplies into the western sectors of Berlin. Truman, determined not to be pushed around, told Marshall, "We stay in Berlin." Almost immediately, the United States launched the "Berlin Airlift," a truly historic undertaking, which lasted until May 11, 1949. During these eleven months, in a highly dangerous operation through air corridors that the Russians could have blocked at any time but chose not to, Truman ordered 278,228 flights to be flown into Berlin with cargoes consisting of 2,326,406 tons of food and supplies and 1,500,000 tons of coal during the winter months. It was an eye-opening show of American power, generosity, and Trumanesque leadership, and it saved Berlin.

But clearly the relationship between East and West was in stunning freefall, each side trying to outmaneuver the other. First was the creation on April 4, 1949, of the North Atlantic Treaty Organization, in which all twelve founding nations, including the United States, concerned about the obvious spread of Soviet power, pledged their military's fidelity to the principle that an attack on one would be considered an attack on all (how different from the U.S. rejection in 1919 of the League of Nations on essentially the same issue!). Then, on August 29, 1949, the Soviet Union announced that it had successfully test fired its first atomic bomb, nicknamed "Joe One," patterned almost exactly after the "Fat Man" bomb that the United States had dropped on Hiroshima (proof if any were needed that Soviet spies had filched America's atomic secrets). Finally, on October 1, 1949, the Chinese communists under Mao Zedong defeated the Chinese Nationalists under Chiang Kai-shek and seized control of the entire mainland, establishing the People's Republic of China and vastly expanding the communist threat not only to Asia but to the rest of the world.

In Washington, on both sides of the political aisle, the startling vision of an expansionist, nuclear-armed Russia in ideological union with a revolutionary China, the most populous nation on Earth, sent an existential shiver down the collective spine of the U.S. government. Truman feared a new war, and the "China Lobby" (led by congressional Republicans and the conservative elements of the news media), sharing his fear but sensing a golden political opportunity, opened a ferocious attack against Truman for the "loss of China," as if it was his to "lose," for abandoning such a friend and ally as Chiang Kai-shek, for being "soft on communism," and for allowing his State Department to be "permeated with Reds and leftists." Rarely did a day go by without vicious criticism of what the China Lobby saw as Truman's collapse before the advancing ideological goliath of Chinese communism. Overnight, several GOP members of Congress, ordinary politicians pursuing ordinary careers, became headline figures—Robert Hale from Maine and Walter Judd from Minnesota, bemoaning Chiang Kai-shek's humiliating retreat to Taiwan, and Senators Bourke B. Hickenlooper of Iowa and Joseph R. McCarthy of Wisconsin, accusing the president of "taking us down the road in shaping policies favorable to the Communist party." They looked for sympathetic reporters to spread their worry about the "domino theory"—that if China could fall to the communists, then Japan, Korea, Vietnam, and all of Southeast Asia could also fall to the communists. And when, on June 24, 1950, North Korea invaded South Korea, the China Lobby felt fully vindicated in directing its fire and anger at Truman for losing China and leaving the United States on the abyss of losing Asia.

The Making of the American Commitment to South Korea

No question about it, the experts say. If South Korea were attacked, the United States would rush to its rescue. The United States has an ironclad commitment to defend South Korea, and it's had one for decades. What was the origin of that commitment? Was it as rock solid as the U.S. commitment, for example, to the North Atlantic Treaty Organization? Did it oblige the United States to fight for South Korea under all circumstances? These were questions worth exploring, for they cut to the heart of the true value (and nature) of a presidential commitment.

When World War II ended in August 1945, the Korean peninsula was split into two parts: the north fell under a brutal communist dictator, Kim Il Sung, who was protected by the Soviet Union, and the south under an equally brutal autocrat, Syngman Rhee, who, by default, became the responsibility of the United States. In May 1948, Rhee established the Republic of Korea, and in December Kim created the Democratic People's Republic of Korea, formalizing the division of the country. Within weeks, as though by pre-arrangement, Soviet troops were withdrawn, and within months American troops followed suit, with Washington believing innocently that a period of peaceful adjustment might be at hand. It was not to be. Skirmishes along the demarcation line became the disconcerting norm, accompanied by a deepening suspicion and hostility between the two parts of Korea.

President Truman, preoccupied by Stalin's aggressive moves in Europe, raised no objection when Dean Acheson, who had succeeded Marshall as secretary of state, speaking at the National Press Club on January 12, 1950, excluded Korea from America's "defensive perimeter" in Asia. Was it a deliberate exclusion? No one was certain, but Kim was quick to pick up on the exclusion—and wonder about its significance. He had been considering different ways of reunifying Korea. One way, he thought, was a North Korean invasion of South Korea. Several times he had flown to Moscow to get Stalin's permission. Finally, after the Acheson speech, Soviet leader Stalin flashed a green light, sensing that communism might, in this way, be able to pick up another trophy without too much danger. According to Nikita Khrushchev's memoirs, Mao had also given his approval to Kim's plan, meaning both Russia and China supported the plan for a North Korean attack on South Korea, an American ally. Kim had assured his colleagues that it would all be over in three weeks. All three communist leaders—Stalin, Mao, and Kim—were soon to learn that they had seriously underestimated Harry Truman.

Korea Explodes

The president was in Independence, Missouri, relaxing for a few days, when he took a late night call from Dean Acheson. "Mr. President, I have very serious news for you," the secretary of state said. "The North Koreans have invaded South Korea." According to his biographer, Robert J. Donovan, Truman was "shocked" by the news, because, in his judgment, this was an "open military attack across an accepted international boundary upon an American-sponsored government." A red line had been crossed. The free world was being challenged by aggressive communist leaders, and Truman thought it was his job to stop them.

The president was a student of history. When he acted in Korea, he was thinking of the Munich Conference in September 1938, when Great Britain made no move to stop Nazi Germany from occupying the Sudetenland in Czechoslovakia. Later, diplomats referred to Munich as a painful example of appeasement leading to the outbreak of World War II. "The fateful events of the 1930's, when aggression unopposed bred more aggression and eventually war," Truman explained to Congress, "were fresh in our memory."

Truman quickly dispatched one army division to South Korea. A few days later he sent four more divisions on an assumption, faulty in the extreme, that the North Koreans, considered to be a band of marauding "bandits," could easily be defeated.

"We are not at war," Truman assured the nation on June 29. There was no need, therefore, for a declaration of war, which was what President Franklin Roosevelt had requested of Congress the day after Pearl Harbor. From Truman to Barack Obama, in fact, no president has felt the need to ask Congress for a declaration of war. The Korean engagement was not, for example, the

War of 1812, when such a declaration would have been considered a requirement for committing American troops to war. The United States, fighting under a UN banner, was engaged, Truman argued, in "a police action . . . to suppress a bandit raid." In this way, Truman became the first president to take the country into a war without any form of congressional authorization. Truman in effect gave to the UN the authority clearly vested in Congress. When Congress first debated the merits of the UN Charter, Truman was in Potsdam negotiating the end of World War II. He sent a cable to Senate leaders, promising that if he ever dispatched American troops to fight in a war, he would first come to Congress to request authority. In Korea, Truman ignored his own pledge, and Congress raised no substantive objection.

Thus, within the context of the cold war, began a historic shift of governmental power: A president, acting on his own, could start a war, or respond militarily to an action he deemed harmful to the national interest, without a declaration of war or even formal consultation with Congress. The U.S. Constitution required a declaration of war, but a president could now ignore this aspect of the Constitution with apparent impunity.

Within a week, it was clear that U.S. forces, unprepared and unfocused, were no match for the North Koreans, who in any case outnumbered them ten to one. Casualties were high, especially among officers. Field reports spoke of "retreat," "rout," "death," and "confusion." One reporter asked: "Could this be the army that only yesterday had thrilled the nation by its victories at Normandy, the Bulge, the Rhine, Guadalcanal? . . . American soldiers chased across rice paddies by North Koreans!"

Observing this unfolding disaster from his headquarters in Tokyo was General Douglas MacArthur, the supreme commander of allied powers in Japan. He did not like what he saw but felt no reason to panic. At any time, he confidently believed, he could destroy the North Koreans, the Chinese, and the Russians. With his corncob pipe characteristically clenched at a cocky angle, attired in splendid khaki regalia, MacArthur looked out over his vast Asian domain like an ancient potentate. He was an American aristocrat, the most powerful figure in occupied Japan.

Born in Little Rock, Arkansas, in 1880, MacArthur grew up believing that no service was more honorable, noble, or patriotic than being a soldier. His father, Arthur Jr., had been a lieutenant general in the United States Army. For his courage under fire, he had been awarded the Medal of Honor. The first sound young Douglas ever heard, he said, was the sound of the bugle. He later recalled that he could "ride and shoot even before I could read or write—indeed, even before I could walk and talk." There was never a question about his life's work. He entered West Point in 1898 and excelled as a cadet, graduating first in a class of 930 in 1903. Indeed, so outstanding was his training and scholarship that he was appointed "First Captain of the Corps of Cadets."

Given the arc of his whole career, it was not surprising that his first assignment would be in the Philippines, his second in Japan (serving in his father's command), and his third in Vera Cruz, Mexico. By the time World War I began, MacArthur was already a brigadier general, one of the brightest stars in the American military constellation. In Europe, where he served gallantly, he won two Distinguished Service Crosses, seven Silver Stars, two Purple Hearts and one Distinguished Service Medal.

In 1930, MacArthur was assigned to Washington, D.C., as Army chief of staff. The year 1932 brought one of his most controversial assignments—the smashing of the Bonus Army, consisting of thousands of World War I veterans who had descended upon the capital with their families, set up shacks, protested, and demanded immediate back pay for their service to the nation. One would have thought that MacArthur would have been sympathetic— after all, these were his compatriots in war; but MacArthur not only showed no compassion, he did not even listen to their complaints. He regarded many of the protesting veterans to be communists and pacifists, though he had no evidence to support his view, and he crushed their protest.

When in 1941 the Japanese attacked Pearl Harbor, MacArthur was sent to the Pacific as "Commander of U.S. Armed Forces in the Far East." By year's end, he was a four-star general, but he was commanding a force badly depleted by heavy losses sustained at Pearl Harbor. He was soon obliged to abandon the Philippines, for him the low point in the war. On October 20, 1944, when he returned to the Philippines with trumpets blaring and reporters in tow to record his triumph, MacArthur suspected the United States was riding a wave of victories that would eventually roll on to the unconditional surrender of the Japanese empire. His projection was accurate. The Japanese surrendered in August 1945, after two atom bombs were dropped on their mainland. On behalf of the United States of America, MacArthur accepted the Japanese surrender, ending World War II and beginning his reign as the ultimate impresario of Japan's transition to democracy.

Until the outbreak of the Korean War in June 1950, MacArthur had performed brilliantly. Even his Japanese critics concede that he acted with sensitivity and respect, especially in retaining the emperor as a symbol of Japanese imperial pride. The outbreak of war in Korea shattered this period of calm and raised questions in MacArthur's mind about whether the United States was pursuing the right strategy in confronting the communist challenge. Like his colleague, the equally colorful and flamboyant George S. Patton, MacArthur believed deeply that the United States had the power to crush Russia and China—and should do so; delay only served to give the communists more time to rebuild their military and re-energize their revolutionary spirit. When the North Koreans attacked, MacArthur sensed that this opportunity was at hand. But there was always this matter of Truman being his commander-in-chief: Would the president, his president, in his mind a small man, an accident of history, a machine politician from Missouri—would this president have the vision and the wisdom to see the world as MacArthur saw it? Would he? Indeed, could he? And if he did not have the vision, what then?

On July 27, MacArthur assumed full responsibility for allied actions in Korea. He flew to the battlefield, conferred with his field commanders, and then issued an order, later famously described as "Stand or Die." Another general, paraphrasing MacArthur, said: "There will be no Dunkirk, no Bataan; a retreat to Pusan would be one of the greatest butcheries in history. We must fight to the end." MacArthur, who had thought four divisions would do the trick, now asked Truman for eight divisions.

The Americans fought gallantly. Many died. Even though reinforced with better-trained troops, they were still being pummeled in one battle after another, forced into further retreat until they gathered in exhaustion and humiliation in the southern enclave of Pusan, preparing for the ultimate humiliation, which would have been an American surrender and the abandonment of the whole of the Korean peninsula to the communists.

MacArthur, conveying the impression of an unhurried military mastermind, came up with the idea of a pincer attack, which surprised the North Koreans. On September 15, 1950, he sent a large amphibious force around the western coast of Korea to Inchon, a port south of the 38th parallel. Though threatening waves made the approach hazardous, his troops reached Inchon and seized the port, rapidly transforming it into a base for reinforcement and redeployment. Wasting no time, MacArthur then sent his troops into a broad flanking operation designed to trap the bulk of the North Korean Army, which was then preparing to pulverize the Pusan perimeter. The North Koreans, suddenly aware they were in deep trouble, changed plans and fled north to escape encirclement. MacArthur's strategic gamble at Inchon succeeded.

Truman then faced a key decision, perhaps his most consequential of the war: whether to kick the North Koreans out of South Korea and re-establish the 38th parallel as the recognized border between the two halves of the country, a modest goal, or to allow MacArthur to invade North Korea, destroy the communist regime and reunify the country, a far more ambitious goal. Truman came under enormous domestic pressure to "finish the job." A midterm election was only weeks away. Dwight Eisenhower, then president of Columbia University, suggested that Truman destroy the communist regime in North Korea. GOP congressman Hugh Scott of Pennsylvania charged that the State Department and especially Secretary of State Acheson were going to "subvert our military victory" by "cringing behind the [38th] parallel." At this point, domestic politics constituted more of a problem for Truman than did battlefield realities. W. Averell Harriman, one of Truman's closest advisers, said: "It would have taken a superhuman effort to say no. Psychologically, it was almost impossible not to go ahead and complete the job." Truman decided to give the green light to MacArthur.

On September 27, the Joint Chiefs of Staff, acting on the president's orders, sent a "directive" to MacArthur. "Your military objective," it said, "is the destruction of the North Korean Armed Forces." It did not say the destruction of the North Korean regime, but that was implied. George C. Marshall, by then secretary of defense, told MacArthur: "We want you to feel unhampered tactically and strategically to proceed north of the 38th parallel." MacArthur replied: "Unless and until the enemy capitulates, I regard all Korea open for our military operations."

With this presidential decision to cross the 38th parallel, the US crossed another landmark, too. Up to this time, foreign policy generally stopped at the water's edge. So it was said—and generally believed. The decision to go to war was seen as a joint enterprise between the executive and legislative branches of government, between the president and Congress. Now, with the start of the cold war, presidents could send troops to fight in foreign wars without a declaration of war or even extensive consultation with Congress. They could make a commitment—and act on it. If things went well, they could assume no problem with Congress. But if things did not go well, they could assume Congress would raise a fuss, even to the point of withholding funds; but this happened rarely.

MacArthur assumed China would not intervene in his destruction of North Korea, a neighboring communist ally. He was wrong, and so were Truman's advisers. Little noticed, it seemed, was a secret cable suggesting strongly that China might intervene in the conflict if the United States threatened North Korea. Chinese foreign minister Zhou Enlai had informed Indian ambassador

K. M. Panikkar in Beijing that if United States troops crossed the 38th parallel, China would come to North Korea's defense. There had actually been reports of Chinese "volunteers" crossing the Yalu River, separating China from North Korea. When Truman asked about these reports, he was assured by the CIA that Chinese intervention was "not probable in 1950." And when he asked MacArthur during their Wake Island meeting on October 15, 1950, whether they would intervene, the general, as always supremely confident, replied: "We are no longer fearful of their intervention." He said the Chinese had 100,000–125,000 troops on their side of the Yalu but no air force, and if they crossed the border, there would be "the greatest slaughter." At this meeting, MacArthur acted as if the president was an unfortunate inconvenience imposed by the Constitution. MacArthur felt like an aristocrat dealing with the rabble of democracy. Truman left Wake Island believing that in MacArthur he was dealing with an arrogant and mercurial personality, but not one who, in the final analysis, would challenge a presidential command.

American forces crossed the 38th parallel in strength, and there was initially little to no resistance. MacArthur said his forces were engaged in a "mopping up operation." Military historian S. L. A. Marshall poetically described the Chinese Army as "a phantom, which casts no shadow." Several Republicans began speculating that MacArthur would make a superb presidential candidate in 1952—he was, some politicians felt, on the threshold of a huge military victory that could well sweep him (and them) into office. MacArthur informed Truman that "organized resistance throughout Korea will be ended by Thanksgiving." He was to learn that predictions during wars can be tricky and embarrassing.

The Chinese communists, in power then for little more than a year, had a different timetable in mind. In early November, as Beijing maintained a curious, calculated silence, Chinese "volunteers" crossed the Yalu and engaged small units of the American and South Korean armies. No one was certain how many "volunteers" were there, but MacArthur was impressed by their persistent hit-and-run approach to the battle. He responded boldly by bombing many of the bridges spanning the Yalu and by ordering the Eighth Army to begin a new offensive to the north.

At this moment, the Chinese mysteriously vanished from the battlefield. Where had they gone? Reconnaissance provided no useful clues. MacArthur's intelligence chief, General Charles A. Willoughby, a gruff Prussian-like officer, assured Washington that the Chinese had no more than 71,000 troops, located, he stressed, on the other side of the Yalu. The Eighth Army pushed further north. There was no resistance. MacArthur issued a war communiqué saying that "for all practical purposes" this U.S. offensive should "end the war." Reporters overheard him confiding to aides, "I hope we can get the boys home by Christmas."

On November 25, more than 300,000 Chinese troops, described as phantoms who cast no shadows, exploded out of the mountains, forests, and ravines of North Korea, opening a climactic battle so catastrophic to American forces and fortunes that Acheson later described it as the worst defeat suffered by an American Army since the Battle of Bull Run. The Chinese announced their sudden appearance with a deafening symphony of bugles, trumpets, and whistles, as they went on a rampage through North Korea, first decimating major South Korean units and then sending the Eighth Army staggering backward through a heavy, howling snowstorm to the 38th parallel. Reluctantly, MacArthur concluded: "We face an entirely new war." A bitterly disappointed Truman told his cabinet: "The Chinese have come in with both feet." In his diary, the president wrote that "overwhelming masses of advancing Chinese" have reoccupied large parts of North Korea. A *New York Times* banner-headline read: "200,000 OF FOE ADVANCE UP TO 23 MILES IN KOREA." *Life* magazine editorialized, "World War III moves ever closer."

And then, a few days later, on November 30, as if things could not get any worse, they did. At a scheduled news conference in the Indian Treaty Room at the White House, Truman raised the possibility that the United States might use nuclear weapons to halt the Chinese advance. For a moment, as the Bible says, the sun stopped.

The news conference started with a routine give-and-take with the media. Then a reporter asked Truman whether MacArthur was seeking permission to strike across the Yalu River, which would mean expanding the war into China.

Truman answered: "We will take whatever steps are necessary to meet the military situation, just as we always have." There was nothing unusual about his answer, but reporters sensed a slight opening.

Another reporter asked: might that include the use of atomic weapons?

Truman could have stopped this line of questioning with an always handy evasion, but he did not. "That includes every weapon we have," he continued.

Yet another reporter asked whether "active consideration" was being given to the use of atomic weapons.

Again Truman could easily have avoided a direct answer, but he chose to confirm the thrust of the question. "There has always been active consideration to its use," Truman snapped, adding, "always has been . . . it is one of our weapons." He left the odd impression that the decision on their use would be made by both him and his top commander in the field—namely, MacArthur.[4]

Within seconds after his news conference ended, United Press International ran the following bulletin: "PRESIDENT TRUMAN SAID TODAY THAT THE UNITED STATES HAS UNDER CONSIDERATION USE OF THE ATOMIC BOMB IN CONNECTION WITH THE WAR IN KOREA." The Associated Press added that the decision could be made by MacArthur. The *Times of India* ran a headline: "No, No, No."

Had Truman made a colossal blunder? Or had he intended to raise the nuclear threat as a way of frightening China into a hurried retreat back across the Yalu? Although historians have argued these questions for decades, it seems as if Truman had at least prepared for the possibility of using atomic weapons. We know now that he had ordered the Strategic Air Command to "augment its capabilities," including the possible use of atomic weapons.

At the time, Truman's "atomic" comments sent a deep, unsettling chill through the world, except perhaps in China, where Mao Zedong was later credited with circulating the rather perverse thought that a nuclear war would still leave China with a population of 400 million people, enough to fight and beat any nation on Earth. Everyone knew that Truman was the only world leader to have actually ordered the dropping of atomic bombs on civilian targets, and he had done so twice against Japan. In his diary, Truman wrote poignantly: "I've worked for peace for five years and six months and *it looks like World War III is here.*"

At this moment in the crisis, Truman must have asked himself whether Korea was worth another war so soon after the end of World War II, another war that could quickly escalate into a nuclear war. Also, he must have wondered whether he was being pushed into another war by an over-ambitious general pursuing an antagonistic political agenda. After a sober reconsideration of his options—political, military, and diplomatic—Truman concluded that he had to change and clarify his policy. Korea was not World War II, he reasoned, and he was not Roosevelt, seeking the "unconditional surrender" of his enemies. He was not going to be locked into an inflexible policy—he could readjust his policy and perhaps even his personnel. He could compromise and limit his war goals to an armistice that would end the war. Truman was aware that such a policy switch would almost certainly enrage MacArthur and ignite a ferocious domestic attack on him and his party, but after many late night arguments with himself and with the ghosts of former presidents, he switched and girded himself for another round of political warfare.

Truman met with an anxious British prime minister Clement Attlee and assured him that American policy in Korea had not changed and that the United States was not going to use nuclear weapons against China, nor open a new front against the Soviet Union. His message, simply stated, was: the United States was not going to widen the war. He sent a similarly soothing message to his allies in Europe and Asia and to his political allies in Congress, and for a time their churning apprehension about America using atomic weapons slipped into a lower gear.

"Old Soldiers Never Die"

Nevertheless, though Truman sang a song of reassurance, MacArthur continued to bellow a different, more aggressive tune, as if he were the sovereign entitled to his own policy and Truman his liege. Suddenly on center stage at this delicate moment in the war was a remarkable tug-of-war between a general and his commander-in-chief—remarkable in part because no one really knew at this time who would prevail.

MacArthur's catechism was clear: North Korea started the war, and North Korea should be punished and defeated; China chose to become a belligerent in the war, sending a huge army across the Yalu, and now it too should be defeated; the Soviet Union should be warned to stay out of the war, but if it entered the war, then it too should be defeated. And MacArthur had no doubt that if he were unshackled by Truman, Acheson, and the "others," and if he were able to use the full power of the United States (read atomic weapons) against its communist enemies, he felt certain he could and would win a decisive and historic victory.

Concretely, MacArthur proposed an immediate blockade and bombing of China, a Nationalist Chinese attack on the mainland supported by the United States, and the deployment of 33,000 Nationalist Chinese troops to the struggle in Korea. The general was pushing for the wider war his president was resisting, and the general was ready to use all of his conservative allies in Washington to win the day. This was a disagreement of historic proportion, a military dissent almost unprecedented in American wars. Major General George B. McClellan, commanding the Union Army during the Civil War, also took on his president—and lost. In key battles, McClellan, an otherwise impressive leader, employed a strange strategy of hesitation that baffled and angered his president, Abraham Lincoln, who twice relieved him of his command. "If

General McClellan does not want to use the army," Lincoln was quoted as saying, "I would like to borrow it for a time."

At this delicate moment in the Korean War, the United States was flashing two diametrically opposite signals to the world—the president with words of caution, the general with words of audacious dissent. It could have been a clever good-guy–bad-guy strategy—but it wasn't.

As the war edged toward a draw, neither side able to achieve a decisive victory, MacArthur lost his patience, and on March 23, 1951, without presidential clearance, he took it upon himself to issue a public ultimatum to China: either negotiate an armistice "in the field" with me (MacArthur) or get blown to bits. Biographer William Manchester said of the general: "He simply could not bear to end his career in checkmate." Truman was dumbfounded—"in a state of mind that combined disbelief with controlled fury," as Acheson recalled. With his ultimatum, MacArthur had broken his promise to Truman, made during their Wake Island meeting, that he would no longer make policy pronouncements from the battlefield without permission. He also shattered a sensitive UN effort to broker an armistice agreement that would have left the 38th parallel as the official dividing line between the two sides.

In the United States, an exasperated MacArthur had many allies, and he calculatedly unleashed them against the president. GOP representative Joseph Martin of Massachusetts picked up one of MacArthur's favorite proposals and advocated a Nationalist Chinese attack on the mainland. "What are we in Korea for—to win or lose?" he asked. "If we are not in Korea to win, then this administration should be indicted for the murder of thousands of American boys." MacArthur sent Martin a letter of encouragement, which the congressman read to the House of Representatives and released to the media, deepening the divide between the general's position and his president's. *Time* magazine, in an editorial by publisher Henry Luce, echoed Martin's call for a second front against China. The United States, Luce said, should take "full advantage of whatever the nationalists can do now to help us now in the struggle for Asia," perhaps in the form of a "limited beachhead invasion, presumably in South China."

Truman lost his cool. "I can take just so much," he exploded, accusing MacArthur of a "double cross." He conferred with his two senior diplomats, Acheson and Harriman, and his two senior military advisers, Marshall and General Omar Bradley, chairman of the Joint Chiefs of Staff, and decided that "our Big General in the Far East must be recalled."

Before actually firing MacArthur, though, Truman checked with the Library of Congress to review the details of the Lincoln/McClellan fracas. What he learned was that it was the opposite of his problems with MacArthur. As historian David McCullough explained: "Lincoln had wanted McClellan to attack and McClellan refused time and again. But then, when Lincoln issued orders, McClellan, like MacArthur, ignored them. Also, like MacArthur, McClellan occasionally made political statements on matters outside the military field. Asked what he thought about this, Lincoln, according to a story Truman loved, said it reminded him of the man who, when his horse kicked up and stuck a foot through the stirrup, said to the horse, 'If you are going to get on, I will get off.' "

On April 11, 1951, at the unusual hour of 1 a.m., the White House released a bulletin—"TRUMAN FIRES MACARTHUR"—that crackled with controversy and ignited a president/general clash unprecedented in the cold war.

In American history, generals had been fired before, but MacArthur seemed larger than life, certainly in his mind larger than the president who had ordered his dismissal. This bulletin sent the whole country into a frenzy of political protestations and excitement: who was going to win this titanic confrontation—Truman, who had the constitutional power to dismiss a dissenting general, or MacArthur, who had, in addition to the stars he carried on his shoulders and the medals he wore on his uniform, the power of congressional conservatives, many in the media and the streets, and the possibility of a presidential campaign?

MacArthur was, to many critics of Truman, an illustrious patriot who had devoted his life to the service of his country. They felt he should be honored and Truman impeached. Joseph McCarthy, on the floor of the Senate, shouted: "The son of a bitch should be impeached." The usually more decorous Senator Robert Taft echoed the same call. The *Chicago Tribune,* which never supported Truman, ran a front-page editorial. "President Truman must be impeached and convicted," it said. "He is unfit, morally and mentally, for this high office." The Hearst, McCormick, and Scripps-Howard newspapers treated MacArthur's firing as a national catastrophe. In San Gabriel, California, Truman was burned in effigy. Truman was booed when he threw out the first pitch at a season-opening baseball game in Washington. In Tokyo, MacArthur told an aide that Truman had conferred with doctors who told him that he "was suffering from malignant hypertension; that this affliction was characterized by bewilderment and confusion . . . and that . . . he wouldn't live six months." This alleged medical diagnosis found its way into many newspapers. The firestorm of criticism was so severe that historians compared Truman's ordeal to that of President James K. Polk, who had his problems with General Zachary Taylor during the Mexican-American War.

Truman's supporters seemed woefully ineffective in their defense of the president. It seemed clear to everyone that MacArthur could openly defy Truman, brazenly proclaim dissenting opinions, and still receive a hero's welcome and an invitation from Republican supporters to address a joint session of Congress, where he continued his assault on a sitting president. "You cannot," he intoned, "appease and otherwise surrender to Communism in Asia without simultaneously undermining our efforts to halt its advance in Europe." Who was surrendering to communism? Truman, of course. "Old soldiers never die," MacArthur concluded, "they just fade away—an old soldier who tried to do his duty as God gave him the light to see that duty."

MacArthur's extraordinary peroration only raised his popular appeal. Were it not for the fact that Eisenhower, a totally unblemished wartime hero, already was the GOP choice for president in 1952, it seemed likely that MacArthur, his anticommunism now unfurled for all to see and hear, might have filled the role. Instead, he withdrew from political temptation and held court in a spacious suite at the Waldorf Astoria in New York until his death in 1964, exercising on occasion only a modest degree of influence in political circles. Truman survived his confrontation with MacArthur to finish his term in office. "I was sorry to have to reach a parting of the way with the Big Man in Asia," he said in a letter to Eisenhower, "but he asked for it and I had to give it to him."

Some conservatives at home drew one other conclusion from this sorry episode. If the Truman administration had decided not to fight the Chinese in Korea, they thought, then the United States ought to get out of Asia. An emergence of old-fashioned isolationism reappeared in newspaper editorials. "We should get our troops out . . . as quickly as possible," advised the *Detroit Times.* "We should withdraw our forces from Asia and after that from Europe," editorialized the *Topeka State Journal.* This theme bounced from one editorial office to another.

The White House absorbed the blows. The president, bowed but undefeated, stood victorious in his battle with a rebellious general, who retreated to the roll of drums and the sound of trumpets, but whose historic dissent would never be echoed again. The system survived. No one questioned MacArthur's patriotism, no one seriously questioned Truman's, either. The cold war seemed to impose new definitions on such words as patriotism, loyalty, and service; it also seemed to impose new limitations on America's place in the world, even though it remained a superpower.

The United States would not widen the war in Korea, and it would tailor its end goal to the achievement of an armistice along the 38th parallel that would leave the aggressor, Kim Il-sung, and his North Korean regime in power. As journalist David Halberstam observed, the Korean War "had reached the point where there were no more victories, only death." For the first time in American history, the United States decided to fight to a draw rather than fight to win. The Korean War ended in "a mutually unsatisfactory compromise." A number of the war reporters were much blunter. They called it "Die for a Tie." Remarkably, the "tie" has survived for decades with the United States committed, even into the 21st century, to the defense of South Korea.

CHAPTER TWO

THE HATCHING OF AN AMERICAN "COMMITMENT"

> "Unavoidably, the U.S. is, together with France, committed in Indochina."
> —DEPARTMENT OF STATE, 1950

> "We are lost if we lose Southeast Asia without a fight.
> We must do what we can to save Southeast Asia."
> —DEAN ACHESON, 1952

WHEN FRANKLIN D. ROOSEVELT died in April 1945 and Harry Truman became president, Vietnam was a problem on the periphery of America's concerns. In time, it was to become the central problem, leading to the only war America ever lost.

How It All Got Started

Through most of World War II, Roosevelt had supported the Wilsonian principle of national self-determination, even though he suspected that a number of his close European allies intended to retain their colonies after the war—the British in the Middle East and South Asia, the French and Dutch in Southeast Asia, and several of the European allies in Africa. As a bridge between his policy of self-determination and the colonial intent of his allies, Roosevelt proposed an interim system of trusteeship, under which colonies such as Indochina, Indonesia, and India would be guaranteed their postwar independence but only after their leaders would first be tutored in responsible governance by their colonial masters—a concept so haughty that it was almost certain to be rejected by the leaders.

Roosevelt himself was appalled by colonial rule; in private conversation, he made no secret of his opposition. He was especially upset by French rule in Indochina. "Indochina should not go back to France," he told Cordell Hull, his secretary of state. "It should be administered by an international trusteeship." His sympathies were obvious. "France," he said, "has had the country—thirty million inhabitants—for nearly one hundred years, and the people are worse off than they were at the beginning."[1]

But in the waning months of the war, and of his life, Roosevelt changed his policy. He dropped his trusteeship proposal. He assured his European allies that if they did in fact decide to reimpose their colonial rule after the war, the United States would not raise any public objections. Why did Roosevelt change his mind? The first reason was national interest. His senior military advisers persuaded him that the United States had to control the sea lanes of the Pacific, from Japan south to Australia, once Japanese militarism was defeated. If unstable regimes, possibly run by communist upstarts loyal to Moscow, were set up in Indochina and Indonesia, they believed, U.S. control would be jeopardized and international trade disrupted. The second reason related to the central importance of Europe in his strategic calculations. Roosevelt worried about a weakening of the wartime alliance over an issue, such as European colonialism, that at the moment he thought was not central to the big prize, which was the "unconditional surrender" of the Nazis. Moreover, as Roosevelt scanned the postwar European horizon, it was clear that he would need the cooperation of the English, French, and Dutch if the Soviet Union were to move aggressively into eastern and central Europe, which was exactly what happened.

Truman, as president, quickly embraced the main outlines of Roosevelt's policy. He himself had no fixed agenda except for the obvious tasks: end the war in Europe; finish it finally in Asia, even if he had to use atomic bombs; create the United Nations; and give the world a chance to take a deep breath after the prolonged horrors of World War II. And, in the meantime, if his European allies wanted to restore their colonial rule in such faraway places as Indochina, then let it happen. The United States would not object, at least publicly—though, in private talks with the French, British, and Dutch, Truman stressed that Washington would prefer a policy of gradual self-determination for their colonies.

At the close of the war, a problem arose in Southeast Asia that was not on Truman's calendar but should have been. On September 2, 1945, Ho Chi-minh proclaimed Vietnam's independence, and he did so with nationalist pride and diplomatic cunning. "All men are created equal," he began, ". . . . endowed by their Creator with certain unalienable rights: among these are Life, Liberty and the pursuit of Happiness." Familiar? He stole liberally from the 1776 American Declaration of Independence and from the 1791 French Declaration on the Rights of Man, as he opened a shrewd play for American (and French) support of Vietnam's independence. At a gala celebration in his capital city of Hanoi, he quoted from UN appeals for national self-determination; many had recently been drafted in San Francisco.[2] He arranged for a national band to play a very original rendition of the "Star Spangled Banner." He made it a point of dining with two members of the Office of Strategic Services (OSS), the predecessor of the Central Intelligence Agency, thanking them for American assistance to his Viet Minh guerrillas during the war and appealing for "fraternal collaboration" between the United States and Vietnam now that the war was over.[3] Clearly, Ho believed that if he had American support, he would gain international recognition and discourage the return of French colonial rule. On that memorable day, however, Ho also warned that the Vietnamese people were "determined to fight to the bitter end against any attempt by the French colonialists to reconquer their country."[4]

Over the next few months, Ho wrote a number of conciliatory letters to Truman and other American officials. In one he proposed a program of "full cooperation" with the United States and in another the start of cultural and educational exchanges between the two countries.[5] Ho often referred to the UN Charter, hoping that its anticolonialist language might generate anticolonialist sentiment in Europe and the United States. "The carrying out of the Atlantic Charter and San Francisco Charter," Ho wrote, "implies the eradication of imperialism and all forms of colonial oppression."[6] Ho was not a naïve revolutionary who believed that European colonialism would wither and die in a rush of UN rhetoric; but he was using every tool at his disposal to persuade Truman to adhere to old-fashioned Wilsonian principles.

Though Truman had this extraordinary opportunity to open a dialogue with the Vietnamese leader, which would probably have changed the postwar history of Indochina, and of America, he rebuffed every overture. He never answered Ho's letters, nor did any of his officials. Truman did not trust Ho (nor any other communist leader), and he had given his word to the French that the United States would not obstruct France's return to Indochina. Ever since Woodrow Wilson's presidency, national self-determination had stood tall, at least rhetorically, in America's pantheon of strategic principles, but it stood nowhere near the top in Truman's pantheon. Trumping all of his concerns was communism. Josef Stalin was expanding his empire into Eastern Europe. Communist parties in Italy and France were gaining political power. The Red Sell, as it was called, was spreading through the Middle East. Marxist guerrilla movements were popping up all over Asia, and Mao Zedong's forces were on the edge of pushing Chiang Kai-shek's troops off the China mainland. Intelligence reports suggested that Mao would then move south toward Indochina.

Truman was a very practical man. France needed American help, and France would get it. Truman recognized France's essential role in Europe. A few days before Ho's declaration of Vietnam's independence, Truman had personally assured Charles de Gaulle, then provisional president of France, during a White House visit that the United States would not support Ho, nor recognize his regime. It was the message de Gaulle wanted to hear.

At the same time, Truman was challenged at home by the rising power of GOP senator Joseph McCarthy of Wisconsin. The junior senator, like many of his Republican colleagues, never missed a chance to criticize the president's foreign policy. A frightening force of nature, for a time an unchecked political charlatan who gave voice to a mid-century anticommunist hysteria called "McCarthyism," the loose-lipped senator saw communists in every closet. Slurring his words, suggesting more than a passing acquaintance with liquor, he fired off unsubstantiated, exaggerated charges of communist subversion and disloyalty at American diplomats, writers, and scholars. As a consequence, McCarthyism spread fear and suspicion throughout the country. For a time, politicians, even presidents, could not ignore the message of the senator's shrill trumpet. It was in this uncertain environment at home that Truman threw American support behind the re-establishment of French colonial rule in Indochina. Even without McCarthy, Truman would likely have adopted the same position; with McCarthy looming in the background, this position was ensured, consistent as it was with the anticommunism of the day.

Ho had promised that the Vietnamese would fight "to the bitter end" any return of French colonial rule, but he did not promise to fight immediately. On March 6, 1946, Ho began an on-again, off-again negotiation with the French, which Washington supported. For a time, it seemed as if they were making progress, but by the summer this illusion passed and war erupted. Ho would not accept French colonialism, and the French would not abandon their colony. In December, the French bombarded Haiphong harbor, killing more than 6,000 Vietnamese, perhaps in retaliation for the communist "massacre" of "many foreigners" in the north and south of the country.[7] Ho fled the capital city of Hanoi, retreating into the hills and mobilizing his guerrilla army once again. He had defeated the Japanese, and he was convinced he could defeat the French. Within a very brief period of time, he established control over two-thirds of the countryside, and his troops began to attack the cities, where the French concentrated their power, modest as it was. Fighting was intense.

France asked for American help, and the United States quickly obliged. Washington arranged a $160 million line of credit for military aid, which was to be sent directly to France, but everyone understood that it would then be funneled to Indochina. At the time, it did not look like the first American step into an Indochina war that was to last thirty years. It was a reluctant first step, offered by one ally to another, each marching to a different drummer: The United States had Europe and the spreading dangers of communism on its agenda. The French had Indochina and the dwindling days of colonialism on theirs.

The situation was grim, according to most observers. John Carter Vincent, who ran the State Department's office of far eastern affairs, wrote a year-end report. "The French themselves admit that they lack the military strength to reconquer the country," he revealed. Under Secretary Dean Acheson told the French ambassador, Henri Bonnet, that "the unhappy situation" in Indochina was "highly inflammatory," adding (rhetorically, as it turned out), "we are ready and willing to do anything" to help.[8] But, in fact, the United States was not "ready and willing to do anything." It still clung to an increasingly untenable position of "neutrality" between supporting the French in Indochina and backing an anticolonial policy in diplomatic forums.

The "unhappy situation" in Indochina continued into 1947. On February 3, Secretary of State George C. Marshall cabled the U.S. Embassy in Paris, expressing "increasing concern" about the war in Indochina. He was frustrated. The French showed a "dangerously outmoded colonial outlook", he wrote; yet, the United States had "only the very friendliest feelings towards France."[9] A few months later, in May, Marshall seemed even more frustrated by the struggle in Indochina. Unless the French could find "true [nationalist] representatives" of the Vietnamese people, who could negotiate an honorable settlement with Ho, the secretary wrote, the struggle would leave a legacy of "permanent bitterness" with "ultra-nationalist or communist" leaders ultimately opening the whole region to Moscow's exploitation. Unfortunately, the French could find no such "representatives." Absorbed with the rising dangers of communist expansionism, evident all over the world, Marshall concluded: "The plain fact is that [the] Western democratic system is on the defensive in almost all emergent nations in Southeast Asia."[10]

By September 1948, Truman's State Department was forced to admit "our inability to suggest any practicable solution to the Indochina problem." In a policy statement, State's diplomats concluded that France was "fighting a desperate and apparently losing struggle in Indochina." They also recognized that

Ho was the "strongest and perhaps the ablest figure in Indochina," and a solution without him was impossible.[11] Yet, they suspected a solution with him would probably open the door to a communist triumph in Indochina certain to damage American interests not only in Asia but in Europe, which was the key battlefield in the developing cold war. What to do? Slowly and reluctantly, seeing no other "practicable solution," the United States increased its support of the French, even as it realized that the French were "losing" the war. It was a quandary Washington was never able to escape.

The French, in their search for an acceptable nationalist leader, finally settled on Bao Dai, who had been emperor of Vietnam during the war, though he commanded little public support. When Ho seized power in September 1945, he unceremoniously demanded Bao Dai's resignation. Remembering, as he later put it, that King Louis XVI had lost his head for resisting the French revolution, Bao Dai agreed. He handed "sovereign power" to Ho and in turn became his "supreme adviser," a title with no power.[12] After a year, Bao Dai went into exile, where he was soon known as "the playboy of Hong Kong." As author Stanley Karnow described the scene, "lonely and powerless, he devoted himself to hunting and wenching."[13] He was a figure of the past, and was so regarded, a pliant piece of the old French colonial furniture, but he was no fool. He had once warned de Gaulle, in vain: "Should you re-establish a French administration here, it will not be obeyed. Every village will be a nest of resistance, each former collaborator an enemy, and your officials and colonists will themselves seek to leave this atmosphere, which will choke them."[14]

This sad figure from Vietnam's imperial past was picked by France to lead the anticommunist forces in Vietnam: Bao Dai was supposed to take on Ho Chi-minh. It was an absurd choice, and it produced an unfair fight, the playboy emperor against the victorious revolutionary. Bao Dai commanded no army loyal to his new regime. He had no authority over the French force of 115,000 troops. He represented no political idea except monarchy at a time when his communist adversary, moving from one victory to another, was preaching revolution.

Bao Dai was a loser; and yet, just as the French had thrown their support behind him, so too did the Americans, though they did it reluctantly. They knew better. In the best of all possible worlds, they would not have included him in any new regime, hoping that Ho would become in Southeast Asia what Tito was becoming in south-central Europe—the nationalist leader of a communist state brave enough to proclaim its independence from Moscow's empire. There were, of course, no guarantees that Ho would become another

Tito; there was just a hunch, among a number of senior officials, that, encouraged in the right way, he might jump at the chance.

Ho was never given the chance to jump because Truman feared that Ho, once in power, would be an uncontrollable force, certain to offend the French, form and then lead an anticolonial government, tighten his ties to Moscow rather than rupture them, and finally feed the McCarthyite barn fire sweeping through the United States. Calculating the odds with the cool detachment of an old-fashioned Missouri politician, Truman concluded that the French (with or without Bao Dai) had no realistic chance of defeating Ho's forces, but he still needed the French in Europe. Indeed, he could not imagine blocking Stalin's advance in Europe without them. Thus, trapped, Truman linked America's fortunes in Asia to a crumbling ally and a cranky ex-emperor.

Slowly, Indochina began to emerge from its former status as a peripheral interest of the United States to its new status as an important but still-not-central front in the global war against communism. This did not mean that Washington would send military aid directly to Indochina, nor that it would send troops to Indochina, nor that it would abandon its paper-thin policy of neutrality in the "dirty war," as the French referred to their unpopular conflict in Indochina. It did mean that, willy nilly, an American commitment to support the anticommunist forces in Indochina was being hatched.

Meantime, within the administration, a strange battle was being fought. On one level, everyone seemed to agree that Soviet communism represented a deadly, spreading threat to American interests, and that it must be contained. But on another level, officials recognized that the United States was sliding into a thoroughly untenable situation in Indochina. Some believed Washington should open a diplomatic channel to Ho, even if such an effort would undercut a European ally. Others felt the United States should stiffen France's anticommunist spine in Indochina by offering more military aid and diplomatic support. Why not recognize Bao Dai's Vietnam? they asked. U.S. policy toward Indochina was, in Acheson's words, a "muddled hodgepodge."[15]

By 1949, the Russian detonation of an atomic bomb and the communist conquest of China had changed the strategic calculus, imposing a new urgency on Washington's "hodgepodge" policy toward Indochina. Acheson still did not want to recognize Bao Dai's regime, believing it would be "unwise" for the United States to support "France as a colonial power" in Indochina. And he still did not want to provide military aid directly to Indochina, believing the French were "blackmailing" the president by warning that if they had to abandon the struggle and the communists won, it would be Truman's fault.

Acheson told a congressional hearing, "We do not want to get into a position where the French say, 'You take over . . . take over the damned country. We don't want it.' . . . The French have got to carry their burden in Indochina, and we are willing to help, but not to substitute for them."[16]

By early 1950, however, Acheson's defenses collapsed. He sympathized with the president, who was being subjected to ferocious GOP attack for having "lost" China and now for providing inadequate help to the French in their desperate fight against Ho's advancing troops. Acheson encouraged Truman to drop America's earlier policy of neutrality in Indochina and take a stronger stand against further communist expansion in Asia, including the dispatch of American military aid directly to French colonial forces in Indochina and then the official recognition of Bao Dai's government. Truman, who was moving in this direction anyway, took his secretary of state's advice. Once again, the United States adjusted its policy. With no joy but feeling it had no other realistic choice, it took another formal step into the Indochina war.

Truman did not have to take this step. Nothing in history predetermined his decision. He could have chosen to fight the Republicans at home and support the French in Europe but not in Indochina. He could have challenged the expanding communist empire in other ways. Not known at the time was the degree of Soviet rot and decay and the huge advantage the United States enjoyed in economic and military strength. But instead Truman made the decision to throw American support behind the French, seeding the ground for a "commitment" that was soon to mushroom into another war involving American forces. Once again, the president proposed the policy, and Congress provided the money. Though conservative Republicans, spurred on by McCarthyism, kept criticizing Truman for supposedly being "soft on communism," they never objected to the idea of a president leading the country into a war without congressional authorization.

In a remarkably candid review of U.S. policy in Indochina, the State Department explained American thinking at the time:

Indochina is "subject to invasion by Red China." Vietnam's "governmental stability is poor," and it controls "less than one-third of the country." The French are "irrevocably committed" to Bao Dai—either back Bao Dai or accept Ho's "communist government," an option the United States considered "unacceptable." Why? Because it would "complete the communist domination of Southeast Asia." The French are spending nearly half of their annual military budget in Indochina—$475 million in 1949 alone. "Unavoidably," the State Department continues, "the US is, together with France, committed in Indochina." [This was the first time the word "committed" or "commitment" was used to officially describe the American involvement in the Indochina war.] Either the United States supports the French or it sees "the extension of communism" through all of Southeast Asia. "There is no other alternative." The French must be supported. It would be a "case of 'Penny wise, Pound foolish' to deny support to the French in Indochina." Support that is necessary now. So long as China does not invade Indochina "in mass," the French "can be successful" there—but only with U.S. help. Then, in its argument, the State Department links Indochina to Europe: "failure to support French policy in Indochina would have the effect of contributing toward the defeat of our aims in Europe." Therefore, we must reexamine "the question of military aid." The State Department concludes: "The United States should furnish military aid in support of the anti-communist nationalist governments of Indochina . . . not including US troops."[17]

What flowed from the State Department's explanation was, first, recognition of the Bao Dai government and, second, direct U.S. military assistance to French forces in Indochina. On January 18, 1950, a few months after Mao's communists seized power in China, they recognized Ho's government in Hanoi as the only "legal government of Vietnam." Twelve days later, the Russians announced their recognition of Ho's government. Quickly, the United States and the United Kingdom responded. On February 7, 1950, they extended diplomatic recognition to Bao Dai's government, and the lines were drawn in Indochina—the communists supporting Ho, and the West supporting Bao Dai. The country was not yet officially divided into two parts—North and South Vietnam. That was to come in 1954.

Once diplomatic recognition was given to Bao Dai, it took only a few months for the United States to open a military supply line directly to him. In April 1950, a White House document called "National Security Council Paper No. 64, 1950, The Position of the United States with Respect to Indochina" stated that Indochina was "under immediate threat," and therefore "the Departments of State and Defense should prepare as a matter of priority a program of all practicable measures designed to protect United States security interests in Indochina."[18] Thus was the spigot of American military aid to Indochina opened, and thus, too, was the United States "committed" to protecting its "security interests" in Indochina. It had never before spoken of such "security interests," nor defined them, and now suddenly these interests had to be protected.

Why the urgency? Why the new and expanding definitions of America's interests in Indochina? Because, according to NSC Paper 64, Chinese communist troops had already advanced to the Indochinese border, making it possible for "arms, material and troops to move freely from Communist China to the northern Tonkin area [of Vietnam] now controlled by Ho Chi-minh." The NSC paper claimed that the "movement of arms" had already begun. "It is doubtful," the paper concluded, "that the combined native Indochinese and French troops can successfully contain Ho's forces should they be strengthened by either Chinese Communist troops crossing the border, or Communist-supplied arms and material in quantity from outside Indochina strengthening Ho's forces."[19] The United States believed that native Indochinese and French troops, numbering 140,000 at the time, "can do little more than maintain the status quo."

On May 8, 1950, Acheson met with French foreign minister Robert Schuman in Washington, and they agreed the situation in Indochina was dire and urgent and required "remedial action." "Economic aid and military equipment" were to be sent to both Indochina and France. They didn't say how much, but by the end of 1950, Washington had already given more than $133 million in military aid to Indochina. One year later, the cost of U.S. military aid had risen to $316.5 million.[20]

All of Truman's advisers supported the president's decisions to recognize and arm Bao Dai and his army, even though none had any confidence in either. They were all absorbed with the global communist threat, which they believed was directed by Moscow, and Ho's insurgency was seen as its lethal vanguard in Southeast Asia. By the fall of 1950, Ho had accumulated a string of military victories from one end of Vietnam to the other; and if the Chinese communists intervened in Indochina, as they had recently intervened in Korea, even if they intervened in small numbers, Washington was convinced that French resistance would crack and Indochina would become a communist satellite. John Foster Dulles, then a State Department consultant, referred to Indochina as a "hopeless military situation."

Looming on the near horizon for the Truman administration was the depressing thought that the United States would soon replace France as the anticommunist anchor in Indochina, or it would watch from the sidelines as the whole region fell to communism.

Truman had always insisted that under no circumstances would he deploy U.S. troops to Southeast Asia. He knew the Joint Chiefs of Staff strongly opposed this option, and so too did his cool-headed secretary of defense, Robert Lovett. But a large, unanswered question hung over the administration's deliberations: if preventing the loss of Southeast Asia to the communists was vital to America's national security interests, as Truman and his advisers insisted, then how could the president accept any limitations on American actions?

Even as late in the Truman administration as March 1952, it was a question still unanswered. At a meeting of the National Security Council (NSC), Lovett stressed that the loss of Southeast Asia to communism would undoubtedly be a "grave danger to US security interests," but he quickly added that he would oppose sending any U.S. troops to Southeast Asia for the purpose of protecting those interests. Like his colleagues, Lovett was still absorbed with the Korean conflict, and World War II was only a recent memory. Yet, Acheson told British foreign secretary Anthony Eden that "we are lost if we lose Southeast Asia without a fight," adding "we must do what we can to save Southeast Asia." It seemed as if the United States wanted it both ways: not to get involved militarily and yet finding no way to avoid such involvement. Acheson, in both his private and public comments, underlined the administration's dilemma: "We must do what we can," he wrote, "but we must not send American troops to Southeast Asia."[21]

For many months, as the situation worsened, the president's senior advisers kept reviewing their options in Indochina with increasing urgency and frustration. That Indochina had to be preserved as a noncommunist bastion against the further spread of communism had become the unchallenged wisdom of the day—no one rose to question this view. But given the cruel realities on the ground—Ho's military superiority over the French, the Chinese communists sending arms and (could anyone rule out?) even troops into Vietnam—how could the United States head off a French collapse in Indochina and protect its newly discovered "interests" in Southeast Asia without a major expansion of its military involvement in Indochina, including the sending of U.S. troops? And, could a Democratic president, who was in office when China fell to the communists, allow yet another Asian country to fall to the communists? And to appear to be doing so little? If only for transparently domestic political reasons, Truman knew he had to do something powerfully persuasive to stop the ongoing communist advance in Indochina. But what? Again, the unanswered question surfaced: If Indochina was in fact "vital" to U.S. national security interests, as everyone insisted, then Washington would eventually have to send troops to defend it; and if the United States did send troops and the Chinese intervened, as they had been threatening to do, the United States would find itself fighting not just Viet Minh troops but Chinese troops, too—twice in two years. And, if it did reengage China militarily, could it be certain that the Soviet Union would not enter this expanded war?

Lovett suggested a novel financial escape, and he was not joking. If the United States really believed that Southeast Asia was "vital" to its security interests, but still refused to send troops to protect those interests, then maybe Washington should be prepared to buy its way out of this dilemma—"perhaps at the rate of a billion or a billion and a half dollars a year" to back the French and their puppet, Bao Dai, much, much more than they had even contemplated sending. "This would be very much cheaper than an all-out war against Communist China, which would certainly cost us fifty billion dollars."[22] This financial approach got nowhere.

Truman was in a tight corner, his options painfully limited. Only one thing was clear: On January 20, 1953, he would leave the White House and return to Missouri. Vietnam would become Dwight D. Eisenhower's headache.

When Truman became president, Vietnam had been a peripheral problem. By the time he left office, it had become a serious problem with no apparent solution, and it was moving closer to the center of Washington's concerns.

CHAPTER THREE

EISENHOWER

"My God, We Must Not Lose Asia!"

"Korea is important, but the really important spot is Indochina."
—JOHN FOSTER DULLES

DURING THE 1952 presidential campaign, the Republicans, led by a popular wartime hero, wanted to put some strategic distance between their candidate's vision of the world and the Truman policy of "containment." They proclaimed a new policy: Once Dwight D. Eisenhower was president, the United States would no longer just contain communist aggression, it would advance democracy all over the world. It would roll back the Iron Curtain. It would liberate people enslaved by Marxist dogma and diktat. It would launch a new era of freedom. Eisenhower played along with his campaign mentors, but once in office, able for the first time to read the secret intelligence about Indochina, he began to realize the complexity and seriousness of the problem. For the next two years, he essentially followed his predecessor's policy in Vietnam and echoed his reassuring rhetoric, at the same time increasing U.S. economic and military assistance to the French and their chosen leader in Vietnam, Bao Dai.

At first Eisenhower offered the aid grudgingly. He was not a great fan of the French, or their leader, Charles de Gaulle, "who," as he later put it in a snide aside, "considers himself to be, by some miraculous biological and transmigrative process, the offspring of Clemenceau and Jeanne d'Arc."[1] Nor was Bao Dai an example in Eisenhower's view of the courageous nationalist leader he knew Indochina then needed to beat back the communists. But, after only a brief time in office, he came to appreciate Truman's dilemma. John Foster Dulles was his instructor. The new secretary of state persuaded Eisenhower that "Korea is important, but the really important spot is Indochina, because we could lose Korea and probably insulate ourselves against the consequences of that loss; but if Indochina goes, and South Asia goes, it is extremely hard to insulate ourselves against the consequence of that."[2] In the 1930s, Eisenhower had been based in Asia, working at the time for General Douglas MacArthur, and he developed an appreciation of the rising tension between Asian nationalism and European colonialism. Conflict between the two, he thought, was unavoidable.

In the early days of his administration, attempting to explain his Indochina policy, Eisenhower often referred to a memo from outgoing secretary of state Dean Acheson, written during the transition between the two administrations, which warned the new president that the United States was already shouldering "between one-third and one-half of the financial burden" of the French "colonial war" in Indochina, that "overt Chinese intervention in Indochina" was a distinct possibility (just as it had proven to be the case in Korea), and that American involvement was inescapable. He also remembered Acheson's somber conclusion: "This is an urgent matter upon which the new Administration must be prepared to act."[3]

Eisenhower, new to presidential politics but not to war, was not eager for the United States to pick up French responsibilities in Indochina. He was, in truth, repelled by the tangled politics of Saigon, Hue, and Hanoi, and he was profoundly disturbed by the prospect of U.S. troops fighting in a colonial war on the Asian mainland.

Years later, while writing his memoirs, he explained his thinking: "The jungles of Indochina . . . would have swallowed up division after division of United States troops, who, unaccustomed to this kind of warfare, would have sustained heavy casualties. . . . Furthermore, the presence of ever more numbers of white men in uniform probably would have aggravated rather than assuaged Asiatic resentments."[4] (How prescient he was about the "casualties"! How revealing that he could imagine only "white men in uniform"! How interesting the use of the word "Asiatic"!)

In his first State of the Union address in February 1953, Eisenhower put his private reservations in a bank vault and spoke approvingly of how European allies had made "costly and bitter sacrifices to hold the line of freedom," including in "the jungles of Indochina and Malaya." He was, in fact, the classic hard-liner, ready at any time to denounce communism as "a hostile ideology—global in scope, atheistic in character, ruthless in purpose and insidious in method," but not eager to engage communism on the field of battle. Like most generals, he understood the costs of war. On his mind was Sun Tzu's classic admonition that war is "a matter of life and death, a road either to safety or to ruin." In Southeast Asia, Ike saw the possibility of ruin, and he recoiled at the prospect of American troops fighting in its jungles and rice paddies. And yet, with each decision, despite his instincts, he stepped more deeply into a colonial war in Asia.

Eisenhower was, for many congressional conservatives, Republican and Democratic, the ideal cold war leader; with Ike as president, the Republicans were back in control of the White House, and the United States was outspokenly determined to save Indochina from the tragic fate that had befallen China. They smiled with satisfaction when the new president promised the French and Bao Dai that the United States would substantially increase its military aid to their cause. Within a matter of months, it was clear that Eisenhower was a man of his word: he approved the earmarking of $785 million in U.S. military aid to the anticommunist cause in Indochina, a huge increase. For a time it seemed as if the fortunes of war had finally begun to turn in favor of the French, and against the communists.[5]

Dien Bien Phu: The Loss of Empire

This talk of France finally on the offensive—and winning—was wishful thinking, and Ike should have known better. The United States was now paying for roughly 75 percent of the war effort in Indochina, but the deeper American involvement did not ensure better results on the battlefield. One bitter example was the battle near the "Seat of the Border County Prefecture" or, in Vietnamese, Dien Bien Phu, a remote mountainous village in the northeastern corner of Vietnam—a battle that proved to be the turning point in the war, up to that point. The White House, by the end of 1953, was receiving contradictory reports about 15,000 elite French troops who were, depending on the report, fighting either gallantly—or desperately—against a surrounding force of Viet Minh guerrillas. Were these reports true? Would/could Dien Bien Phu be held? The president, who had been following events closely, thought that the French were actually gaining the upper hand, hurling back one Viet Minh assault after another, and were almost certain of victory.

But Ike wanted an on-the-ground check. He sent General John O'Daniel to Indochina on a fact-finding mission. Dien Bien Phu: What was the situation there? Who was winning? The general returned with a very optimistic report: The fortress at Dien Bien Phu, he told Eisenhower, could "withstand any kind of attack the Viet Minh" was "capable of launching." Eisenhower was relieved. He was about to make a major decision, and he needed reliable information. But, as events unfolded, it was clear he did not get it.

Eisenhower had to decide whether to take the next big step in America's deepening involvement in Indochina. It just so happened that the French were at that moment pressing the president for the first time to undertake a direct combat role in Indochina. Up to this point, the United States had been sending military aid to the French. Truman had recognized the Bao Dai government and soon thereafter had even begun to send military aid directly to Bao Dai's ragtag army. But now the United States was being asked to face— and cross—the Rubicon. The French wanted twenty-five B-26 bombers and, more important, 400 Air Force personnel to fly and service them *in combat*. If General O'Daniel was right and Dien Bien Phu was not in danger, then Eisenhower could have rejected this unprecedented French request and kept the United States out of a direct combat role. But, not for the first time, he went against his better judgment—he decided to split the difference. He sent ten B-26 bombers and 200 Air Force personnel. The president, who knew from experience that "in for a penny" could quickly mushroom into "in for a pound," had just made a historic decision—and he knew it, and he was uncomfortable with it. He had lifted the lid on an American combat role in Vietnam, and he did so without congressional authorization. He neither asked for, nor got, a supporting resolution. He had criticized Truman for waging the Korean war without specific congressional authorization. Now he was beginning to do the same thing in Vietnam.

In February 1954, at a meeting with Republican senators, Eisenhower was put on the spot by Leverett Saltonstall, the rangy aristocrat from Boston. Why were American servicemen being sent to Indochina? Was the United States getting involved in another war when the last one, in Korea, was only just ending? No, Eisenhower insisted. Then, reluctantly, the president crossed another line. He lied to the senator. He said the pilots were not being sent to a combat zone, even though he knew that they could become engaged in the battle for Dien Bien Phu. Why else would bombers be sent to a combat zone except to bomb! "Don't think I like to send them there," Ike tried to explain, "but we can't get anywhere in Asia by just sitting here in Washington and doing nothing—my God, we must not lose Asia—we've got to look the thing right in the face."[6] He promised the senators that the planes and the pilots would be removed from Indochina by June 15, 1954. Eisenhower would not be the only president to mislead or lie to Congress to cover his actions in Indochina.

A month later, CIA director Allen Dulles brought two depressing bulletins to the president. The situation at Dien Bien Phu had suddenly worsened: The Viet Minh had launched a devastating assault against the French garrison.

Complicating matters, the French had decided to accept a Soviet proposal for a Geneva Conference about Indochina in April, even though they knew the United States opposed it. The French prime minister, Rene Pleven, tried to explain his government's decision by saying that "there was no longer the prospect of a satisfactory military solution." That being the case, Eisenhower wondered, why did the French keep asking for more military aid and now even troops? Why had they failed so abysmally in their effort to transform the anti-communist Vietnamese army into a legitimate fighting force? One reason was that the French had no respect for Vietnamese history or capacity, frequently belittling Vietnam as a "country, which, for 1,500 years, has never had any sovereignty," a phrase attributed to Foreign Minister Georges Bidault.

On March 23, 1954, the French Army chief of staff, Paul Ely, flew to Washington on an emergency shopping trip, assuming he would get a sympathetic hearing. He met with Eisenhower and John Foster Dulles and, unsurprisingly, requested additional military aid. He left dissatisfied with the president's response. After checking an extravagant listing of France's needs, which amounted in effect to France asking the United States to join the war in Indochina, Eisenhower nodded affirmatively to only one item: He agreed to send an unspecified number of C-119 Flying Boxcars to Indochina for the purpose of dropping napalm, "which would burn out a considerable area and help to reveal enemy artillery positions," but he stipulated a set of strict conditions on further U.S. involvement.

The conditions were:

—France had to grant full independence to Indochina, ending its colonial rule;

—Britain had to be part of any military operation in Indochina;

—Southeast Asian nations had also to be part of military operations;

—Congress had to grant "full and clear prior approval";

—France had to yield total authority to the United States for all future military operations in Indochina, including command of French combat troops; and, finally,

—France had to "prove" its dedication to this new arrangement, whatever that meant.

Eisenhower knew that most of these conditions could not be met: The French were not going to admit defeat in Indochina, nor to yield full operational command of their combat troops to the United States. The British were opposed to sending their exhausted armed forces to yet another battlefield.

And Congress (if asked, and it wasn't) would have little interest, if any, in authorizing another war in Asia—Korea was enough. So, why these conditions? Eisenhower needed political cover. He suspected that when Dien Bien Phu fell, his conservative Republican colleagues might begin to beat the drums for U.S. intervention in Indochina not only to spare France, a NATO ally, from further humiliation but also to save Southeast Asia from collapsing to communism; and he did not want to go that far. Eisenhower believed only in limited U.S. intervention. Like being only a little pregnant, he was to learn that limited intervention almost surely would lead to an all-out commitment to war. Moreover, he did not want to jeopardize the "standing of the United States as the most powerful of the anticolonial powers," and he refused to "engage the prestige of the United States," unless, as Secretary Dulles often said, the United States "expected to win." At the time, winning was not a realistic outcome.

As Dien Bien Phu was falling to Ho Chi-minh's forces, Eisenhower's National Security Council (NSC) drafted a battle plan to use nuclear weapons against the communists. NSC adviser Robert "Bobby" Cutler tried running it past the president. Eisenhower exploded. "You boys must be crazy," he said. "We can't use those awful things against Asians for the second time in less than ten years. My God!"[7] On an almost daily basis, the president's senior advisers—including his vice president, his NSC adviser, his chairman of the Joint Chiefs of Staff, his adviser on mutual security, and sometimes his secretary of state—would urge Eisenhower to bomb communist forces at Dien Bien Phu with atomic or conventional weapons, but he refused. Maybe only a wartime hero, who had once commanded Allied forces in World War II, could have withstood the pressure.

Eisenhower was well aware that his administration was filled with angry, impatient hawks ready to fly into the nearest war. His secretary of state, John Foster Dulles, always suspicious of China's ultimate intentions, pushed for American intervention in Indochina—but only under certain conditions. He explained: "If you are scared to go to the brink, you are lost."[8] The chairman of the Joint Chiefs of Staff, Admiral Arthur Radford, also enjoying life on the brink, proposed not just intervention but the use of nuclear weapons. In his actions, the chairman went even further. He reached a private understanding with French general Ely, later called "Operation Vulture," for a massive air strike against communist forces at Dien Bien Phu, including the use of two or three atomic bombs.[9] Radford and Ely both assumed that the president, though reluctant, would ultimately give his blessing to such an attack, once it became clear that the communists were on the edge of victory. Radford was wrong. Eisenhower killed Operation Vulture, saying such an air strike, without clear congressional approval, would be "completely unconstitutional and indefensible." The president listened to his advisers but walked his own path. "Without allies and associates," the commander-in-chief told his staff, "the leader is just an adventurer, like Genghis Khan."[10] For a long time, many American scholars painted a portrait of Eisenhower as a detached leader more absorbed with his golfing scores than with policy deliberations. Not true, according to recently available evidence. In his first term, before he was struck by serious medical problems, he was deeply engaged in politics and diplomacy.

The siege at Dien Bien Phu was a big news story, and it dominated the front pages for fifty-six days, long enough to spark controversy on both ends of Pennsylvania Avenue and to engage the interest of two politicians who were already scanning the political horizon for a presidential run. (No account of the Dien Bien Phu siege is better than Bernard B. Fall's *Hell in a Very Small Place*, published by J. B. Lippincott Company in 1967.) Democratic senator John F. Kennedy of Massachusetts, usually a hawk, sounded remarkably dovish about the wisdom of sending more U.S. military aid to the French. "To pour money, materiel and men into the jungles of Indochina without at least a remote prospect of victory," he warned, "would be dangerously futile and self-destructive." Kennedy, who had visited Indochina two years earlier, spoke of the "futility of channeling American men and machines into that hopeless internecine struggle. . . . No amount of military assistance in Indochina can conquer an enemy that is everywhere and at the same time nowhere, 'an enemy of the people' which has the sympathy and covert support of the people."[11]

Vice President Richard Nixon, after first supporting vigorous action against communist expansion in Indochina, softened his stance, apparently finding safer political ground backing both sides of the argument. The Vietnamese people wanted their "freedom and independence," he said.[12] "Military strength, mutual defense treaties, military assistance operating together will not do the job alone," the vice president said, "unless the people are on your side." And he did not believe the "people" were on the side of the French. In fact, he added, with uncharacteristic candor, Ho Chi-minh seemed to be a "far more appealing . . . popular leader" than Bao Dai.[13] As the situation in Indochina worsened, however, most senators lacked the courage to strike an independent path and ended up following the president's lead.

On April 23, three days before the opening of the Geneva Conference, Secretary Dulles cabled Eisenhower. "France is almost visibly collapsing under our eyes," he said. "Dien Bien Phu has become a symbol out of all proportion to its military importance," but Dulles added the obvious—it was leading to "the collapse of French will." From Paris, Dulles sought aggressively to resurrect Operation Vulture. Whether by "massive B-29 bombing" or dropping "three atomic bombs," he urged decisive and immediate action, but Eisenhower still refused. "Armed intervention by executive action is not warranted," the president said. He then added a crucially important factor generally overlooked in the public anguish and political controversy surrounding the struggle for Dien Bien Phu: "The security of the United States is not directly threatened." Eisenhower kept his eye on the sparrow's fall. The loss of Dien Bien Phu was important, but not crucial to American security.

At Dien Bien Phu, the surrounded French garrison, led by General Henri-Eugene Navarre, fought bravely, but defeat was all but certain, probably within a week—unless, he pleaded, the United States dispatched immediate military assistance. He had shades of Operation Vulture in mind. With U.S. assistance, Navarre said, he was certain he could beat back the communist challenge. Without it, he warned, he would lose the battle, and France's colonial grip on Indochina would be loosened and eventually slip into oblivion. And then what? Eisenhower, the general, was sympathetic to Navarre's plea, but Eisenhower, the president, saw no immediate benefit for the United States to enter the Indochina war. He had put a toe into the Indochina war when he sent ten bombers and 200 pilots to help the French at Dien Bien Phu, but he would not put in his entire foot. An election loomed on the near horizon, and he felt the American people, so soon after the bloody conflict in Korea, wanted the benefits of peace.

The Birth of South Vietnam

On April 26, 1954, when the Geneva Conference opened, Eisenhower decided the United States would play an essentially passive role, an odd position for a great power. The United States was present, little more, as Britain, Russia, and China mediated a cease-fire between the French and the Viet Minh that "temporarily" partitioned Vietnam at the 17th parallel, creating two rump entities, neither with an established national identity. Ho objected to the partition, but Russia and China persuaded their stubborn partner to accept it. The Viet Minh would control the north, Bao Dai the south. Nationwide elections would take place in two years. Only naïve foreigners thought they would ever be held. Eisenhower had assumed, correctly, that the French would use the conference as diplomatic cover for their defeat in Indochina, effectively ending their colonial rule there, and he refused to sign or endorse the agreement. His secretary of state would not even shake hands with the Chinese foreign minister, Zhou Enlai, a slight the Chinese would not forget. Eisenhower already had other strategic plans, and they coalesced around the idea of "collective security," an idea Nixon had suggested in late 1953.

Because the president, like John Foster Dulles, did not believe that Dien Bien Phu was the linchpin of the anticommunist effort in Indochina, he looked for another way to continue the battle. He found a model in the North Atlantic Treaty Organization, a group of like-minded states, led by the United States, engaged in the global struggle against communism. On September 8, 1954, Washington and its allies created SEATO, the Southeast Asia Treaty Organization, an Asian "concert of nations," designed, interestingly, not to roll back communism, which would have been consistent with Republican Party policy, but rather to keep it from advancing any further; in other words, to "contain" communist expansion, which had been the Truman approach to managing the cold war. SEATO, unlike NATO, did not have a joint military command, because it did not have forces specifically assigned to it, and the language of its founding documents was deliberately vague. One reason was that SEATO, when it was founded, consisted of eight countries—the United States, France, Britain, Australia, New Zealand, the Philippines, Thailand, and Pakistan—each with its own needs and capacities. They came together as an anticommunist alliance, and when the United States deepened its military involvement in the Vietnam War, it served as an excellent rationale for action against North Vietnam.

The creation of SEATO fit a pattern of American pactomania: all over the world, it seemed, the United States was setting up anticommunist alliances and mutual and collective defense treaties, consistent with Truman's containment policy. After NATO was established, Japan was brought into this global anticommunist crusade in 1951; the Philippines also in 1951; ANZUS, consisting of Australia, New Zealand, and the United States in 1952; South Korea in 1953; and CENTO, or the Baghdad Pact, in 1955. SEATO and CENTO did not survive the tests of time, challenge, and change, but the others did.

At a news conference on April 29, 1954, NBC reporter Joseph Harsch asked Eisenhower to explain his use of the term "modus vivendi" to describe the new reality in Vietnam. The president said he was attempting to "steer a course between two extremes, one of which . . . would be unattainable, and the other unacceptable." The "unattainable" was a Bao Dai victory over Ho

Chi-minh, and the "unacceptable" was a communist victory over all of Vietnam. With divided Germany, Berlin, and Korea on his mind, he suggested: "The most you can work out is a practical way of getting along . . . one with the other, no more."[14] By this reasoning, Eisenhower shrewdly sidestepped the politically explosive charge that he had acquiesced in the loss of another Asian country to communism. Half was still noncommunist, he asserted in many different ways, and that half was to assume increasing importance for the rest of his time in office. But that "half" was not really a nation; it was more a geographic entity with a flag. What gave it a special distinction was that the United States was slowly becoming its benefactor, its spokesman, its shield against North Vietnam.

Subtle but important changes in American policy flowed both from the results of the Geneva Conference and the founding of SEATO, which the Senate approved and Eisenhower eventually signed in February 1955. First, the United States began to treat what the Geneva Conference called "the free territory under the jurisdiction of the State of Vietnam" as a separate country, which it had never done before. Thus, in official American parlance, was "South Vietnam" born. "Free territory" was an expression carrying heavy freight in official Washington. It meant membership in the "free world"—the country in question deserving the honor and support such membership entailed. Second, American economic and military aid would henceforth be sent directly to "South Vietnam," rather than through French middlemen, as though by this new method of delivery a new nation was consecrated.

Then, because every new "nation" needed a new leader, Bao Dai anointed Ngo Dinh Diem, a cranky, clannish, Catholic politician, whom he detested, to be the new premier of South Vietnam. As an apparent sign of his confidence in the survivability of South Vietnam, Bao Dai left for exile on the French Riviera. Diem proved tough to manage, and the U.S. Embassy in Paris circulated the rumor that Diem was really a "Yogi-like mystic, [who] appears too unworldly and unsophisticated to be able to cope with the grave problems and unscrupulous people he will find in Saigon."[15] Nevertheless, for many American politicians, including the respected Democratic senator from Montana, Mike Mansfield, Diem was seen as the "George Washington" of his country. The French, who knew Diem, objected to his arbitrary rule, but they no longer had the power to contest America's newly dominant role in Vietnam. Diem was now America's client. That Francis Cardinal Spellman of New York also embraced and blessed him added to the special halo of legitimacy that quickly glowed around this spoiled scion of Saigon's aristocracy. The Catholic

Church was a powerful force supporting Diem and South Vietnam. If the United States had chosen to play a more active role in Geneva, it might have been able to set up a better governing arrangement for Vietnam. Unfortunately, Washington knew little about the corrupt world of Vietnamese politics and never seemed eager to learn anything. The French in those days described Saigon as a "panier de crabes," a "basket of crabs," each struggling for power, each associated with a different power center, such as the new prime minister Diem, the old emperor Bao Dai, the religious sects of the Cao Dai and Hoa Hao, the Mafia sect of Binh Xuyen, and the disjointed parts of the Vietnamese army. It was a mess, and the United States now owned it, though Eisenhower was uncomfortable with the new arrangement. He tried, in effect, to limit American ownership, but he failed.

On October 23, 1954, Eisenhower sent Diem a private letter of support, later cited by President Lyndon Johnson as the "start" of America's "commitment" to defend South Vietnam. Actually, it was more a hope on Eisenhower's part that a U.S. aid program, properly administered, could become the basis for a new bilateral relationship. He began by expressing his satisfaction that the United States was able to move and resettle "several hundred thousand loyal Vietnamese citizens" fleeing the North Vietnamese "political ideology which they abhor." He then crafted his vision of an "intelligent" American aid program that can "assist Vietnam in its present hour of trial, provided that your government is prepared to give assurances as to the standards of performance it would be able to maintain in the event such aid were supplied."[16]

Clearly Eisenhower had been briefed on Diem's many shortcomings, including corruption at every level of governance. "The purpose of this offer is to assist the Government of Vietnam in developing and maintaining a strong, viable state, capable of resisting attempted subversion and aggression through military means," the letter stated. "The Government of the United States expects that this aid will be met by performance on the part of the Government of Vietnam in undertaking needed reforms." Eisenhower had been told about the pervasive graft in Diem's family, but he had no way around this Mafia-like clan. Diem, who now controlled the levers of power in Saigon, assured Eisenhower that he would open a broad program of reform, and Eisenhower had little choice but to take him at his word. In Eisenhower's pleas and in Diem's promise were early indications of what was to become an American "commitment" to defend the "Government of Vietnam," but at the time Eisenhower was still trying to contain the expanding boundaries of the commitment.

On January 1, 1955, the U.S. Military Aid and Advisory Group, known as MAAG, took over the training and equipping of the South Vietnamese army from the French, who were delighted to shed this responsibility. By the end of 1955, the French withdrew all their troops. A succession of senior American officials began descending on Saigon, filling each visit with wildly exaggerated praise of Diem and his government, even though several, in private venues, expressed strong reservations. "The militant march of communism has been halted," proclaimed Nixon after conferring with Diem in Saigon. Usually a shrewd judge of foreign entanglements, Nixon must have known that his optimism was little more than boiler-plate jargon for the accompanying press corps, reporting his optimistic anticommunist melody to his GOP base at home. Another victory for the United States! Another victory for the Republican Party's management of global affairs! Hooray!

But these words conveyed more than misleading political bombast; they also produced diplomatic consequences utterly unforeseen. They were often interpreted by diplomats around the world as the solemn policy and pledge of the United States. And one consequence was that in the aftermath of the French collapse in Indochina, the United States inherited the role of protector of Western interests in the area. Slowly but surely, the Eisenhower administration embraced its new responsibilities in Vietnam with an odd enthusiasm more innocently attuned to the needs of American politics than to the complex realities of postcolonial Vietnam. Diem had no interest, for example, in the nationwide elections promised in Geneva. Nor, in fact, did the United States. Both Diem and Eisenhower suspected that if there were nationwide elections, the communists would win. Because Eisenhower had reluctantly tied America's fortunes in South Vietnam to the one-man rule of Diem, he could entertain no alternatives to Diem, who threw his political opponents into prison or killed them.

U.S. officials embraced Diem with varying degrees of enthusiasm and sincerity, but the effect was the same. Every year, Washington sent hundreds of millions of dollars in military aid to Diem's army of 150,000 troops. Eighty-five percent of their salaries, equipment, and training came from the U.S. Treasury. In addition, seven hundred U.S. military advisers were sent to South Vietnam to train Diem's soldiers, but their effort had only minimal effect. Corruption was as endemic to Saigon's military as it was to its society and politics. And despite American help in villages throughout South Vietnam, the communist insurgency was gaining strength in 1957 and 1958—roads were being cut, bridges blown up, local officials assassinated—and Diem could find no way to blunt its advance. His regime was embarrassingly ineffective; yet the United States tightened its embrace of it.

For example, on May 8, 1957, Eisenhower himself stood under a hot sun at Washington's National Airport to greet Diem, who had accepted an official invitation for a state visit. Normally, the greeting would have been at the White House. The visiting leader of South Vietnam was arriving for a four-day festival of lavish receptions and meetings, none more spectacularly staged than his address to a joint session of Congress. Everywhere Diem was hailed as a "tough miracle man" and "savior" of his country. He had, after all, survived since 1954. Few members of Congress questioned his rule; in fact, except for one hearing, devoted to alleged corruption in the management of American aid to Saigon, it's an amazing fact that Congress never met, formally or informally, to discuss and help formulate U.S. policy in Vietnam. Whether Republican or Democratic, no senator or representative rose to oppose Eisenhower's policy in South Vietnam. No one asked about Congress's power to authorize the use of American forces in Indochina. Having approved of SEATO's broadly defined mission in Southeast Asia, Congress apparently felt it had done its duty and could now hide behind the president's skirt.

For several tense months in 1956 and 1957, Eisenhower also had to focus on the consequences of a war in the Middle East, involving two close NATO allies, France and Great Britain, and an anxious friend, Israel. The Suez Crisis was brought to an end only when Eisenhower, in a series of diplomatic exchanges with Israeli prime minister David Ben-Gurion in early 1957, took the unprecedented step of committing the United States to helping Israel in the event of a similar crisis in the future. In this case, as in so many of Eisenhower's actions in Vietnam, Congress was not consulted.

"The Clack and Rattle of Falling Dominoes"

On April 4, 1959, Eisenhower, scanning the strategic horizon in Southeast Asia, delivered a major speech at Gettysburg College in Gettysburg, Pennsylvania, in which he unmistakably linked America's "national interests" to the survival of South Vietnam as a free and independent nation. This commitment had been implied in the bilateral relationship for almost a decade, but here for the first time it was publicly pronounced by an American president to be the policy of the nation. Clearly and carefully, it tied America's security to South Vietnam's survival, one unmistakably linked to the other. There were distant echoes of Munich in Eisenhower's message, but there were also more recent memories of China going communist, and then intervening in Korea, of the Soviet Union becoming a nuclear power and extending its domain over Eastern Europe, of the world being split into two spheres, one free, the other communist, of a cold war creating new dangers in every corner of the world. Eisenhower, like other presidents of his era, tended to hear dominoes falling, one after another, and he did not want to hear any falling on his shift. Back in 1954, he had spoken of the 'falling domino' principle: "You have a row of dominoes set up, you knock over the first one, and what will happen to the last one is the certainty that it will go over very quickly."[17] Listen to his words now—to the context and rhythm of this speech:

> "Because of the proximity of large communist military formations in the North, Free Vietnam must maintain substantial numbers of men under arms. . . .
>
> "Unassisted, Vietnam cannot at this time produce and support the military formations essential to it, or, equally important, the morale, the hope, the confidence, the pride—necessary to meet the dual threat of aggression from outside and subversion within its borders.
>
> "Still another fact! Strategically, South Vietnam's capture by the Communists would bring their power several hundred miles into a hitherto free region. The remaining countries in Southeast Asia would be menaced by a great flanking movement. The freedom of 12 million people would be lost immediately and that of 150 million others in adjacent lands would be seriously endangered. *The loss of South Vietnam would set in motion a crumbling process that could, as it progressed, have grave consequences for us and for freedom* [italics added].
>
> "Vietnam must have a reasonable degree of safety now—both for her people and for her property. Because of these facts, military as well as economic help is currently needed in Vietnam.
>
> "We reach the inescapable conclusion that *our own national interests demand some help from us in sustaining in Vietnam the morale, the economic progress, and the military strength necessary to its continued existence in freedom*" [italics added].[18]

This speech, much more than the letter of support he had sent to Diem in 1954, effectively tied America's "own national interests" to the survival of Vietnam as a "free," anticommunist bastion in Southeast Asia. This was the "inescapable conclusion" Eisenhower had reached. When a popular wartime hero and two-term president reached such a conclusion, which of his successors had the courage to say he was wrong and demand a change in policy? None, as it turned out. Which journalist had the courage to explain what had just happened? None, as it turned out. The journalists were in Ike's hip pocket.

In 1954, the connection between the United States and South Vietnam came as easy rhetoric. By 1959, it was becoming the stuff of policy, already sanctified by American casualties: 108 killed, 486 wounded. The accepted wisdom of the day was that as a domino South Vietnam would not be allowed to fall. That it would fall four administrations later was, at the time, an unimaginable consequence of the gradually deepening American engagement in Southeast Asia. If the struggle in Vietnam were reduced simply to a military struggle, the result would have been foreordained. With a degree of arrogance typical of the time, neither Eisenhower nor his immediate successors believed that the United States could possibly lose in Vietnam. With American military supplies and training, the South Vietnamese army, they assumed, would carry the day. And if, armed and determined, South Vietnam still could not prevail, the United States had only to come out of the shadows, flex its muscles, growl once or twice, and if the enemy did not flinch, run and hide, then the United States would crush it. It was not within America's mental horizon to entertain the possibility that, once engaged, the United States could actually lose the war.

Nixon, who was already looking toward the 1960 presidential campaign, picked up the theme of the Eisenhower speech and explained the importance of South Vietnam as a fragile domino that, if allowed to fall, would endanger all of Asia, including Japan. Domino visions were everywhere. "If Indochina falls, Thailand is put in almost an impossible position," he told a radio audience in 1959. "The same is true of Malaya. . . . If Indochina goes under Communist domination, the whole of Southeast Asia would be threatened, and that means that the economic and military security of Japan will inevitably be endangered also."[19]

Kennedy and Johnson, in their time, also pledged their allegiance to the domino theory of history, as though it were beyond questioning. As president, Kennedy told a television interviewer: "I believe it. I believe it. I think that the struggle is close enough. China is so large, looms so high just beyond the frontiers, that if South Vietnam went, it would not only give them an improved geographic position for a guerrilla assault on Malaya but would also give the impression that the wave of the future in Southeast Asia was China and the Communists. So I believe it."[20]

Johnson went even further. "The battle against communism must be joined in Southeast Asia with strength and determination to achieve success there," he stated starkly, "or the United States, inevitably, must surrender the Pacific and take up our defenses on our own shores. Asian communism is compromised and contained by the maintenance of free nations on the subcontinent. Without this inhibitory influence, the island outposts—Philippines, Japan, Taiwan—have no security, and the vast Pacific becomes a Red Sea."[21] Johnson then added the absurdly hyped description of Diem as "the Winston Churchill of Southeast Asia," a description that later he hoped people would forget. Slowly, through expanding rhetoric, no journalistic inquiry, little-to-no congressional debate, and no public stirring, the United States was binding itself to Vietnam—and its political leadership.

Eisenhower was a World War II hero, a general who had commanded allied forces in Europe; Kennedy was "the best and the brightest," representative of a new wave of forward-looking American politicians and public officials; Johnson was a superior manipulator of congressional politics, an astute judge of power. And yet all three presidents, when confronted with the dilemma of South Vietnam, could come up with nothing more sophisticated than the two simplistic, sound-bite choices they had set before themselves and the nation: either to defeat communism in South Vietnam or to fight the last battle for American freedom on the California shores. They substituted dominoes for serious deliberation. They succumbed to a depressing set of strategic nightmares, none more alarming than if China could fall to communism, then so too could the rest of Asia. They had become bewitched by the ghostly clack and rattle of falling dominoes. When, in fact, South Vietnam did collapse to communism in April 1975, the neighboring dominoes, Thailand, Malaysia and Indonesia, not only did not fall but—height of ironies!—the victorious North Vietnamese reached out for trade deals and diplomatic relations with their defeated enemy.

CHAPTER FOUR

KENNEDY

The Coup That Failed

"To pour money, materiel and men into the jungles of Indochina without at least a
remote prospect of victory would be dangerously futile and self-destructive."
—SENATOR JOHN F. KENNEDY, 1954

ON JANUARY 19, 1961, when Dwight D. Eisenhower, the last of the presidents born in the nineteenth- entury, was preparing to yield power to John F. Kennedy, the first of the twentieth-century presidents, he spoke a language both used and understood. It was the language of the cold war. For more than an hour, Eisenhower shared the secrets of presidential power with Kennedy, who, in one day, at age 43, would become the second youngest president in American history. When they were finished, trade secrets disclosed and presumably absorbed, the two men walked from the Oval Office into the Cabinet Room, where senior advisers from the outgoing and incoming administrations waited for them to lead the careful choreography of political transition in a democracy. Whether of the old guard or the new, all of the advisers shared essentially the same view of the world and of America's place in it. The cold war dominated their calculations. The Soviet Union led an empire of communist countries, all dedicated to an ideological doctrine aimed at global conquest. The United States had a solemn obligation—indeed, a commitment—to meet this existential challenge and defeat it, even in such faraway places as Southeast Asia. Freedom itself depended on American resolve, on America's word.

If there was a difference between the old and the new, it was that the outgoing officials were tired—some had been in office for eight years and desperately needed a break—and the incoming officials were bursting with vigor and enthusiasm: "action intellectuals," as they were called, ready for any challenge. One of them, historian Arthur M. Schlesinger Jr., later remembered: "Euphoria reigned; we thought for a moment that the world was plastic and the future unlimited."[1] Journalist David Halberstam described them, in a book, as "the Best and the Brightest." "A remarkable hubris permeated the entire time," he wrote.

At the very top of their list of foreign policy problems, composed by two staffers representing the two sides, was not Berlin, which Soviet leader Nikita Khrushchev described as "a bone in my throat;" not Cuba, ninety miles off the Florida coast; not the celebrated "missile gap," a major topic in the presidential debates of 1960; not the dangerous contest for power in the Congo—at the very top of their list was the "deteriorating situation in Southeast Asia." And, interestingly, the focus was not on Vietnam but on Laos. According to notes taken by Clark Clifford, who had been an aide to President Harry Truman and served as an adviser to Kennedy: "President Eisenhower said, with considerable emotion, that Laos was the key to the entire area. He said that if we permitted Laos to fall, then we would have to write off all of the area. He stated that we must not permit a communist takeover. . . . It was imperative that Laos be defended. He said that the United States should accept this task with our allies, if we could persuade them, and alone if we could not."[2]

When Eisenhower and Kennedy met earlier on December 6, 1960, to discuss the transition, they "hit the high spots," as Eisenhower noted in his official account: "Berlin, the Far East and Cuba," but he never specifically mentioned Laos.[3] Why in one meeting he did not mention Laos and why in the follow-up meeting six weeks later he spoke of it as Kennedy's most urgent task has never been explained. Nothing of significance happened in Laos from December 6 to January 19.

"Alone if we could not." In 1954, Eisenhower had promised economic and military aid to Vietnam's leader, Ngo Dinh Diem, on the assumption that it would be properly administered and the communist challenge would be met and defeated. In 1959, Eisenhower had gone considerably further, stating in a public address that the "national interests" of the United States were linked to the survival of a free and independent South Vietnam. Now, in an amazing escalation of the rhetoric of commitment, though conveyed confidentially, he informed the new president that the United States should "defend" Laos, a neighbor of Vietnam in what used to be French Indochina, and, if necessary, do it "alone."

Kennedy asked how long it would take to move a division of American troops to Laos. Two weeks, if the troops were moved from the United States, he was told; obviously less time, if they were already in the Pacific. Kennedy asked no other questions, but he was, national security adviser Walt W. Rostow later reported, "profoundly shaken" by "Ike's recommendation."

Departing secretary of state Dean Acheson had warned Eisenhower eight years earlier about communist dangers in Southeast Asia, and now Eisenhower was warning Kennedy about the need to go it "alone," if need be, to defend Laos.

One reason for Kennedy's strong reaction was his recollection of a chilling speech delivered a few weeks earlier, on January 6, by Nikita Khrushchev. The ebullient Soviet leader had mentioned Cuba and Berlin, two prominent trouble spots, but he focused primarily on what he termed "wars of national liberation." Because both superpowers possessed nuclear weapons, the working assumption in both Washington and Moscow was that "world wars" and "local wars" were too dangerous for either country. "The living would envy the dead," Khrushchev once said of the aftermath of a nuclear war. But, he went on, "uprisings of colonial peoples against their oppressors," which often developed into "guerrilla wars," would be supported "wholeheartedly and without reservation" by the Soviet Union. In the Soviet leader's mind, then, such "guerrilla wars" were not only acceptable to the Soviet Union; they would be supported by the Soviet Union. "They march in the vanguard of the peoples fighting for liberation," Khrushchev added with the rhetorical flourish heard often in communist propaganda. Where might these "wars of national liberation" occur? He mentioned three places: Cuba, Algeria, and—Vietnam.

Khrushchev had Kennedy's attention. The new president read the speech over and over again—in his office, at Cabinet meetings, at dinners with friends, alone. Sometimes he read it aloud, and then asked his aides to comment. Walt Rostow opined that this new kind of warfare was an "international disease . . . designed, initiated, supplied and led from outside an independent nation." Up to this point, wars had been fought between or among states; now Khrushchev was introducing a new concept: Guerrilla groups could be formed in one state but could fight in another, functioning in a hazy zone above the politics of their hosts in blatant disregard of national boundaries or obligations.

Dean Rusk, the new secretary of state, essentially agreed with Rostow's opinion. Ever since his Rhodes Scholar days at Oxford in the 1930s, Rusk had told friends that if Mussolini had been stopped in Ethiopia, or Hitler in the Sudetenland, World War II could have been avoided. And, by this reasoning, if Ho Chi-minh could now be stopped in Laos, or Vietnam, World War III might be avoided. "I am not the village idiot," Rusk exploded during one meeting. He understood there were profound differences between the Sudetenland and South Vietnam, but he believed deeply that aggression by any other name was still aggression and that it had to be stopped. Rusk had long ago accepted the power and logic of Eisenhower's recommendation that the United States might have to apply force to stop the spread of communism in Southeast Asia.[4]

Though, as a senator, Kennedy had entertained doubts about an American commitment to the defense of South Vietnam, believing all of Indochina ought to be free and independent of French colonial rule, clearly as president he did not have the courage of his doubts. Nor, for that matter, did fortune smile kindly on his opening months in office. There were obvious questions about whether this young senator could master his new responsibilities as president. Berlin was a danger of migraine dimensions. The Congo, the dark giant in the heart of Africa, was a new playing field of superpower competition. The Bay of Pigs invasion of Cuba, which Kennedy had sanctioned, proved to be a disgrace and a disaster. And, now, there was the baffling problem of landlocked Laos: Should the president send American troops to Laos, as Eisenhower had recommended? Or should he push for the neutralization of the country, which could lead to a communist takeover? Neither course was inviting.

Two of his closest advisers—Rostow and General Maxwell Taylor—supported the thrust of Eisenhower's recommendation: They urged Kennedy to intervene militarily in Laos if the Pathet Lao communists resumed their attacks. That struck Kennedy as wrong, muddle-headed, and highly dangerous. He did not want to openly challenge Eisenhower on Laos, but he instinctively objected to sending American troops to Indochina. He had questions for which there were no apparent answers. What would Khrushchev do? Would Laos become one of his "wars of national liberation"? At a White House meeting, Kennedy quoted French president Charles de Gaulle as warning "with feeling" that the United States should not send combat troops to the Asian mainland, and he emphasized "the reluctance of the American people and of many distinguished military leaders to see any direct involvement of U.S. troops in that part of the world."[5] But then what should he do? Showing political courage by not embracing Eisenhower's recommendation, Kennedy decided to negotiate: The United States would not fight for Laos, but it would negotiate energetically for the neutrality of Laos. He got British prime minister Harold Macmillan to persuade Eisenhower to sit tight and await the outcome of the negotiation before expressing his unhappiness, and he arranged for retired general Douglas MacArthur to lecture congressional leaders on the inadvisability of deploying American troops to Indochina.

In April 1961, the United States joined the Soviet Union, China, and other major players in Geneva; this time, different from their negotiations in 1954, their subject was not Vietnam; it was the future of Laos. It took more than a year of negotiating, but, in June 1962, they reached the only agreement all the parties could accept: A coalition government would be created in Laos. It would be neutral, and no foreign military bases or forces would be allowed. Everyone in Washington knew that "coalition" was a dirty word, widely interpreted as a slippery step toward a communist government. Kennedy argued that it was either a coalition government, which had the advantage of buying time, or a war possibly involving American troops, and no one in Kennedy's Camelot wanted to send American troops to fight in Southeast Asia. Coalition was Kennedy's concession to reality, his way of avoiding the charge that he had lost another Asian country to communism.

Within six months, the North Vietnamese and the Americans were violating the agreement with distressing but predictable regularity, both sides sending arms and advisers into Laos to help their allies. The communists also were using Laos to transship men and arms into South Vietnam. Neither side chose to raise a fuss: the Americans, because they didn't want a deeper involvement in Laos; the communists, because they were convinced that in time they would control Laos and soon thereafter Vietnam. In this way, an uneasy and unsatisfactory *status quo* was established, and it held, even though in private conversation in Geneva, Rusk kept warning Soviet foreign minister Andrei Gromyko that the United States was "deeply committed to South Vietnam and cannot and will not accept its destruction."[6] His thinking was that if Laos fell to the communists, after its time as a neutral state, then the North Vietnamese would likely move against South Vietnam, and he wanted Gromyko to know that that was a no-no.

Kennedy knew, after his Laos coalition concession and after the Bay of Pigs calamity, that he ran the serious risk of looking and acting weak. He felt he had to take a stand somewhere, and he chose South Vietnam. Defeat, he stressed to his staff, was not an option, though he refused to send troops to Vietnam to ensure victory. Again, as was the case repeatedly with Truman and then Eisenhower, when in doubt about a next step, add to the kitty. Kennedy launched an eye-catching aid program for South Vietnam in the spring of 1961. It showed Kennedy as an activist, an optimist, a can-do president. It caught Moscow's eye, because it was quickly criticized. It reassured Diem of Washington's backing. Soon Saigon's harbor was filled with cargo, transport, and war ships carrying more advisers, another 400 Green Berets, and an added $42 million in military and economic assistance. In a move with even deeper resonance, Kennedy ordered the CIA to organize commando raids into North

Vietnam in an effort to fire up the enthusiasm of the South Vietnamese armed forces and to throw the communists on the defensive. Kennedy once asked his NSC staff: "How do we change morale? How do we get [South Vietnamese] operations in the north? How do we get moving?"[7] Kennedy even persuaded SEATO to declare publicly that it would refuse to "acquiesce in [a] takeover of [South Vietnam by] . . . an armed minority . . . supported from outside. . . ."

In May, Diem assured a visiting Vice President Lyndon B. Johnson that his forces could now go on the offensive. Other Saigon officials spoke with similar optimism. But Diem's assurance proved to be of flimsy stuff. Within a few months, it was clear that it was not his forces who were going on the offensive; it was communist forces, striking almost at will throughout the country. According to the Pentagon, 58 percent of South Vietnam was already under communist control.

Kennedy imagined that if he could sit down with Khrushchev and explore the testy U.S.-Soviet relationship, they could both come up with logical ways of defusing global tensions. What he was to learn in June, at their first summit meeting in Austria's baroque capital, Vienna, was that logic did not travel between Washington and Moscow. For example, Kennedy raised Khrushchev's speech about "wars of national liberation." He did not dispute that such wars could exist—he had one in mind in South Vietnam—but he was hoping that they would not be allowed to interfere with the quest for better relations between the two superpowers. The president raised the subject of communist guerrillas in South Vietnam. "We do not believe they represent the popular will," he said.[8]

But, if Kennedy hoped such candor would strip away the ideological bark and open an opportunity for practical solutions to real problems, he was sadly mistaken. Khrushchev, showing ideological conviction and confidence in every cadence of his speech, stated boldly that the Soviets had to support such "wars of national liberation" because they were the only way "oppressed peoples" could overthrow "the yoke of colonialism." And he then warned the president that if the United States continued to meddle in such wars, it might inadvertently trigger the "terrible prospect of mutual destruction." Khrushchev seemed to be warning Kennedy that, if handled poorly, "wars of national liberation" could lead to nuclear confrontations.

Kennedy was shaken by the Vienna summit. His dreams of a better relationship with the Russians suddenly seemed terribly naïve. Looking ahead and thinking about Berlin, he told *New York Times* columnist James Reston that it was going to be a "cold winter," and Khrushchev told an aide that he had taken the measure of the new president and found him to be "impression-able" and "weak." (The aide was interpreter Viktor Sukhadrev, who conveyed Khrushchev's immediate impression of the Vienna summit to the author and presumably other reporters covering the event.)

Back at the White House, Kennedy began a major reassessment of his global policy. He concluded that if Khrushchev had indeed misjudged his mettle at the summit, he had to take strong, "visible" action to discourage the Russian leader from miscalculating his resolve to defend Western interests around the world, and not just in South Vietnam. He quickly bolstered the American military position in West Berlin, which was a serious move, and he ordered hundreds of U.S. military advisers in Laos, who had been pretending to be civilians, to put on their uniforms as a show of American determination. This last step was, as biographer Richard Reeves noted, "a costume change in a comic opera war."[9] It was not serious.

When Kennedy contemplated his next steps in South Vietnam, he realized that he had very little reliable information. Was Khrushchev right? Did his guerrilla fighters represent a determined majority of the people? Or were they a minority? How bad was the military situation? Who was the real enemy in South Vietnam? Was it the newly formed National Liberation Front, backed by North Vietnam? Was Diem capable of defending his regime? What could (and should) the United States do? Johnson had recently returned from Saigon with the pathetically simplistic judgment that Washington had either to "commit major United States forces to the area" or "cut our losses and with-draw." Or, as he later put it, "help these countries to the best of our ability or throw in the towel in the area and pull back to San Francisco and a 'Fortress America' concept." Such either-or talk irritated Kennedy. He was not about to "throw in the towel," nor did he think it advisable to "commit major United States forces." But, realistically, aware of the commitments made by former presidents, what could—should—he do?

In the summer of 1961, Kennedy went outside the "family" to seek the advice of Douglas MacArthur. He invited the former general to Washington. According to Robert Kennedy, MacArthur told senior staffers that "we would be foolish to fight on the Asiatic continent and that the future of Southeast Asia should be determined at the diplomatic table." Aide Kenneth O'Donnell remembered a meeting between Kennedy and MacArthur. "There was no end to Asia," the general told the president, "and even if we poured a million American infantry soldiers into that continent, we would still find ourselves outnumbered on every side." Alexis Johnson, the deputy undersecretary of state, was skeptical of MacArthur's judgments. "Nevertheless, it made a very deep impression on the president," he said. "I think that for the rest of the time that he was in office this view of General MacArthur's . . . tended to dominate very much the thinking of President Kennedy with respect to Southeast Asia."[10]

A few months later, in the fall of 1961, Diem interrupted the president's deliberations to confess that his troops were on the defensive, the result of a tripling of communist attacks from north to south. Out of desperation, not desire, he requested a mutual defense treaty with the United States, which he was unlikely to get, and the dispatch of U.S. combat troops to South Vietnam, which was then under consideration. Before reaching any decision, the president sent General Taylor, by then chairman of the Joint Chiefs of Staff, and Rostow of the NSC, two of his closest advisers, to Southeast Asia for a detailed investigation of the growing crisis. They concluded after a two-week journey that South Vietnam was the essential domino and that it was in deep trouble—that "if Vietnam goes, it will be exceedingly difficult if not impossible to hold Southeast Asia."[11] Specifically, they recommended not only a boost in the number of U.S. military advisers but, for the first time, the dispatch of 8,000 U.S. combat troops plus three squadrons of helicopters manned by American pilots. Though their recommendation could be considered radical (there had never been U.S. combat troops in South Vietnam), Defense Secretary Robert McNamara startled everyone by belittling the 8,000-troop recommendation. To show "we mean business," McNamara proposed sending six U.S. divisions, or roughly 200,000 men.

Kennedy was shocked by McNamara's proposal. He rejected it, instituting, by presidential decision, what national security adviser McGeorge Bundy later called his "no-combat-troop policy."[12] The idea of a rapid escalation of American troops in Vietnam was, to Kennedy, repugnant and unwise. Ever since he visited Vietnam in the early 1950s, he believed that a foreign army could not win a colonial war, whether it was a French army or an American one. "The troops will march in, the bands will play, the crowds will cheer," he told Schlesinger, and "then we will be told we have to send in more troops. It's like taking a drink. The effect wears off, and you have to take another."[13] Journalist Stanley Karnow, who wrote a classic work on Vietnam, believed that the president's restraint was, in fact, "illusory." By this time, he wrote, the United States was already committed, at least by presidential rhetoric, to the defense of South Vietnam. Kennedy confided to Rostow: "I can't take a 1954 defeat today," referring to the French defeat at Dien Bien Phu and suggesting that he might have a different view in a second term.[14] He might even consider pulling out.

The president's advisers broke essentially into two groups. One believed that if the United States intended to save South Vietnam from a communist takeover, which was Kennedy's stated aim, it would have to send a substantial combat force to do the job—and the sooner the better. The others argued logically that if the United States could accept the likely establishment of a coalition government in Laos, then it could accept the same negotiated outcome in South Vietnam—and the deployment of American troops would then become unnecessary.

Taylor and Rostow, joined by Rusk and McNamara, the secretaries of state and defense, built their argument around the domino theory. They all recommended that "the United States should commit itself to the clear objective of preventing the fall of South Vietnam to Communism." If South Vietnam fell to communism, they went on, the rest of Southeast Asia "would move to a complete accommodation with Communism, if not formal incorporation, within the Communist bloc." They wrote: "We should be prepared to introduce United States combat forces" and, if necessary, "strike at the source of the aggression in North Vietnam."[15] Neither Rusk nor McNamara took any pleasure in recommending the dispatch of American troops to Vietnam, but they were absolutely persuaded that the march of communism in Asia had to be stopped and South Vietnam was the place to stop it.

Opposing this powerful quartet of presidential advisers were such old Democratic Party stalwarts as Chester Bowles, the under secretary of state; W. Averell Harriman, the former U.S. ambassador to Moscow who was chief negotiator at the Laos Conference in Geneva; and John Kenneth Galbraith, the Harvard economist serving as U.S. ambassador to India. Bowles, after checking the intelligence from Saigon, thought the United States was "headed full blast up a dead end street." Harriman had no confidence in Diem and sought to expand his Geneva assignment into a broader negotiation aimed at neutralizing all of Southeast Asia. Galbraith, in a series of private letters to Kennedy, was scathing in his criticism of Diem's "ineffectuality" and "unpopularity." Galbraith wrote: "He holds far too much power in his own hands, employs his army badly, has no intelligence organization worthy of the name, has arbitrary or incompetent subordinates in the provinces and, some achievements notwithstanding, has a poor economic policy."[16] Their criticism was endorsed by Sterling Cottrell, head of the State Department's Vietnam task force. "Since it is an open question whether [South Vietnam] can succeed even with U.S.

assistance," he wrote, "it would be a mistake for the United States to commit itself irrevocably to the defeat of the communists in South Vietnam." George Ball, then under secretary of state for economic affairs, told the president that if the United States committed itself to Diem, it would be obliged to send combat troops to South Vietnam, a point of view Kennedy dismissed as "crazy."[17] The underlying message of these advisers was that it would be smarter in Southeast Asia to negotiate than to fight.

With his back to the wall, not choosing to abandon the fight and yet unwilling to commit troops to the battlefield, Kennedy picked a middle position, not surprising for any leader facing a difficult choice. If the communists were to rely on "wars of national liberation," as Khrushchev had warned, then the United States would engage them not with combat troops but with a new and imaginative strategy called "counter-insurgency." Actually, it was not new; it was an American copy of British strategy in nearby Malaya, where economic and social reform took precedence over the military struggle, where the task of winning the "hearts and minds" of the peasantry was considered more important than winning a battle.

Counter-insurgency worked in Malaya, though it took a long time; but in South Vietnam, it was a problematic strategy from the beginning. For one thing, the Pentagon ran things in South Vietnam; counter-insurgency was clearly a job for the State Department. (Interesting fact: McNamara visited South Vietnam many times, Rusk never once.) The Malayan effort was run by British officers, not, as in South Vietnam, by a mix of American generals, CIA agents, and French-trained Vietnamese autocrats. The British political system gave the strategy enough time to bear fruit; the American system demanded quick solutions—it lacked patience for long engagements—and none was available on short notice. Finally, the enemy in South Vietnam was far more resourceful and determined than the enemy in Malaya; Ho Chi-Minh was an experienced, totally dedicated revolutionary who probably understood the essence of the counter-insurgency strategy better than Kennedy. At the end of the day, Kennedy's counter-insurgency effort in South Vietnam came up short, but he employed it with characteristic gusto. Counter-insurgency was absolutely worth the effort, he felt. As Bundy later explained: "It was felt that if you applied the techniques used in Malaya and really put your mind to it and operated with energy, you had a darn good chance. At the very least, you couldn't say you couldn't do it, and that the level of commitment you were undertaking, which was carefully limited, below what Taylor and Rostow recommended, had quite a sufficient promise of success so that it didn't make sense to quit."[18]

Kennedy's counter-insurgency plan was ambitious, and it was expensive. It involved forty separate projects of social, economic, and military reform. The plan was the brain child of Air Force brigadier general Edward Lansdale, an almost legendary figure who had a long record of supporting Diem, no matter his shortcomings. Lansdale's plan included setting up what were called "strategic hamlets," or small villages designed to protect the inhabitants from being influenced by the roving communist insurgents. It was the American way of going on the offensive without committing combat troops to the war. "We have to show him by deeds, not words alone," Lansdale stressed, speaking of the average peasant, "that we are his friend."[19] Kennedy was an early fan of the plan. He expanded CIA operations. He quadrupled the number of military advisers—from 700 to some 3,000 and by the time of his assassination to roughly 18,000.

One of those early military advisers was a 25-year-old Army captain, named Colin Powell, who was later to become chairman of the Joint Chiefs of Staff and secretary of state. He arrived in Saigon on Christmas day 1962. Like his buddies, he was gratified to be part of a U.S.-led, anticommunist crusade. "We were all so excited," he recalled many years later. "We believed that we were sent there to help the Vietnamese people against these bad communist Vietcong." At the time, he said, reflecting a uniquely American innocence about the world, "this was the noble thing to do, to help a country that was fighting the communists." Of course, the advisers knew very little about the country they were helping. "The South Vietnamese political situation was a mess, and we didn't know who these people were."[20]

Kennedy also sent many more helicopters, planes, and armored vehicles to South Vietnam. He significantly increased economic aid to Diem's government, which he seeded with so many advisers that reporters began to write about the "Americanization" of the war. And, most important, though the president continued to reject the idea of sending ground combat troops to South Vietnam (that's only a "last resort," he told McNamara), he did approve of American pilots flying combat missions out of Bienhoa, an air base north of Saigon. Kennedy thus ignored the danger that a small commitment could expand into a much larger one. (Galbraith, in one of his letters, advised: "Keep up the threshold against the commitment of American combat forces. This is of the utmost importance—a few will mean more and more and more. And

the South Vietnamese boys will go back to the farms. We will do the fighting.")[21] Obviously, Kennedy was taking a series of important half-steps, each
one deepening the American involvement in South Vietnam, but he refused to
sanction a full-scale U.S. combat role in Vietnam. Without the total engagement of the Vietnamese people and government, he kept telling his staff, the
United States could not win this war on its own.

By March 1962, it was apparent even to the usually optimistic Kennedy
crowd that the strategic hamlet program was not succeeding. The president
himself described the program cautiously as "very much up and down . . .
[making] it impossible to draw any long-range conclusions." That was a polite
way of saying it was not living up to its advance billing. One reason was that
Diem had no following among the Buddhist peasantry. He was an urban, corrupt, Catholic politician, who was engaged in widespread repression. Another
reason was a Vietcong offensive, which disrupted many of Diem's plans. A
third reason was a flowering of American news reporting on the complexity of
the entire war effort. David Halberstam of the *New York Times,* Neil Sheehan
of United Press International, and Malcolm Browne of the Associated Press
found official sources who pointed them to stories of government corruption
and of the oppression of Buddhist monks. Their stories, spread out on the
front pages of American newspapers, severely challenged White House spin
about "progress" in Vietnam. The president was furious, complaining to editors and publishers, but to little avail. Compounding his problem were stories
on the three big American networks showing pictures illustrating the corruption and oppression. Suddenly questions were raised on Capitol Hill and in
state houses around the country: What are we doing there?

The Joint Chiefs of Staff, which never had any confidence in the strategic hamlet program, pressured the president to send combat troops to South
Vietnam—the only way, the chiefs insisted, that the communists could be
stopped. During the Truman administration, they had opposed sending
troops, but during the Eisenhower administration they began to change their
minds. Call it arrogance or poor intelligence, but they now truly believed that
if the United States sent combat troops to South Vietnam, they would quickly
defeat the communists, establish a solid anti-communist regime, and then
they would be able to go home. Rusk and McNamara agreed with the Joint
Chiefs, but the Cuban missile crisis cut into their Vietnam calculations. For
a few months in the early fall of 1962, Kennedy faced an existential threat to
the United States from Soviet missiles discovered in Castro's Cuba. The possibility of a nuclear exchange with the Soviet Union was real, and Vietnam, by

comparison, shrunk to its proper dimension—a serious problem but hardly an existential threat. By the end of the year, when the president was again able to focus on Vietnam, he learned that the military situation there had worsened considerably and Diem was again asking for an infusion of American aid, including combat troops. Hadn't he seen this movie before? Was it possible, his political aides wondered, that a messy political crisis in South Vietnam could damage his re-election prospects?

Kennedy again decided he needed fresh intelligence. He sent Senator Mike Mansfield to Saigon. Kennedy respected the Montana Democrat and valued his advice. Mansfield returned with a blunt message, different from his earlier ones: He told the president that the United States was being sucked into a long and probably futile war. Political scientists labeled this "entrapment." Mansfield saw little evidence of progress, and he thought the United States ought to consider a coalition government in South Vietnam.[22] The president trusted NSC analyst Michael Forrestal and State Department official Roger Hilsman, both knowledgeable about Vietnam, and he sent them back to Saigon once more. They returned in January 1963 with the lukewarm assessment that the United States was "probably winning" but that the war would take "longer . . . [and] cost more in terms of both lives and money than we had anticipated."[23] By early 1963, Kennedy realized that the United States had poured hundreds of millions of dollars in economic and military aid into Diem's shaky regime, and, like Mansfield, he too saw little progress. He told a few of his closest friends that, maybe, after the 1964 election, assuming his re-election, he might begin pulling American advisers out of South Vietnam. Might. Much would depend on whether a pullout would lead to a communist takeover.

On May 8, 1963, the day many Vietnamese celebrated the birth of the Buddha, a problem of a distinctly less ethereal nature arose. Diem's police stupidly decided to enforce a previously ignored nationwide ban on the public display of religious flags. Buddhist monks protested the ban in the old imperial capital of Hue. Thousands of people joined them. The police asked them to disperse, and when the monks refused, the police fired wildly into the crowd, killing nine of them. Burning Buddhist discontent with the Diem regime boiled to the top. All over the country, in city after city, Buddhist monks in their saffron-colored robes demonstrated against their Catholic head of state. Reporters noticed that they were remarkably well organized. One Buddhist leader, Thich Tri Quang, briefed foreign journalists, produced a journal, and organized three-monk-cells in pagodas, not usually a place for political activity and agitation. He warned American officials: "The United States must either make Diem reform or get rid of him. If not, the situation will degenerate."[24] A national crisis seemed only days away.

At a busy intersection in Saigon, on June 11, an elderly monk named Thich Quang Duc sat down in the middle of the traffic, a small circle of monks and nuns gathered around him. He pressed his palms together in prayer. Then one of the other monks poured gasoline over him and still another ignited him with a lighter. As a crowd watched this self-immolation, new to American sensibilities but a traditional if extreme form of protest in Vietnam, a monk read a plea to Diem left by the dying, 66-year-old monk asking for "charity and compassion" for all religions. Pedestrians, overwhelmed by this fiery sight, prostrated themselves in reverence. Traffic stopped.

The AP's Browne, tipped off by a Buddhist friend, rushed to the scene with a camera. His photo of the burning monk quickly appeared on American television and in newspapers everywhere—proof, it any were needed, that South Vietnam was itself burning. In the next few weeks, other monks engaged in self-immolation. Anti-Diem demonstrations broke out all over the country. The Buddhist protest in one form or another was now the big story.

U.S. Embassy officials pleaded with Diem to seek some form of reconciliation with the Buddhists. They worried that the war effort was being adversely affected. Diem refused. His brother and closest collaborator, Ngo Dinh Nhu, who was in charge of security, argued that the protests in Hue, a center of Buddhist learning, had been inspired by the communists. Madame Nhu, Diem's arch sister-in-law, told one reporter that the recent run of Buddhist self-immolations amounted to nothing more than a "barbecue." She then added with a smirk: "Let them burn, and we shall clap our hands."[25] Her cruel and insensitive comments further inflamed the crisis and deepened the mutual suspicion between the United States and Diem's regime. The air was heavy with rumors of plots, coups, and assassinations.

In early July 1963, whether wittingly or not, Kennedy embarked on a treacherous path, discussing with several of his senior advisers the possibility of a coup d'état against Diem, not necessarily one that the United States would organize but one that Washington would not "thwart." ("Thwart" became the operative verb.) On the same day, perhaps coincidentally, a veteran CIA operator named Lucien Conein met in Saigon with an influential South Vietnamese general named Tran Van Don. They, too, discussed a possible coup. Don, representing a small number of rebellious generals, had a very specific question: "What will the American reaction be if we go all the way?" Conein had no answer, but he and Don agreed to meet again and again, constituting the only real link between the United States and the coup-plotters. At any time, Conein, on instructions, could have killed the plot, but he did not, and the secret anti-Diem scheming continued.

On August 21, Nhu's troops, known to be loyal to both him and Diem, attacked the Xa Loi pagoda in Saigon, the most prominent in the capital. The CIA, which had the job of tracking Nhu's tricky and unpredictable maneuvers, was totally surprised. Truckloads of heavily armed troops swooped down on the ornate pagoda in the dead of night, ransacked the place, and arrested 400 monks and nuns, among them the 80-year-old patriarch. In Hue, Nhu's troops also struck, but the monks and nuns there resisted the onslaught, barricading themselves into their pagoda, while thousands of townspeople gathered on the outside to protest against the Diem regime. Within hours, more than a thousand monks, nuns, students, and civic leaders were arrested in a nationwide crackdown, many battered and bruised while others were whisked away and never seen again. Presumably they were killed.

In Washington, Kennedy was furious and puzzled. Why this anti-Buddhist crackdown? And why now? He wondered whether Diem could any longer be trusted. Nhu, the brother, had to go—that was everyone's advice to the president. Hilsman, now head of the State Department's Far East bureau, proposed giving Diem one last chance to dispose of his brother, if at all possible. On August 24, after getting Kennedy's approval, he cabled Ambassador Henry Cabot Lodge Jr., a Republican from Massachusetts, newly appointed to the post, that Diem could hold on to his American backing, but only if he fired his troublesome brother; but if he refused to fire Nhu, then "we must face the possibility that Diem himself cannot be preserved."[26] Hilsman also told Lodge that the dissident generals could be assured of America's "direct support" for their planned coup if Nhu remained in power. This was later to be interpreted as a historic cable—the United States opening the door to a coup against the leader it had supported for ten years.[27]

The top echelons of the Kennedy administration were split on the wisdom of sending the August 24 cable. Hilsman had the support of State Department colleagues Harriman, Forrestal, and Ball, but Rusk's support was offered with conditions. Roswell Kilpatric, the deputy secretary of defense, gave his approval only after being assured that the president had cleared it. Vice President Johnson and CIA director John McCone strongly disapproved of the cable, as did General Taylor. When Kennedy, on Monday morning, opened a four-day review of his Vietnam policy, he was stunned by the obvious disarray among his top advisers. "My God," he confided to a friend, "my government is coming apart."

In Saigon, the generals refused to share the details of their plot with Conein. They feared betrayal at every corner—by other South Vietnamese generals not in on the plot, by American generals who disapproved of the plot, by one of their own. They wanted proof of American support, and proof in their minds would be a slowdown or a stop in U.S. aid to the Diem regime. Kennedy was not yet ready for such a step, but his ambassador in Saigon wanted to accelerate the plot to dislodge Diem from power, believing the longer he stayed in power, the more likely there would be a communist takeover. Lodge at first had been reluctant to join Hilsman's bandwagon, but soon he became one of its most ardent supporters.

On August 29, Lodge tried to push the president toward a final decision. In a cable, he wrote: "We are launched on a course from which there is no respectable turning back: the overthrow of the Diem government. . . . There is no turning back, because there is no possibility in my view that the war can be won under a Diem administration." He urged an "all-out effort" to encourage the dissident generals to "move promptly." Otherwise, he warned, Saigon could explode in anti-Diem violence that could bring a "pro-Communist or at best a neutralist set of politicians" to power. Lodge, sensing an administration reluctance to interfere in a client state's internal affairs, argued with passion that the United States had paid for the right to interfere. "Our help to the regime in past years inescapably gives us a responsibility that we cannot avoid."[28]

If Kennedy had been receiving reliable reports of genuine progress, as McNamara wanted him to believe was the case, then he would never have given his blessings, however vaguely phrased, to plans for an anti-Diem coup. But he had not been receiving such reports. Quite the contrary. Paul Kattenburg, a veteran of many years in the U.S. Embassy in Saigon, had just reported that anti-Diem sentiment in South Vietnam was so powerful that if the United States continued to back him, it would be forced to leave the country within six months. A better plan, he stressed, would be "for us to make the decision to get out honorably" and leave behind a coalition government. Nonsense, interjected Rusk, "we will not pull out . . . until the war is won." Another disturbing report (one of many on the subject) suggested that Nhu, with Diem's quiet backing, was trying to work out a political accommodation with the North Vietnamese, which, if implemented, could have undercut the entire American effort in South Vietnam. Such a deal could also have hurt Kennedy politically.

Already, in anticipation of the 1964 presidential campaign, Republicans who had been supporting the president's policy in Vietnam began criticizing it. Indecisiveness, Kennedy recognized, could be as harmful as defeat. No novice at hard-knuckled politics, Kennedy decided to back his Republican ambassador's recommendations. He gave Lodge full authority to cut American aid to Diem, however and whenever he chose.[29]

On September 2, Kennedy took advantage of a CBS television interview with Walter Cronkite to explain his policy to the American people and to the presidential palace in Saigon. "Unless a greater effort is made by the [Diem] government to win popular support," he did not believe the war could be effectively prosecuted. Diem, he added carefully, has "gotten out of touch with the people," and there had to be changes in "policy and personnel."[30] Kennedy did not specify what changes, but Diem suspected the president had him and his brother in mind. The anti-Diem generals read Kennedy's comments as encouragement to move forward with their planning.

Kennedy sent another fact-finding mission to South Vietnam, almost as if he didn't believe the reporting of the U.S. Embassy or of the U.S. Military Command. When in doubt, send another fact-finding mission—that seemed to be Kennedy's style. General Victor Krulak, who had worked for Taylor, and Joseph Mendenhall, who worked with Hilsman, spent four days there. They talked with many officials, American and South Vietnamese, and returned with different impressions: Krulak spouting optimistic claptrap about military progress, and Mendenhall concluding pessimistically that the Diem regime was near collapse. Kennedy listened and quipped: "You two did visit the same country, didn't you?"[31]

In late September, Kennedy, unable still to make up his mind, sent McNamara and Taylor to Saigon. They returned after ten days with a report riddled with compromises and contradictions. On the one hand, to flatter the U.S. military in South Vietnam, they raved about "great progress" in the field, even to the point of suggesting that 1,000 advisers could be pulled out of South Vietnam by the end of the year and predicting that the "bulk" of the troops could be withdrawn by the end of 1965. This prediction was clearly designed to help Kennedy prepare for his re-election campaign in 1964. On the other hand, they ripped into Diem's intransigence and raised the possibility that, as a form of punishment, the United States might begin to reduce its flow of aid to him—but not by much.[32]

And, on October 2, that was exactly what the United States proceeded to do. Kennedy ordered a series of "selective pressures" against Diem, each interpreted by the rebellious generals as a green light to proceed with their coup. A number of future economic aid shipments were cancelled. Threats were heard to cut military aid to Nhu's special forces unless they were redeployed out of the capital. The CIA station chief, considered too close to Nhu, was recalled. Finally, the Pentagon announced that 1,000 advisers would be withdrawn from South Vietnam by the end of 1963 and all advisers would be withdrawn by the end of 1965, provided the war continued to go well, which, in fact, was not the case. Kennedy conferred with congressional leaders, but he never asked them for a resolution authorizing his policy in South Vietnam. In fact, in this respect, his consultation with Congress had the appearance of a pro forma routine.

In this context, it was not at all coincidental that only a few days later, on October 5, General Don and Conein resumed their secret talks. They met in a dentist's office, not a likely spot for plotting a coup. The South Vietnamese general said his colleagues did not expect overt American support but hoped the United States would "not thwart" their coup. They also wanted a pledge of continued U.S. economic and military support, which was running at about $500 million a year, after they seized power.

Lodge sought and got Kennedy's approval for the convoluted formula that Washington "will not attempt to thwart" the coup, but Kennedy added, self-protectively, that the United States would not be directly involved in the coup. "While we do not wish to stimulate a coup," he stressed, "we also do not wish to leave the impression that the United States would thwart a change of government. . . . But we should avoid being drawn into reviewing or advising on operational plans, or any other act that might tend to identify the United States too closely."[33] Kennedy, in other words, wanted the coup, but he didn't want it to look as if he wanted the coup.

And yet, in high-level meetings with his advisers, Kennedy could not disguise his ambivalence about the buildup to the coup. He had many questions. Did the coup plotters have enough troops? Were they reliable? Responsible? Were they properly positioned? Was Conein really the only U.S. contact to the plotters? Might Diem still control enough troops in the capital to forestall a coup? Was the U.S. Embassy in Saigon organized to manage the aftermath of a coup? Were U.S. nationals in jeopardy? Kennedy wanted answers.

On October 25, national security adviser Bundy, in a long cable to Lodge, conveyed the president's anxieties and raised many questions, but his main message was that Kennedy did not want to "thwart a coup"—he just did not want to appear to be supporting a coup. He worried about "substantial possibility serious and prolonged fighting or even defeat," "important Saigon units still apparently loyal to Diem," "deeply concerned" from "operational standpoint," "badly need some corroborative evidence," "question of protecting US nationals at once arises," and "post-coup contingencies." Bundy shared Kennedy's fear that the Saigon coup could end up becoming another Bay of Pigs disaster. "We reiterate burden of proof must be on coup group to show a substantial possibility of quick success," he stressed. "Otherwise we should discourage them from proceeding since miscalculation could result in jeopardizing U.S. position in Southeast Asia."[34] In retrospect, it is clear that Kennedy and Bundy operated in an unreal world, as if they thought they could turn a coup on and off like a spigot of water, as if once the coup got started, they could still control the flow of events.

Lodge replied immediately, admitting that the risks were considerable but stating that delaying or stopping the coup would be to assume "an undue responsibility for keeping the incumbents in office."

On October 28, Conein was back for another visit with Don in the dentist's office. This time Don gave Conein the actual plans for the coup—which units would be moved where and when. He said he could give Conein only four hours notice. Conein informed Lodge, and Lodge informed the White House that the coup was "imminent."

On October 29, Kennedy showed clear signs of having second thoughts. He convened a National Security Council meeting. Taylor was furious about the coup planning. He distrusted Conein and thought Don was "either lying or playing both sides against the middle." He thought Lodge was fundamentally wrong on the war—"we are gaining in the contest," he asserted. "There is a basic difference apparently between the Ambassador's thinking and mine." Harkins, the U.S. military chief in Saigon, cabled his strong misgivings. "There are no generals qualified to take over," he warned. Robert Kennedy wondered if the coup "risks so much," was it worth supporting?[35]

Bundy, in another urgent cable to Lodge, reflected the deep anxiety so obvious at the NSC meeting. He raised the key question on everyone's mind: could the coup be stopped? The president, he wrote, was "deeply concerned." He left the confusing impression that the administration favored postponement or cancellation of the coup.

But, once again, Kennedy left the final judgment to Lodge. "If you should conclude that there is not clearly a high prospect of success, you should communicate this doubt to the generals in a way calculated to persuade them to desist at least until chances are better. But once a coup under responsible leadership has begun . . . it is in the interest of the US government that it should succeed."[36]

On November 1, just as Lodge sat down for a meeting with Diem, the coup began. It was 10 a.m. Diem told Lodge that he had heard reports of a coup. What had the ambassador heard? Lodge responded that he had heard nothing about a coup. He was lying. Then, after an exchange of diplomatic pleasantries, Lodge returned to the embassy for lunch and an afternoon nap.

At 4:30 p.m., Diem telephoned Lodge. He was clearly agitated. He informed Lodge that a coup was in fact under way, that it appeared to be succeeding, and he demanded to know the U.S. position. In diplomacy, there are times when a lie can be an ambassador's best answer.

Lodge again lied. He told Diem that he did not "feel well-enough informed to be able to tell you." It was 4:30 a.m. in Washington, he continued fatuously, and no one high in the government was available.

Diem replied: "I am a chief of state. I have tried to do my duty."

Lodge tried to sound sympathetic. "I admire your courage and your great contribution to your country." Then he added: "I have a report that those in charge of the current activity offer you and your brother safe-conduct out of the country if you resign." "Current activity" was the ambassador's way of referring to the coup.

Diem did not choose to pick up the resignation offer. "I am trying to re-establish order," he said, and hung up.[37]

The fighting continued into the night.

On November 2, at 3 a.m., Diem and his brother Nhu escaped from the presidential palace and fled to Saint Francis Xavier, a French church in the Cholon suburb of Saigon. There, as dawn approached, the two brothers realized that their situation was desperate. At 6 a.m., Diem telephoned Duong Van "Big" Minh, one of the rebel generals. He told Minh that he was prepared to negotiate. He would resign, he said, but only if his designated successor, the vice president, could take charge of the government. The generals conferred briefly and rejected Diem's condition. However, they agreed to allow Diem and Nhu to leave the country. At 6:30 a.m., when informed he could leave, Diem asked for the "honors due a departing president." No, replied the generals.

But now the rebel generals had a different problem, a tactical one. Once they held Diem and Nhu, where would they send them? And how would they get them there? They conferred with Conein, he with Lodge, and Lodge with the White House. The United States had no plane readily available, Conein was told, and the United States would not grant asylum to either brother. The United States was saying, in effect, that it no longer wanted to have anything to do with the brothers; they were now the coup leaders' problem. But if they could not be sent to the United States, where else? Arrangements would take time, and the generals would have to assume responsibility for their safekeeping while a destination was determined.

First, though, they had to transfer the brothers from the Cholon church to staff headquarters in Saigon. That tricky assignment went to a general, a major, and a captain. At the church, Diem and Nhu shook the general's hand and reluctantly climbed into an armored car. They drove toward Saigon. At a railroad crossing, they stopped. What happened then was that the major shot the brothers with an automatic weapon, the captain continued the twin assassinations by spraying them with bullets, and then he repeatedly stabbed their already dead bodies with a knife. When the assassins returned to staff headquarters, they saluted and declared: "*Mission accomplice.*"[38]

News of Diem's murder reached Kennedy while he was meeting at the White House with Taylor and a few other aides. The president jumped to his feet and, as Taylor later recounted, "rushed from the room with a look of shock and dismay on his face." Schlesinger remembered that moment, too. "He was somber and shaken," Schlesinger wrote of the president. "I had never seen him so depressed since the Bay of Pigs."[39] Kennedy thought he had a deal with the generals that Diem and Nhu would be overthrown but not killed. He imagined, naïvely, that the coup would be clean and contained and in the end reveal no American fingerprints.

On November 4, Kennedy dictated a private memo about the assassination, in which he admitted "we must bear a good deal of responsibility" for the coup. "I was shocked by the death of Diem and Nhu," he said. The president seemed torn by admiration for Diem, whom he called an "extraordinary character," and the "particularly abhorrent" way he was murdered. "While he became increasingly difficult in the last few months," the president continued, "nevertheless he held his country together, maintained its independence, under very adverse conditions." The question "now," Kennedy wondered, was whether the "generals can stick together" or whether the country will fall apart.[40]

The White House demanded a full explanation from Lodge. The ambassador commissioned Conein to talk to Minh. The general explained that Diem and Nhu both committed suicide. Conein said he did not believe the explanation, nor would anyone else. "There is a one-in-a-million chance that people will believe your story," Conein told Minh.[41] Perhaps for this reason neither the U.S. government nor the Saigon regime ever conducted an official, public inquiry into Diem's murder.

For a time, it was a popular murder. Nightclubs reopened, political prisoners were released from prison, official Diem portraits were torn up and burned, strategic hamlets were demolished, and Lodge invited the triumphant generals to a congratulatory party at the American Embassy.

Then, a few days later, the ambassador cabled the president that, in his judgment, the coup had been a Vietnamese affair that "we could neither manage nor stop after it got started. . . . It is equally certain that the ground in which the coup seed grew into a robust plant was prepared by us, and that the coup would not have happened as it did without our preparation." His conclusion: "The prospects now are for a shorter war."[42]

Kennedy was assassinated three weeks later, and the war continued for another eleven years.

CHAPTER FIVE

JOHNSON
"Let Us Continue"

"I am not going to lose Vietnam. I am not going to be the president who saw
Southeast Asia go the way China went." November 24, 1963

"I don't want to be known as a war president." Summer 1965
—LYNDON B. JOHNSON

"LET US CONTINUE," proclaimed the new president, Lyndon B. Johnson, two
days after John F. Kennedy had been assassinated in Dallas on November 22,
1963. What Kennedy had begun, Johnson would continue—and finish. He
saw himself as a tough Texan standing tall at the Alamo of America's Vietnam
policy; he did not want others to see him as a country bumpkin who knew
little about the world. Moreover, there was that "commitment," to which his
predecessors had pledged the nation. He was not going to be a president who
went back on his country's word.

"I am not going to lose Vietnam," he told Ambassador Henry Cabot Lodge
Jr. "I am not going to be the president who saw Southeast Asia go the way
China went."[1] Lodge had just briefed the new president on the situation in
South Vietnam. It was spinning out of control. Lodge emphasized that "if
we don't do something, it'll go under—any day."[2] With Kennedy, Lodge had
been moderately optimistic about post-coup Vietnam. With Johnson, just
weeks later, he had become decidedly pessimistic. It was the new president's
introduction to the uncertain intelligence and the fluctuating judgments of the
American brass in Saigon, many of whom knew little about Vietnam's history,
politics, culture, or religion.

Texas chronicler Ronnie Dugger explained that as Johnson began to consider his Vietnam options, two words from the 1930s kept "flashing" through
his mind—"Munich" and "appeasement."[3] He would have none of either.
The new president remembered that Kennedy, in one of his last public pronouncements on Vietnam, had stressed that "we are not there to see a war
lost." Johnson would not see it lost either. He knew that he had inherited "a

hell of a mess," as Defense Secretary Robert McNamara had told him, but he actually believed at the time that the United States could "win the war."[4] Unfortunately, no one urged the president to define what "winning" meant in a guerrilla war.

While it was true that Johnson had inherited the war, it was equally true that by the time he left office in January 1969, the war had become his. As Abe Fortas, a close friend and adviser, analyzed the president's early predicament: "Johnson pursued the Vietnam war because of Dwight Eisenhower's position and Kennedy's position."[5] They had both "committed" the United States to the defense of South Vietnam, and Johnson, the newest member of the president's Vietnam club, would not abandon what they had embraced as American policy.

In April 1965, during a talk at Johns Hopkins University, Johnson tried to explain his thinking. He raised the question—"Why are we in South Vietnam?"—and then answered in a broad cold war context. "We are there," Johnson said, "because we have a promise to keep. Since 1954, every American president has offered support to the people of South Vietnam. . . . Over many years, we have made a national pledge to help South Vietnam defend its independence. And I intend to keep that promise." It was a moral undertaking. "To dishonor that pledge," he went on, ". . . would be an unforgivable wrong." It would "shake the confidence" of people "from Berlin to Thailand" in the "value of an American commitment and in the value of America's word." For this president, "the central lesson of our time is that the appetite for aggression is never satisfied. To withdraw from one battlefield means only to prepare for the next. We must say in Southeast Asia—as we did in Europe—in the words of the Bible: 'Hitherto shalt thou come, but no further.'"[6] He invoked the Bible to restate a presidential "commitment" to resist communist expansion—in this instance, in South Vietnam.

As Johnson was to learn all too painfully, South Vietnam marched to its own drummer. It did not necessarily accommodate its destiny to the "word" or "commitment" of a U.S. president, nor to his plans or dreams. The assassination of South Vietnam's leader, Ngo Dinh Diem, three weeks before Kennedy's murder, opened a period of extreme instability, one general overthrowing another, while the Vietcong strengthened its position throughout the countryside. Johnson, who had not supported the coup, understood immediately that Diem's blood would forever stain America's hands. He knew that for a flickering moment before the coup, Kennedy had toyed with the notion of a "complete military withdrawal from Vietnam." A Boston aide, Kenneth

O'Donnell, quoted Kennedy as saying: "I'll be damned everywhere as a communist appeaser, but I don't care. If I tried to pull out completely now, we would have another Joe McCarthy red scare in our hands, but I can do it after I'm re-elected."[7] But, for Johnson, new to the presidency and pledged to continue Kennedy's policy, withdrawal was out of the question, and it was probably never a real option for Kennedy either, though a cottage industry has emerged in recent years focusing on the single question of whether Kennedy, in his second term, would have withdrawn from the Vietnam War. McGeorge Bundy, his national security adviser, and McNamara, his secretary of defense, later spoke confidently about his "no-combat-troop policy" in Vietnam, his determination to keep American combat troops off the Asian mainland. That might well have been his intention. But others have offered a more compelling case: that Kennedy would never have allowed South Vietnam to go communist on his shift! As a Democrat, mindful of a generation of Republican attacks on Harry Truman's "loss of China," Kennedy would have deepened the American involvement in Vietnam, not ended it. His rhetoric about the evils of communism and his decisions, however reluctantly made, to increase the number of military advisers in South Vietnam, to initiate commando raids into North Vietnam, to allow American pilots to fly combat missions out of Bien Hoa airbase—all suggested a president who would not allow America's word to be tarnished, nor its reputation to be damaged, by the collapse of a client state to the communists. Again, not on his shift.

In late December 1963, Johnson sent McNamara to South Vietnam for a hard look at the "mess" he had inherited from his now sainted predecessor. The defense secretary returned with a very depressing report. If the situation did not improve within ninety days, he told the president, it would "lead to a neutralization at best and more likely to a communist-controlled state."[8] A new president in office for less than two months, Johnson was not of a mind to listen to such news. He wanted to focus on "the woman I really loved," as he affectionately termed his plans for a "Great Society," his ambitious domestic agenda, and not on that "bitch of a war on the other side of the world."[9] Yet the "bitch of a war" demanded more and more of his time. He had to make decisions, and he leaned heavily on McNamara for advice.

"It really boils down to one or two decisions," Johnson said, balancing his unhappy options of "gettin' out or gettin' in." He could not imagine "gettin' out"—and leaving South Vietnam to the communists; he therefore seemed to be stuck with the "gettin' in" option.[10] Like Kennedy, Johnson was flanked by hawks and doves—those who wanted to commit U.S. ground troops to the war and finish it once and for all, and those who wanted to negotiate an American withdrawal, believing the war was unwinnable. By instinct, Johnson was in both camps; by his actions, he was becoming more of a hawk. The United States was already "in" South Vietnam. The question for Johnson was how much more deeply would he "get."

A few weeks later, the Joint Chiefs of Staff, sensing a hardening in the president's position, recommended that "additional US. troops" be sent to South Vietnam and that "as necessary . . . actions against North Vietnam" be readied. Johnson was not yet ready for military action against the north. There was an election to be won in 1964 and a domestic agenda to be prepared for 1965. He decided for the moment to put the military options on hold—waiting for the right moment, which he assumed would come after his election.

In the early months of 1964, as Johnson sought the legitimacy that would flow from his own election as president, he conferred with key Senate allies about what he should do in Vietnam. Although Majority Leader Mike Mansfield advised him to go for the neutralization of Southeast Asia ("we do not want another China in Vietnam," he warned), most of the senators were ready, though joylessly, to support the president's policy, whatever it was going to be. Georgia's Richard Russell, who had been Johnson's mentor in the Senate, told the president: "I didn't want to go in there, but now that we're in there, I don't know how to get out. . . . As a practical matter, we're in, and I don't know how the hell you can tell the American people you're comin' out. . . . They'll just think that you've just been whipped and you've been run—you're scared. It'd be disastrous."[11]

Johnson felt increasingly trapped by the bleak choices he faced in Vietnam. Journalist David Halberstam described the President as "restless, irritable, frustrated, more and more frenetic, more and more difficult to work with." But also, he wrote, "not a man to be backed down. Lyndon would not cut and run . . . no one was going to push Lyndon Johnson around." The president divided Washington insiders into men and boys. The men were tough, activist doers; the boys were talkers, writers, journalists, intellectuals. Not surprisingly, Johnson sympathized more with the McNamaras than with the George Balls.[12] The McNamaras rejected neutralization, considering it a step toward a communist takeover; they supported more military action to head off such an outcome. It was not that they had a specific strategy for conducting the war; in fact, they had no strategy—they just could not imagine losing. McNamara said: "The stakes in preserving an anticommunist South Vietnam are so high that, in our judgment, we must go on bending every effort to win." That made sense to the president.

In early March, McNamara returned to South Vietnam, basically to tell General Nguyen Khanh, the new Saigon strongman, that Johnson wanted no more coups and a much more aggressive offense against the communists. The president wanted six months of good news before the November election. Then, assuming his election, he would make the big decisions about Vietnam. As he told his advisers, "we're not getting it done; we're losin'." The public, of course, got another story—that the United States was heading toward victory, though victory was never defined.

McNamara's report to the president, dated March 16, 1964, painted a grim picture, indeed. It was Vietnam reality banging up against official rhetoric. Unless South Vietnam holds the line against communist expansion, it said, "almost all of Southeast Asia will probably fall under communist dominance," meaning Vietnam, Laos, and Cambodia. Burma would make an accommodation with the communists. Thailand would fight "for a period" but then succumb. The Philippines "would become shaky, and the threat to India on the West, Australia and New Zealand to the South, and Taiwan, Korea and Japan to the North and East would be greatly increased." In Johnson's White House, the "domino theory" was alive and well. For this reason, McNamara continued, South Vietnam had to be supported and strengthened. How? The United States had to be put on "72 hours' notice" to "initiate" "Border Control Actions" to protect Laos and Cambodia and "30 days' notice" to "initiate the program of 'Graduated Overt Military Pressure' against North Vietnam." It was naïvely assumed that increased military pressure on North Vietnam would gradually end the communist insurgency in South Vietnam. Neither program was described in detail, but it was clear that, except for the "use of US combat forces," every option was "on the table."[13]

In his autobiography, Johnson allowed no crack to appear between his policy on Vietnam and Kennedy's. "My first major decision on Vietnam," he wrote, was "to reaffirm President Kennedy's policies." Which he did, it seemed, on every public occasion. "My second major decision," he continued, was "to order retaliation against the Tonkin Gulf attacks and to seek a congressional resolution in support of our Southeast Asia policy."[14] The resolution was what Johnson had wanted all year. White House aide Jack Valenti described Johnson as "very, very disgruntled and discontented with the fact that we were messing around in Southeast Asia without congressional approval." The president quoted GOP senator Arthur Vandenberg as saying, "By God, if you want us in on the landing, we sure as hell better be in on the take-off." Johnson realized that if, after the election, he was to start bombing North Vietnam and sending combat troops into South Vietnam, he had to educate Congress and the American people about why such an escalation was necessary. Johnson, unlike his immediate predecessors, believed that if he was to lead the United States more deeply into a war, he had to have congressional authorization. He did war by the book.

The Tonkin Gulf Resolution

The Tonkin Gulf "attacks" came in early August 1964, at the height of Johnson's presidential campaign against Republican senator Barry Goldwater. The timing was fortuitous. Often, Goldwater would flex his rhetorical muscle, demanding a stronger anticommunist policy and suggesting Johnson, a former Senate colleague, was soft on communism, a liar, and unworthy of the office. Johnson, a canny opponent, would portray himself as a tough commander-in-chief dedicated to peace and Goldwater as a reckless extremist who, if elected president, would probably stumble into a nuclear war with the Soviet Union.

When, at 3:08 p.m., on August 2, 1964, North Vietnamese PT boats attacked the USS *Maddox,* a destroyer on a spying mission eight miles off shore, Johnson knew instinctively that a providential moment had arrived. He needed public approval for military action, and he had to look strong but flexible and always committed to peace. According to political lore, he had been carrying a copy of a congressional resolution authorizing military action in his inside jacket pocket for months, knowing that one day soon he would have to strike at North Vietnam and he wanted congressional approval. For Johnson, such approval was crucial—it would later be considered the functional equivalent of a "declaration of war." He had always believed that Truman made a terrible mistake by going to war in Korea without some form of congressional authorization. "He could have had it easily," Johnson declared, "and it would have strengthened his hand. I had made up my mind not to repeat that error."[15]

What happened in this case was that the USS *Maddox* was engaged in a dangerous mission—perhaps, in the view of its skipper, Captain John Herrick, too dangerous. It spied on the enemy coastline, checking on military maneuvers, naval exercises, and troop movements. He had warned Washington of "unacceptable risk" and "possible hostile action" if the mission continued, but Washington was not listening. When the North Vietnamese attacked, on August 2, Herrick immediately summoned air support from a nearby aircraft carrier, the USS *Ticonderoga*. One Navy pilot, James Stockdale, who years later gained special notoriety as Ross Perot's running mate in the 1992 presidential election cycle, flew into action. His view was amazing. "The gun flashes of the PT boats were very visible," he told me. "The ricochets of our bullets off the PT boats flashed, and I—could be detected clearly in bright sunshine. . . . One boat was sunk. The other two I would have given, as I reported later, a 50/50 chance of either of them getting home—they were full of bullet holes but were still making headway." But, as suddenly as the attacks began, they ended. The remaining North Vietnamese PT boats retreated from the area of combat, and the USS *Maddox* returned to its reconnaissance duty.[16]

Johnson, who had ignored Herrick's earlier warning, described the August 2 exchange in the Gulf of Tonkin as an "unexpected crisis." After meeting with his senior advisers, he ruled out military retaliation, placing blame for the incident on an "overeager North Vietnamese boat commander" who had "miscalculated."[17] He ordered another destroyer, the USS *Turner Joy,* to join the USS *Maddox* in the Gulf of Tonkin as an additional sign of American resolve. Of course, Johnson could have pulled the *Maddox* away from the North Vietnamese coastline and ended its spying mission, but no Texan was going to turn tail and flee from a fight—not this one, anyway, and certainly not during an election campaign. The spying mission continued.

August 4 was different. It proved to be a day of confusion, crisis, controversy—and opportunity. Washington began receiving reports of another North Vietnamese PT boat attack on the *Maddox* and the *Turner Joy*. In the darkness of a tropical storm, which whipped the Gulf of Tonkin into a fury, shipboard radar picked up odd signals. Sailors call them "skunks." Pilots sometimes call them "ducting" or "bogies." Either way, they can convey misleading impressions. Both the *Maddox* and the *Turner Joy* interpreted the "skunks" as approaching boats or torpedoes, and, mindful of what had happened only two days earlier, they opened fire.

"Under continuous torpedoes attack," Herrick urgently wired Washington. "Successfully avoided at least six torpedoes. Four torpedoes in water, and five torpedoes in water." At the time, he was certain an attack was under way.

Stockdale, back in action, looked for the enemy from his cockpit. "The scene down below was not hard to follow," he told me. "It was easier because it was so dark, because it was only the luminescence of these wakes, of the florescence of the water, which was just a spotlight in a dark pit." He saw the destroyers firing into the stormy seas, but he saw no attacking boats. "It was just a matter of them turning and firing, and ceasing firing, and I asked them where I should fire. I couldn't see anything. I'd go out there and spray bullets around where they should have been."

Just then, in Washington, McNamara picked up a strange signal from a North Vietnamese naval base. "Have engaged the enemy," it read, "and shot down two planes. Morale is high. Men have seen damaged ships." McNamara knew this information was inaccurate—no U.S. planes had been shot down, no ships had been damaged. Yet, though he knew better, he told Congress that the signal was "unimpeachable evidence" of the North Vietnamese attack— the first in a long string of official misstatements, misjudgments, and misunderstandings that marked the long American descent into Vietnam.

In the Gulf of Tonkin, the "battle" continued. Herrick never saw a North Vietnamese PT boat, though he kept telling Washington about approaching torpedoes. After two hours and thirteen minutes, he began to doubt the thrust of his own reporting. He decided, as a naval experiment, to put the *Maddox* into a series of swift, intricate turns, which kicked up high waves that slapped against the side of the ship. What he learned was what he was beginning to suspect—that the ship's sonar was picking up false signals, nothing more than the sounds of its own engine and propellers. Embarrassed, he wired Washington: "Review of action makes many reported contacts and torpedoes fired appear doubtful. Freak weather effects and overeager sonar man may have accounted for many reports. No actual visual sightings by *Maddox*. Suggest complete evaluation before further action."[18]

Stockdale recalled events that night with a sad clarity. "I had the best seat in the house to see that patch of water," he told me, "for two or three miles in radius around these two ships, as they conducted all of this firing and evading. There were no wakes, there were no ricochets, there was nothing but American firepower."

In Washington, at 6:15 p.m., the National Security Council met in emergency session. Everyone knew Johnson had decided to retaliate. Calls for caution, doubts, countervailing evidence—they were all being ignored. The *Ticonderoga* and another aircraft carrier, the *Constellation,* were put on high alert for a "reprisal raid." Stockdale, one of the pilots readied for the raid, expressed shock and bewilderment. "I said, reprisals for what? Of course I knew that nothing had taken place the night before. A very, very poignant moment in a man's life to realize the enormity of it all. . . . If I had a telephone, I'd like to tell the president that he's gone off half-cocked."

At 11:36 p.m., no longer prime time, Johnson told the American people "that renewed hostile actions against United States ships on the high seas in the Gulf of Tonkin have today required me to order the military forces of the United States to take action in reply. That reply is being given as I speak to you tonight."

George Ball told me that "there was a good deal of question as to whether there was an August 4th provocation." During the war, Ball had always been a dove on American involvement. "As the reports began to come in hour by hour," he said, "grave doubts arose as to whether there had been an attack or simply a confusion of radar signals. And the president himself said to me, 'I just think those dumb sailors were shooting at flying fish. I don't think there was any, any attack.' " Because, according to the U.S. Constitution, a president has the right and the power to order even "dumb sailors" into battle, Ball did not object at the time, and McNamara and other senior officials went along with the president's decision. They knew—and Johnson knew—that nothing had happened on August 4 and, in addition, that the reprisal raid in the early morning hours of August 5 would be seen as a U.S. combat operation in Vietnam. With a perfect opportunity to stand up and shout, "Stop!" they sat down and nodded in agreement.

"You have to be there to realize that the world has turned a corner," Stockdale said, remembering the raid. "We are now locked into the Vietnam war—there is no question about it." He paused for a moment: "I'm no whistle blower. I'm a soldier, and it didn't give me any conscience pangs to go ahead and carry out [the raid] at that time. It's not my conscience that irks me. It's just the stupidity of it that irks me." He added with genuine disappointment, "just the mere fact that it was an illegitimate birth made that war a bastard."

The raid completed, Johnson summoned congressional leaders to the White House. He confirmed what they already knew: He wanted congressional authorization for any further action in Southeast Asia, and he was assured he would get it quickly. House Speaker John McCormick, a Massachusetts Democrat, spoke of the importance of a "united front to the world." And McCormick and his colleagues produced: The House vote was 416 to 0, the Senate vote was 88 to 2. Johnson said he was "encouraged by this show of solidarity."[19] Though a congressional resolution, it was drafted by a team of presidential advisers, and it specifically authorized the administration "to take all necessary measures to repel any armed attack against the forces of the United States and to prevent further aggression."[20] Two phrases were written into the text to meet any eventuality: "all necessary measures," meaning, any military action the president deemed necessary; and "to prevent further aggression," meaning, in a most expansive way, any threat to American interests in Southeast Asia. The president was satisfied. As he later explained, he was not going "to commit forces and undertake actions . . . unless and until the American people through their Congress sign on to go in. If the President's going in, as he may be required to do, he wants the Congress to go in right by the side of him."[21] Johnson was Congress's man in the White House. If he as president was going to go to war, he wanted Congress to be there with him. And he didn't want to be second-guessed. Johnson told reporters, with the delight of hindsight, "anybody who has read the resolution" could see that it authorized the President "to take all—all—all necessary measures."[22] He hammered away at "all, all, all" to eliminate all doubts about his authority to go to war, if he deemed it necessary.

Johnson had considered but quickly rejected the idea of a formal "declaration of war," he explained years later, because if he had to go to war with North Vietnam, he did not want to find himself in a wider war that might also have included China or Russia. "I didn't know what treaty China might have with North Vietnam, or Russia might have with North Vietnam," he told Senator Wayne Morse of Oregon, one of the two senators who voted against the resolution. Unwittingly perhaps, Johnson had now set a precedent for war-making powers that would bedevil the executive and legislative branches of government for decades to come: With only a congressional resolution, however loosely drafted, however hurriedly approved, a president could now *commit* American men and women to combat and ignore the inner calling of the Constitution for due deliberation by Congress of a presidential decision to take the country to war, which a "declaration of war" would, by definition, entail.

Before the 1964 presidential election, Johnson repeatedly struck the same public note of extreme caution about sending American troops to South Vietnam. His pitch during the campaign was that he, not Goldwater, was the man of peace. "We are not about to send American boys nine or ten thousand miles to do what Asian boys ought to be doing for themselves," he said.[23]

After the election, in which Johnson obliterated Goldwater, he seemed to drop all pretense of caution: He ordered a speedier buildup of American forces in Vietnam. He was determined, as he kept telling his advisers, that he would not be the first president to lose a war. His basic problem was that he did not know how to win this war, either.

Armed now with both a congressional resolution and a resounding election victory, Johnson began the true Americanization of the Vietnam War. Within a matter of months, much sooner than he wanted or expected, he faced the most fateful decision of his presidency: whether he should send U.S. combat troops to South Vietnam. It was, as he later described his state of mind, a "lonely" decision—the problems in Southeast Asia posing an extraordinarily heavy burden for one man to carry. "A president searches his mind and his heart for the answers," he wrote in a clear effort to evoke sympathy and understanding. "When I was alone and sleepless at night . . . when I sat alone in the Aspen Lodge at Camp David, when I walked along the banks of the Pedernales River. . . . In those lonely vigils, I tried to think through what would happen to our nation and to the world if we did not act with courage and stamina—if we let South Vietnam fall to Hanoi." In his loneliness, he sought solace in those advisers, such as Dean Rusk, who shared his view that South Vietnam had to be defended by the United States. "If the communist world finds out that we will not pursue our commitments to the end," Rusk was quoted as saying, "I don't know where they will stay their hand." Johnson was "convinced" that "they would not stay their hand" and "if we ran out of Southeast Asia . . . our retreat . . . would open the path to World War III."[24]

In January 1965, McNamara and Bundy wrote their famous "fork in the road" memo to Johnson. They saw only "eventual defeat" if the United States continued its policy of half-way measures. They outlined two options: either "use our military power . . . and force a change of communist policy" or go all out on "a track of negotiations, aimed at salvaging what little can be preserved." They recommended the first option, but with only moderate enthusiasm.[25] The memo had a strong impact on Johnson—it forced him finally to realize that he had kicked the can down the road for a long time and he had now run out of road. Should he send more troops to Vietnam, and, if yes, how many? And, should he change their mission from advisory to combat? White House aide Douglass Cater recalled: "I'd never seen the man in as dejected a mood—he said, 'I don't know what to do. If I send more boys in, there's going to be killin'. If I take them out, there's going to be more killin'. Anything I do, there's going to be more killin'."[26]

By late spring 1965, the South Vietnamese army, never a hardy band of warriors in the best of times, began to deteriorate under withering communist assault. Five combat regiments and nine battalions disintegrated in a brief time. A presidential decision was swiftly approaching. On April 1, Johnson took a big step toward Americanizing the war. He decided to increase U.S. troop strength in South Vietnam by 18,000 to 20,000 troops and to deploy two additional Marine combat battalions and a Marine air squadron. Perhaps even more significant, he changed the Marine mission from base security to offensive combat operations against the Vietcong. On April 13, he reached an even more significant decision: He sent the 173rd Airborne Brigade to South Vietnam. Even after these momentous decisions, he did not want them to be translated into newspaper headlines. He wanted to avoid what Bundy delicately referred to as "premature publicity." He settled for what he hoped would be escalation on the sly, hoping the American people and Congress would not notice. How absurd!

At a news conference on April 27, reporters, still unaware of the expanding American escalation, asked if Johnson could imagine "circumstances" involving American troops "fighting" instead of just "advising" the South Vietnamese. The president deflected the thrust of the question by answering curtly and deceptively that "our purpose in Vietnam is to advise and assist those people in resisting aggression."

On June 7, General William Westmoreland, the new U.S. commander in Vietnam, told McNamara that he needed a force of 175,000 troops to hold off the communists. A week later, in a back channel cable, he explained to Johnson that "the South Vietnamese armed forces cannot stand up to this pressure without substantial U.S. combat support on the ground." At this time in his presidency, the important question for Johnson was whether he could have both guns and butter. Could he substantially expand the American military role in Vietnam and at the same time build his Great Society at home? His first instinct was that if any president could persuade Congress to provide the funding for both his Great Society and for a major U.S. combat operation in South Vietnam, it would be he, the master manipulator of congressional purse strings. And, actually, for a time, Congress cooperated, and the funding flowed. The costly Great Society agenda got off the ground just as the president was deciding to send U.S. combat troops to South Vietnam.

Johnson, though, was not a happy warrior. "Every time we have gotten near the culmination of our dreams," Johnson lamented, "the war bells have rung." He thought about "the woman I really loved," domestic programs such as civil rights, voting rights, education, and realized they might all have to be scuttled or at least shelved for the duration of an unwanted war in Vietnam. "If I have to fight, I'll do that. But I don't want to be known as a War President."[27]

Johnson's Big Decision: From an Advisory to a Combat Role

On July 2, 1965, as Johnson neared another milestone decision, he paused for a moment to consult Eisenhower. "Do you really think we can beat the

Vietcong?" he asked. Ike ducked a direct answer, claiming he was not up to speed on current intelligence, but in response to the more meaningful question about American policy in Vietnam, he replied that the United States did not really have a choice. "We are not going to be run out of a free country we helped to establish," he replied. Ike recalled his groundbreaking decision in 1954 to support the creation of South Vietnam and to link its survival to the national interest of the United States.

On July 14, Johnson told a gathering of rural electrical managers in the Rose Garden that "three Presidents—President Eisenhower, President Kennedy and your present President—have made a commitment in the name of the United States, and our national honor is at stake in Southeast Asia. And we are going to protect it, and you just might as well be prepared for it, and we can do it better if we are united. We do not expect the road to be smooth, and you just be sure it is not going to be short. But we do intend that the end result will be a better world."[28] Johnson believed that the "commitment" of the United States and the "word" of American presidents were compelling enough reasons to stay the course and fight in South Vietnam.

On July 25, having essentially decided to send "American boys" to do "what Asian boys ought to be doing for themselves"—which might have been a genuine change of heart or merely confirmation of what he had always believed he would do after the election—Johnson met in the morning with his Joint Chiefs of Staff; in the afternoon with Rusk, McNamara, Ball, Bundy, Clark Clifford, as well as John McCloy and other civilian advisers; and in the evening at Camp David with a small, select group of advisers, including McNamara, Clifford, and UN Ambassador Arthur Goldberg. He wanted everyone to be part of his decision.

Clifford told the president, "I don't believe we can win in South Vietnam." Before them was a Joint Chiefs recommendation to send 50,000 combat troops to South Vietnam. "If we send in 100,000 more men," Clifford continued with the sadness of voice and demeanor that he summoned for such occasions, "the North Vietnamese will meet us. If the North Vietnamese run out of men, the Chinese will send in volunteers. Russia and China don't intend for us to win the war." In a remarkably prescient comment, Clifford told the president: "If we lose 50,000-plus [men], it will ruin us. Five years, billions of dollars, 50,000 men, it is not for us." Instead of sending more men, the government should "quietly probe and search out with other countries—by moderating our position— to allow us to get out." Clifford added: "I can't see anything but catastrophe for my country."[29]

Ball had earlier made the same point in a paper: The South Vietnamese "are losing the war . . . no matter how many hundred thousand *white, foreign* (U.S.) troops [Ball's italics] we deploy." He was apocalyptic in his prognosis. "Once large numbers of U.S. troops are committed to direct combat, they will begin to take heavy casualties in a war they are ill-equipped to fight in a non-cooperative if not downright hostile countryside." Usually a man of few words, Ball continued: "Once we suffer large casualties, we will have started a well-nigh irreversible process. Our involvement will be so great that we cannot—without national humiliation—stop short of achieving our complete objectives. Of the two possibilities I think humiliation would be more likely than the achievement of our objectives—even after we have paid terrible costs."[30] Ball proved to be an adviser of remarkable prescience.

On the table were all of the depressing factors involved in committing U.S. combat troops to Vietnam: escalation, casualties, Vietnamese nationalism, further escalation, domestic dissent, congressional opposition, possible widening of the war to include Russia and China, even *in extremis* a nuclear war. Lurking in the background of all of these deliberations was the essentially optimistic belief that if the United States took this next big step and committed its combat troops to fight in South Vietnam, the war might soon be over, though the cost in casualties would surely be high. The United States would win, and the communists would lose. Rarely addressed at that time was the belief of a number of prominent U.S. generals that if the United States was to commit combat troops to the Vietnam War, it ought to have a clear-cut strategy for victory. It ought to know first how to define victory in a guerrilla war, how many troops would be needed, what the end game would look like. But the United States did not have such a strategy; it had only the goal of preventing South Vietnam from falling to the communists.

The president's wife, Lady Bird, often found him in a depressed mood, preoccupied by a war he feared the United States might not be able to win. According to her secretly recorded tapes, she remembered him saying: "Vietnam is getting worse every day. I have the choice to go in with great casualty lists or to get out with disgrace. It's like being in an airplane, and I have to choose between crashing the plane or jumping out. I do not have a parachute."[31] It was the same gloomy view he had shared four months earlier, on March 6, 1965. His old Senate mentor, Richard Russell of Georgia, had told him that there was no way out of Vietnam and meantime American troops were dying, and Johnson responded: "That is exactly right, and we are losing more every day. We're getting in worse. A man can fight if he can see daylight down the road somewhere, but there ain't no daylight in Vietnam. There's not a bit."[32]

On July 27, at an emergency meeting of the National Security Council, Johnson asked McNamara for a summary of the military options. The defense secretary was candid and comprehensive. The Vietcong was getting stronger. The North Vietnamese were already powerful. The communists controlled much of the countryside. A dozen provincial capitals were surrounded. South Vietnamese troops desperately needed American help, or, he pronounced grimly, their country would fall to the communists.

Johnson listened and then outlined five possible courses of action:

—Saturation bombing of North Vietnam by the Strategic Air Command;
—Pack up and go home;
—Stay there, "as we are";
—Go to Congress, ask for "great sums of money," call up the reserves, "increase the draft" and "go on a war footing"; or, finally,
—"Give our commanders in the field the men and supplies they say they need."

Unsurprisingly, Johnson settled on the fifth and final course of action. "We should do what was necessary to resist aggression but we should not be provoked into a major war." Johnson wanted everyone's approval. He went around the room. "I questioned each man in turn. Did he agree? Each nodded his approval or said 'yes.' " Everyone in the room understood that the president had just made a historic decision. The Joint Chiefs had been pushing for a U.S. combat role. Eisenhower had resisted. Kennedy had resisted. Johnson now agreed, but only because he feared that without more American troops, South Vietnam would fall to the communists.

In this way, in late July 1965, Johnson reached the "painful conclusion," as he put it, that he had no choice but to increase the number of U.S. ground troops in South Vietnam and to commit them to a combat role.[33] It was in a way a logical next step, given the rhetorical spadework of previous administrations, the commitment of earlier presidents, the pervasive influence of the "domino theory," and his determination not to be the first president to lose a war. And always in Johnson's considerations, there was China. Would the Chinese again surprise everyone and intervene, as they had done in Korea? Would they be deterred from intervening when they saw American combat troops being deployed to South Vietnam? Johnson had intelligence that 300,000 to 500,000 Chinese troops had been positioned near the Vietnamese border. Chinese warships maneuvered in the North China Sea, and Chinese diplomats hinted about a bigger war.[34]

Johnson acted. He ordered an initial increase of 75,000 troops, not the 50,000 the Joint Chiefs had requested. He noted that North Vietnamese regular army units were being deployed in the Central Highlands in a move probably intended to cut the country in two. McNamara urged Johnson to send another 100,000 troops to meet this new emergency. The president's national security adviser, Bundy, who earlier had been gung ho about the war, raised a yellow flag. "If we need 200,000 men now," he cautioned, "may we not need 400,000 later?" Ball, the president's gadfly, proposed a "tactical withdrawal" rather than a troop increase. "Politically, South Vietnam is a lost cause," he had said in his memo, challenging the prevailing wisdom of the administration. "A deep commitment of United States forces in a land war in South Vietnam would be a catastrophic error." Johnson would have been wise to listen to Ball, but instead he once again listened to McNamara.

"I have today ordered to Vietnam the air mobile division and certain other forces," he told a noontime news conference on July 28, "which will raise our fighting strength from 75,000 to 125,000 men almost immediately." He tried to soften the impact of his announcement by lumping it in with other news. By year's end, the number of U.S. troops in South Vietnam would jump to 184,000.[35]

The president did not want to make too much of a public splash about his decision to escalate the American role in Vietnam. "I don't want to be dramatic and cause tension," he told his advisers. He was apparently hoping that the escalation could go forward without stimulating a domestic uproar that would affect his Great Society program. He felt he still had enough time to gain the upper hand in Vietnam before he lost it at home.

The Lessons of the Ia Drang Battle

Realizing that he was going to be making a number of major decisions about the war, Johnson decided to visit Vietnam. He flew to the new American base at Camranh Bay—the first time an American president had visited a war zone since Franklin Roosevelt journeyed to Casablanca in 1943. Johnson was deeply touched and proud. His own military service in World War II had been brief and relatively safe. Now he saw a different reality. "I have never been more moved by any group I have ever talked to," he observed, "never in my life." When he returned, he became even more absorbed with the costs of the war, once quoting a prayer attributed to George Washington: "Good God, what brave men must I lose today?"[36] Early in the morning, before dawn, he would call the Operations Center at the White House and ask about casualties suffered in an operation he had been briefed about the night before. During his working day, *Time* observed, he would often become "strangely silent," his mind thousands of miles away from whatever meeting he was supposed to be chairing. Vietnam was his omnipresent preoccupation.

Shortly after his return, in November 1965, the first major battle of the war involving U.S. combat forces took place in the Ia Drang Valley. The First Cavalry Division fought magnificently, defeating the "cream" of the North Vietnamese army. The Pentagon was thrilled, and the president was relieved, but the battle began to raise questions in McNamara's mind about the ultimate wisdom of American policy. One reason was the high casualty rate—the United States lost 240 soldiers in the battle, which saddened and surprised the defense secretary.[37] This was now to become the pattern of McNamara's reporting on the Vietnam War—optimism in public, doubts in private. The defense secretary, impressed by the endurance and tenacity of the communist forces, then surprised the president by proposing that even though the United States won this initial battle in the Ia Drang Valley, it should seek a "compromise solution" to the war and, as a step in that direction, initiate a "bombing pause" of three to four weeks.[38] Everyone in the administration understood that the secretary's proposal would lead to a "coalition government," including the communists. To Johnson, this sounded like slow surrender.

At a meeting with Rusk, McNamara, and other aides, Johnson challenged his defense secretary, suggesting he was beginning to question his judgment: "The military says, a month's pause would undo all we've done," the president said.

McNamara responded: "That's baloney, and I can prove it."

Johnson: "I don't think so. I disagree. I think it contains serious risks."

McNamara said that in his view a military solution was no longer feasible.

The president was shocked: "Then no matter what we do in the military field, there is no sure victory?"

McNamara: "That's right. We've been too optimistic. We need to explore other means."[39]

McNamara's dissent heartened the few doves in Johnson's coterie of advisers but distressed the many hawks, who wondered what was happening to the usually forceful and determined secretary of defense. Johnson wondered, too.

By December 1966, a year later, U.S. troop strength rose to 385,000, a boost of more than 200,000. By this time in the war, 6,500 U.S. troops had been killed and another 37,000 wounded, and there was little to show for their sacrifice. The South Vietnamese army tried but failed to take the offensive. Increasingly U.S. troops assumed the major share of the fighting, and the communists showed no sign of abandoning the fight.

McNamara, an official with growing doubts, began to search for a face-saving way out of the war. He sent another proposal to the president, containing three startling recommendations, which, if accepted and implemented, would have represented a drastic change in U.S. policy:

—Cap all further troop increases;
—Stop all bombing of North Vietnam;
—Set up a coalition government, including the Vietcong.

Years later, after the United States had been defeated in Vietnam, a tired McNamara returned to this proposal in a book he called *In Retrospect: The Tragedies and Lessons of Vietnam*. He wrote, with a deep regret enveloping each word: "We should have begun our withdrawal from South Vietnam. There was a high probability we could have done so on terms no less advantageous than those accepted six years later without any greater damage to U.S. national security and at much lower cost to America and Vietnam."[40]

At the time, McNamara sounded like a budding heretic, and Johnson rejected his proposal.

In private, officials later disclosed, McNamara suffered from an acute form of depression, brought on by the war. In public, though, he struck a totally different pose, sometimes of almost giddy optimism, at other times, more guarded. "I can tell you that military progress in the past twelve months has exceeded our expectations," he told reporters late in 1966.[41] That was untrue. The president spoke of "an unbroken series of military successes."[42] That too was untrue.

As the war escalated in intensity, the administration played a public relations game of statistical warfare, in which the United States always won and the Vietcong always lost. It was the president's way of buying time by deceiving the American public. "At the beginning of 1965," Johnson wrote years later, "the ratio of enemy to allied casualties was estimated at 2.2 to 1. The next year this ratio was 3.3 to 1, and in 1967 it was 3.9 to 1. The number of Vietcong who went over to the South Vietnamese government's side increased from 11,000 in 1965 to just over 20,000 in 1966 and more than 27,000 in 1967. . . . The number of people controlled by the communists has dropped from 3.2 million in June 1966 to 2.4 million in January, 1967."[43]

And yet, despite these statistical victories, the Johnson administration still felt the need to increase its troop strength in South Vietnam. In August 1967, Johnson decided to increase American troop strength to 525,000. He knew that more than 9,000 had already been killed, and another 60,000 wounded, but he still could not imagine an American defeat. Another escalation, another tweak here or there, he and others reasoned, and there would be "light at the end of the tunnel."[44] Actually, by some measurements, the United States *was* winning the war—it was killing more Vietcong, it was holding more territory, it was bombing and destroying enemy installations at a fierce rate. Even so, the Vietcong and their North Vietnamese allies, though battered and bruised, continued their guerrilla and conventional struggle against this mighty super-power with a fierce nationalistic will and determination. Under relentless American attack, they bent, but did not break. These "little men in black pajamas," as U.S. troops disparagingly referred to the Vietcong guerrilla fighters, this "raggedy ass little fourth rate country," as Johnson called North Vietnam, proved to be a formidable foe.

"I did underestimate the tenacity of the North Vietnamese," Rusk told me many years later. "Despite . . . their staggering losses, the North Vietnamese did persist until they engaged in effect the war weariness of the American people and succeeded in winning politically what they could not win militarily. They showed remarkable persistence."[45] "Tenacity" and "persistence" were the two words Rusk often employed after the war to describe the enemy, but publicly they never crossed his lips during the war. Unlike McNamara, his doubting colleague, Rusk succeeded with scotch and aspirin to suppress his doubts and support the president.

A Year of Trial and Illusion

1967 was a tough year for everyone. The United States faced an eruption of challenges that staggered the administration. Nothing, it seemed, was more important than the exponential rise in American casualties, the result of more troops engaged in more battles. For the first time, the middle class began to feel the sting of sacrifice it had managed to avoid up to this time. Now its young men and women were also being killed and wounded in battle, sharing with poor minorities, mostly blacks, the increasing pain of an increasingly unpopular war. In the last week of August, for example, 24 Americans died in Vietnam. In the last week of September, 128 Americans died in Vietnam. In the last week of October, 193 died. In the last week of November, 212 died.[46]

And so the casualty rate climbed, each week affecting more families from all segments of society and adding a new, somber texture to the antiwar movement. It was then no surprise that Congress found itself bombarded with urgent parental appeals for an end to the war or at least for a radical change in policy. It was no surprise, either, that antiwar demonstrations mushroomed in the nation's capital. On one occasion more than 30,000 angry, placard-waving protesters marched on the Pentagon, frightening authorities into sending armed troops to block their path. Violence ensued. It was rifles against placards, Americans against Americans—the unsettling image that filled TV screens across the country that evening and the front pages of newspapers the next morning.

Journalism was joining the domestic battle. Many editorial writers, who had been generally supportive of administration policy, changed their minds, as it became increasingly clear that the cost of the war and the cost of the Great Society were getting to be too much of a burden for the American economy. The *New York Times,* in a series of editorials that reflected the rising anxiety of the American public, described the war as a "bottomless pit . . . in which nothing succeeds like failure." Here was a major metropolitan daily questioning the president's basic assumption that he could have both guns and butter. The *Times* touched a raw nerve in Johnson, who truly loved his Great Society "woman" but worried about whether he could still afford her. The paper expressed widespread "concern that the rebuilding of slums and other domestic tasks . . . are being sacrificed to the necessity for spending upward of $2 billion a month to feed the Vietnamese conflict."[47]

Johnson was beginning to realize that the Vietnam War was an angry cancer eating away at his domestic programs and that, in the end, he might lose both the war and his Great Society. But to admit this possibility was to acknowledge his failure as president, and he was not ready to do that. He needed more time. He pleaded for more understanding. He sent his new under secretary of state, Nicholas deB. Katzenbach, to tell a group of skeptical reporters that "guns and butter" was still an achievable objective. Katzenbach struck me and other reporters, however, as being less than enthusiastic about his assignment. "Is he on dope?" a colleague asked, and he was not joking. What was it going to take to persuade the White House that it could not at the same time prosecute a stubborn war and sustain a massive domestic program such as the Great Society?

Complicating Johnson's agenda even more was a crisis in the Middle East that exploded in early June into a dangerous six-day war between Israel and its Arab neighbors that almost led to a confrontation between the United

States and the Soviet Union. Egypt's President Gamal Abdul Nasser arbitrarily blockaded the Straits of Tiran in the Gulf of Aqaba on May 23, 1967, choking Israel's access to the Red Sea. The U.S. position was that Israel had a legal right to such access and called Egypt's move "disastrous to the cause of peace."[48] The United States tried diplomacy to end the blockade, but failed.

Israel's Prime Minister Levi Eshkol reminded Johnson of a pledge by Eisenhower in 1957 to keep the Straits of Tiran open to all "free and innocent" passage, including Israeli ships. But Johnson was so absorbed with the war in Vietnam and the threat to his Great Society program that, though his sympathies lay with Israel, he could not at that time take any military action in the Middle East to back up earlier U.S. promises to Israel. The upshot was Israeli feelings of betrayal.

In Vietnam, Israel's ally, the United States, was not winning. That was clear to the president, to the Pentagon, to the Vietcong, and to Senator John Stennis of Mississippi, chair of the Armed Services Committee. Should there be a change in American policy? In late August, Stennis summoned eleven witnesses to a special hearing of his Preparedness Subcommittee: ten admirals and generals—and McNamara. The military brass, without exception, proposed a program of heavier bombing. The brass wanted to carry the war into North Vietnam. The defense secretary took a totally different tack. Hanoi, he said, could not be "bombed to the negotiating table." He patiently explained that in his view a "new kind of air campaign" would be "illusory." It would "not only be futile but involve risks to our personnel and to our nation that I am unable to recommend."[49]

To hawks in the Senate, McNamara was talking pure heresy. To the increasing flock of Senate doves, he was talking plain common sense. To Johnson, McNamara was crossing a red line—he was bucking administration policy and had to be replaced. On November 28, the White House announced that McNamara would become president of the World Bank. McNamara later said, with probably unintended humor, "I do not know to this day whether I quit or was fired. Maybe it was both."

For Johnson, this was a time of cruel, unrelenting pressure—his experiment with buying both guns and butter in serious question, blacks in spreading protest in American cities, peace in the Middle East hanging by a thread, the campuses aflame with anger, the public increasingly uneasy about the war—and CIA director Richard Helms telling him in a "for your eyes only" memo that a withdrawal from Vietnam would not be as consequential as previously thought. What? Withdrawal? That had not been among the options Johnson allowed himself even to consider. Confiding to historian Doris Kearns Good-win, Johnson said, "I felt that I was being chased on all sides by a giant stampede coming at me from all directions—the rioting blacks, demonstrating students, marching welfare mothers, squawking professors and hysterical reports."[50]

And now, in addition, the ugly, festering disputes within his own admin-istration about his wartime strategy were bursting into the open, especially after McNamara's congressional testimony. If there was to be a rethinking of policy and personnel, Johnson wanted the advice of his Special Advisory Group on Vietnam, known to reporters with a dollop of sarcasm as The Wise Men, The Old Men, or The Council of Elders. They had been meeting once or twice a year since 1965. On November 1, they met again: career diplomats, retired generals, admirals, scholars, and lawyers. With only one exception, namely George Ball, the president's licensed in-house critic, they all seemed to share the president's public optimism that the war was going well.[51] "All the challenges have been met," Johnson proclaimed. "The enemy is not beaten, but he knows that he has met his master in the field." General Westmoreland was even more upbeat. "I've never been more encouraged during my entire almost four years in country," he said. "I think we are making real progress. Everybody is very optimistic."[52] However, McNamara, still defense secretary, sounded very pessimistic. "Continuation of our present course of action in Southeast Asia," he said, "would be dangerous, costly in lives and unsatisfac-tory to the American people."

The Shock of the Tet Offensive

Johnson's Wise Men were, as it turned out, not all that wise, certainly not about the shifting realities of the Vietnam War. On January 30, 1968, as tens of thousands of South Vietnamese troops trekked home in happy anticipation of the Lunar New Year holiday, called Tet, the communists launched a sudden, massive, surprise offensive throughout South Vietnam. It was, wrote Stanley Karnow, an offensive of "extraordinary intensity and astonishing scope."[53] An estimated 70,000 troops attacked more than 100 cities and villages; entered Saigon by stealth, several thousand in civilian garb, and even for a brief time occupied U.S. Embassy grounds; captured Hue; penetrated villages such as Ben Tre, Mytho, Cantho, and Soc Trang; and caught U.S. forces totally off guard. Westmoreland, so confident a few months earlier that he had the com-munists on the run, found himself engaged in a defensive struggle up and down the spine of South Vietnam. "We are now in a new ball game," he told the Pentagon, a judgment eerily similar to MacArthur's "we face an entirely new war" after China burst into the Korean War.[54]

At home, the euphoria, so tenderly nurtured by Johnson, collapsed, the light at the end of the tunnel suddenly extinguished. Senators, some of whom had trusted Johnson, felt betrayed. They demanded a drastic overhaul of policy—either go all out and destroy North Vietnam, or withdraw from South Vietnam. In the so-called fishbowl of the CBS Evening News, anchor Walter Cronkite checked the rush of wire copy in absolute disbelief. "What the hell is going on?" he asked. "I thought we were winning this thing." A few weeks later, Cronkite went to Vietnam and, when he returned, told the American people that in his judgment the United States was stuck in a no-win situation in Vietnam. And he, unlike Johnson, enjoyed a roughly 80 percent approval rating. "If I've lost Cronkite," Johnson fretted, "I've lost middle America." Henry Kissinger, who was a Harvard professor at the time, put it in more scholarly language, but his message was clear to everyone: "The Tet offensive overthrew the assumptions of American strategy."[55]

A besieged president tried to put the Tet offensive in a more favorable perspective. On February 2, Johnson told reporters that "responsible military commanders" in Saigon had informed him that the communists paid a "very dear price" for their nationwide attacks. "They say ten thousand died, and we lost two hundred and forty-nine, and the South Vietnamese lost five hundred. That doesn't look like a communist victory." In fact, he added, the Tet offensive was a "complete failure."[56] From a strictly military point of view, it was. Thousands of Vietcong troops were killed and entire units destroyed by American air and artillery power. But even if the Vietcong was shattered as a fighting force during the Tet offensive, the communists always had the North Vietnamese regular army troops to engage the South Vietnamese army (the ARVN) and the Americans. It took a while for Johnson to understand that in this very special kind of guerrilla war, such as the one being fought in Vietnam, the regulars lose if they don't win and the guerrillas win if they don't lose. Meaning, by the end of the Tet offensive, even though the communists had lost tens of thousands of troops, dead or captured, they were still considered the victors. Their strategy was never based on the expectation of a military victory at that point. It was based on the belief that in time the Americans would tire of Tet offensives—that after years of rising casualties and costs, the Americans would become increasingly fatigued and eventually would go home.

In 1975, shortly after the communists forced the United States to abandon South Vietnam, two officers met, one North Vietnamese, the other American.

The American insisted that, from a strictly military point of view, the communists had never defeated American troops in a major battle. "That is correct," the communist replied. "It is also irrelevant."[57]

Nothing better illustrated the administration's fatigue with the war than a birthday party for Secretary Rusk on February 9. It was his fifty-ninth birthday, and a small group of reporters regularly assigned to the State Department gathered outside his office for an informal toast. The secretary of state looked exhausted. The strain of recent days showed in the dark lines under his eyes. Usually the ultimate southern gentleman, this time, in response to a question about the failure of U.S. intelligence to anticipate the Tet offensive, he erupted with angry words that no reporter present could ever forget. "There gets to be a point when the question is: whose side are you on?" he asked, turning on ABC reporter John Scali. "Now, I'm secretary of state of the United States, and I'm on our side." Scali was shocked. "You're not implying—" Scali began, but Rusk brusquely and uncharacteristically brushed him aside. "During World War II," he continued, "there was never a time when you couldn't find a reason to bitch at your allies or at intelligence or at the commander of the adjoining unit or the quartermaster who wasn't giving you your portable toilet seat at the right time. There wasn't a time when you couldn't find something to bitch about." Rusk took a swallow of his scotch. "But what do you talk about?" he asked, his words edged with a bitter resentment. "Do you talk about how to win this thing? Or do you throw this thing in and say everything is lost?" "This thing" was obviously the Vietnam War, and Rusk was unwittingly reflecting the inner battles of the administration, but he still tried to sound optimistic. He pressed his right thumb on top of the coffee table. "When the United States applies pressure on something," he said, almost as a warning, "that something gives." He nodded several times and then repeated, "That something gives." But Rusk was to learn that North Vietnam did not give.

Scali protested that Rusk was not answering his question, which related only to the possibility of an intelligence failure. But Rusk was not to be stopped or diverted. "On my fifty-ninth birthday, forgive me if I express myself on these matters because none of your papers or your broadcasting apparatuses are worth a damn unless the United States succeeds. They are trivial compared to that question. So, I don't know why, to win a Pulitzer Prize, people have to go probing for the things that one can bitch about when there are two thousand stories on the same day about things that are more constructive in character."[58]

Rusk, who once jokingly described himself as the "friendly bartender," had obviously been rattled by the Tet offensive. He was no longer the man reporters affectionately called the "beaming Buddha." Rusk understood that America had suffered a huge defeat within the context of a guerrilla war. But what should the United States do? That was the unspoken question, for which he did not have an easy answer. Nor did anyone else in the administration.

On February 14, General Westmoreland announced that since the start of the Tet offensive two weeks earlier, the communists had lost 33,000 troops dead and another 6,700 captured, and the Americans had lost 1,100 troops, meaning more than 500 a week—more than the United States had suffered in any week of this long war. If this was ever a war measured solely by statistical milestones, the United States would clearly have been declared the winner years before; but, as the communist officer told the American officer in 1975, statistics in this war were "irrelevant."

Overnight, it seemed, America's emotional pendulum had swung from an artificially stimulated euphoria to a deep skepticism about the war. True, as Rostow told reporters, the communists had suffered terrible losses, they failed to hold a single provincial or district capital, and if they had intended to ignite a popular uprising against the Saigon regime, they came up short in this regard too. But all over the world, especially in the United States, the headlines told a different story. They spoke of an American defeat.

On March 26, Johnson growled, "Somebody poisoned the well." But it was not a "somebody" who poisoned the well. It was a guerrilla army. Johnson still refused to accept the idea of an American defeat. Though deep in a guerrilla war, he still acted like a president fighting a conventional war. He sent an urgent message to Westmoreland—if you need more troops, say so; if you need more planes, more ships, just say so. Reflecting Westmoreland's collapsing strategy, Johnson still saw the war as a matter of numbers, of attrition rates, of kill ratios, of statistics. In moments of utter delusion, he imagined himself to be Lincoln during the Civil War, or Roosevelt during World War II—as a leader pressed and pressured, but still proud and strong, who would never accept defeat and who, no matter the difficulties, would ultimately "nail the coonskin to the wall," as once, during his visit to Vietnam, he had tried to inspire his troops to do. "Tet," pronounced Johnson, now filled with historical parallels, was "an all-out Kamikaze attack, an assault with everything they've got, with their entire stack in for the purpose of trying to roll over us and have another Dien Bien Phu."[59] He bolstered his spirits (and the nation's) by comparing Ho with Hitler, communists with Nazis, Vietnam with World War II. In the dead of night, all alone, he might have considered the option of withdrawal, but in the Oval Office, during the day, he would allow himself to project only an outcome resembling a military victory.

And initially his Joint Chiefs of Staff did nothing to alter his outlook. Nor did Westmoreland. The general responded to the president's entreaties by asking for an additional 206,000 troops. His request had the force of a rocket hitting the White House. When it was leaked to the *New York Times,* appearing on the front page, it ignited a new round of criticism and recrimination. But there was more. Astonishingly, Westmoreland also proposed that the United States invade North Vietnam, perhaps inspired by the example of MacArthur's surprise Inchon landing behind enemy lines north of the 38th parallel dividing Korea. In a state of utter bewilderment, Clark Clifford, the newly named defense secretary, wondered, what's on Westmoreland's mind? Where on earth does he think the troops would come from? Would the president pull them out of Europe? Would he call up another 300,000 reservists? Would he borrow helicopters from the British? Would he add another $10 billion to the already astronomic cost of the war?[60]

Clifford's desk, a marvelous example of one man's effort to manage a crazy world, reflected the depth and breadth of the challenges he faced. It was a wonder to behold. It was unusually large, and it was always covered with neat clusters of notes, memos, or documents, each held down by a heavy glass paperweight, and organized with meticulous care in rows running from the bottom of his desk to the top. The clusters nearest him contained the most urgent problems; those further from his reach were problems for tomorrow or next week. During this time of big decisions, Clifford invited his senior officials to gather around his desk for long discussions about possible changes in American policy in Vietnam. Among them were Paul Warnke, his assistant secretary of defense for international security affairs, and General Robert Pursley, his military assistant. Though American and South Vietnamese troops had recovered from the initial shock of the Tet offensive and imposed huge losses on Vietcong forces, Clifford, Warnke, and Pursley quickly concluded that America's approach to the Vietnam War had to be drastically changed. No, for example, to Westmoreland's request for an additional 206,000 troops. For them, an easy decision. Far more important, they realized that the United States had no real military strategy for winning the war or disengaging from it. Grimly they concluded that the war could not be won unless the United States decided to go all out and, with the use of nuclear weapons, destroy North Vietnam and then run the risk of a wider war involving China and the Soviet Union. It was the Korea calculation all over again.

Clifford shared this grim assessment with the president, whose first response was to summon another meeting of his Wise Men. They met, and they deliberated: should there be another bombing pause? Should they formally reject Westmoreland's wild appeal for more than 200,000 additional troops and offer only 13,500 troops? Should they focus on building up the Vietnamese army (what was initially called deAmericanization or, as it was later called, Vietnamization)? Should they emphasize diplomacy and go for a coalition government, including the communists? There were many more questions than answers. Johnson, not hearing a firm recommendation, withdrew to the Oval Office, where he sought his own counsel in the splendid isolation of presidential responsibility.

Five days later, on March 31, Johnson announced a new peace plan and then, having lost his credibility in the bloody battles of Tet, and worse, having lost his political fire and ambition, unimaginable in this Texas politician prior to Tet, he proclaimed to the nation and the world that he would not run for another term in office. "I shall not seek and I will not accept the nomination of my party for another term as your president," he told the nation. Johnson had always worried that he would die in office, the victim of a massive heart attack, and a number of his friends later said that he had decided not to run for re-election for fear of heart failure and that he had made the decision months before. The more likely reason was his growing frustration with the war.

Thus did Vietnam consume a president and his presidency. Jack Valenti tried to explain the corrosive power of the war. "Vietnam was a fungus," he said, choosing his words carefully, "slowly spreading its suffocating crust over the great plans of the president, both here and overseas. No matter what we turned our hands and mind to, there was Vietnam, its contagion affecting everything that it touched, and it seemed to touch everything."[61] Another presidential adviser, David Lilienthal, made essentially the same point in purely medical terms. This "pinpoint on the globe [Vietnam]" was "like an infection, a 'culture' of some horrible disease, a cancer where the wildly growing cells multiply and multiply until the whole body is poisoned."[62]

Johnson recognized that he was losing popular support for a war he seemed unable to win. Katzenbach put the president's dilemma in the form of an Aesopian question: "Can the tortoise of progress in Vietnam stay ahead of the hare of dissent at home?" They both recognized that if they were to head off a total collapse of support at home, they would have to demonstrate progress on the battlefield; and yet progress on the battlefield depended in part on popular support at home.

Complicating the tortoise/hare question still more was the opening of peace talks in Paris in May. After deciding not to run for re-election, Johnson accepted the idea of negotiating a de-escalation of the war with North Vietnam. He sent veteran negotiator W. Averell Harriman to Paris to see what was possible. From North Vietnam's point of view, the new negotiations made perfect sense; it was consistent with their overall strategy of "fighting while negotiating." From Washington's point of view, it was a necessary step to contain domestic opposition to the war, but it had the unintended effect of intensifying the internal disagreements in the president's cabinet. The president, in an apparent effort to outstrategize the communists, started a "full-scale fighting while negotiating" policy. The Pentagon got the president's permission to launch an "all-out" offensive against retreating North Vietnamese forces, but U.S. negotiators Averell Harriman and his deputy Cyrus Vance objected strenuously—they argued that the offensive would be seen as a major escalation of the war and thus discourage any possible progress in the Paris talks.

The old splits in administration war-gaming became more apparent and more embarrassing. The Pentagon, supported now by Rusk, Rostow, Westmoreland, and Ambassador Ellsworth Bunker, believed the United States had the enemy on the run after Tet and ought now to clobber them in both North and South Vietnam. Bunker insisted: "We can afford . . . to be tough, patient and not too anxious in our negotiating stance." But Clifford, Harriman, Katzenbach, Deputy Defense Secretary Paul Nitze, and Warnke were of the view that the war could no longer be won and the United States should be seeking mutual de-escalation and disengagement in Paris. Johnson watched from the sidelines, refusing to make timely decisions. "The enemy is using my own people as dupes," he complained.[63] Speechwriter Harry McPherson urged Johnson to take a more active role in resolving the internal disputes. "You are the commander-in-chief," he said, gently chiding the president. "If you think a policy is wrong, you should not follow it just to quiet the generals and admirals." Clifford joined McPherson in trying to re-energize Johnson. You are acting more like a "legislative leader, seeking a consensus among people who are often irreconcilably opposed than like a decisive commander-in-chief giving his subordinates orders."[64]

Warnke and Pursley, for the first time in the war, produced in May a strategic formula for slowly shifting responsibility for the conduct of the war from the Americans to the South Vietnamese. It was left to the next president to give life to this change in policy. It was outlined in a secret letter Warnke drafted for Clifford's attention on May 3. Choosing to extract the most optimistic nuggets from the post-Tet battlefield, Warnke expressed delight that the South Vietnamese government had not "collapsed" after LBJ decided to begin negotiations with North Vietnam—and, by the end of the year, to "level off" and ultimately "reduce" American troop strength in South Vietnam. The administration's "highest priority item" must now be providing the South Vietnamese army with "improved equipment and training."

This deAmericanization of the war would take "years," but it would begin the process of extricating the United States from the "bottomless pit" of its "commitment" in Vietnam. "The American public cannot and should not be expected indefinitely to accept the loss of 300 Americans lives a week and the expenditure of over \$2 billion a month," Warnke wrote.[65] Clifford bought the Warnke-Pursley argument and sold it to Johnson, but the president was never happy with the conclusion that the United States could not finish the job in Vietnam. He continued negotiating in Paris, fighting in South Vietnam, and bombing in North Vietnam, and so it continued through the summer.

With the Democratic presidential candidate, Vice President Hubert Humphrey, in a close struggle with the Republican candidate, Richard Nixon, Johnson decided under mounting pressure from the Democratic establishment to stop the bombing of North Vietnam. He was trying to help Humphrey—so his aides told reporters, who did not quite buy the story. They thought Johnson worried that Humphrey was in less than full-throated support of his policy. Finally, Hanoi and Washington decided to resume serious peace talks in Paris on the Tuesday of the presidential election. However, South Vietnam's President Nguyen Van Thieu refused at the last minute to attend the talks and the opportunity died—and with it whatever chance Johnson might have had to break the negotiating impasse in Paris while he was still president. In a telephone conversation with GOP senator Everett Dirksen of Illinois, Johnson said that he had heard that Thieu was "waiting on Nixon," that he had been persuaded by Republican conservatives to "wait on Nixon" for a better deal.[66] If Johnson had not waited until the last minute to restart the Paris talks, many political observers believed that Humphrey might have won the election. Was it possible that Johnson had deliberately stalled? There was speculation at the time that Johnson did in fact stall, because he wanted Humphrey to lose and Nixon to win—perhaps because he thought Nixon would be tougher on the North Vietnamese. No one knew, and Nixon won by a whisker, in part because he cultivated the popular impression that he had a plan, "a secret plan," to end the war.

CHAPTER SIX

NIXON

"There Is No Way to Win This War"

"I've been saying 'an honorable end to the war,' but what the hell does
that really mean? There is no way to win this war, but we can't say that,
of course. In fact, we have to seem to say just the opposite."
RICHARD NIXON, 1969

IT HAS BEEN argued by Otto von Bismarck, Henry Kissinger, and others that
the business of statecraft should not be seen as a showcase for a nation's morality—in fact, that morality might even be an impediment to a cold assessment
of the facts. A nation, to survive, might have to engage in immoral acts, only
to argue later that the highest form of morality was ultimately the survival of
the nation.

In 1968, an assessment would have to start with the Tet offensive, which,
by any objective judgment, changed the landscape of the war. Up until Tet,
Lyndon B. Johnson still entertained the thought that somehow he could "win"
the war or at least manufacture an outcome that could be camouflaged as an
acceptable end to the war. After Tet, the war began to look hopeless, to him, to
many of his advisers, and to the American people. Casualties, first. How many
killed-in-actions (KIAs) would Americans accept? Fifty a week? A hundred a
week? Five hundred? At the beginning of 1968, an especially bloody year in
Vietnam, 15,979 Americans had already been killed in the war. By the end
of the year, shortly after Richard Nixon won the presidency, the number had
spiked sharply to more than 30,000. In one year, the number of American
deaths in Vietnam had nearly doubled. And by the time the war ended on
April 30, 1975, the United States having suffered the first military defeat in
its history, the number had climbed to 58,191.[1] In other words, an additional
27,623 Americans died in the last years of a war that the new president privately conceded was unwinnable.

"In Saigon the tendency is to fight the war to victory," newly elected President Richard M. Nixon told Henry Kissinger, the Harvard professor whom he

had just selected as his national security adviser. "But you and I know it won't happen—it is impossible. Even General [Creighton] Abrams [General William Westmoreland's successor as supreme allied commander in South Vietnam] agreed."[2] Kissinger later wrote that Nixon "entered the presidency convinced . . . that a clear-cut victory in Vietnam was no longer possible, if it ever had been." He understood that "destiny had dealt him the thankless hand of having to arrange a retreat and some sort of exit from a demoralizing conflict."[3]

But if Nixon believed from the very beginning of his presidency that "victory" in Vietnam was "impossible," then why did he continue to prosecute the war? Why sacrifice so many more young Americans and Vietnamese to a cause he already considered lost? Was Nixon being simply immoral, or even amoral? Or did he have a definition of morality that he thought justified his policy choices—namely, the survival of America as a vibrant democracy in an unstable world, which, according to Nixon, could not be achieved if the United States suffered an embarrassing defeat in Vietnam.

One day, shortly after his election, the new president turned to Richard Whelan, one of his speechwriters, and wondered aloud, "I've been saying, 'an honorable end to the war,' but what the hell does that really mean?"[4] Nixon answered his own question. "There's no way to win this war," he acknowledged, "but we can't say that, of course. In fact, we have to seem to say just the opposite, just to keep some degree of bargaining leverage."[5] So, as he began to juggle his negotiating tactics—an overture to Hanoi, a carefully crafted warning to Moscow, a news conference in Washington, a comforting word to Saigon—he was supremely confident that he could bring the war to an end on roughly his terms and timetable. No more than a year was what he had in mind.

Nixon saw himself as a master of the universe, as a president who, with American power and prestige, could control the tempo of the war and manage the diplomatic process in such a way that the United States could emerge from this costly, damaging struggle with its head held high, its people proud, and its credibility intact. In this way, he told the many audiences only a president can command, he would achieve his exalted "peace with honor," a phrase he never really defined but assumed the American people would understand.

With some sympathy, Nixon looked back at Johnson's extended agony in Vietnam and concluded that the war had to be brought to a quick end, and he thought he knew how to end it. In America, he could see during his own presidential campaign that the public's patience with the war was wearing thin and presidential authority was ebbing. "I'm not going to end up like LBJ, holed up in the White House, afraid to show my face in the street," Nixon told

Bob Haldeman, his principal White House confidant. "I'm going to stop that war. Fast."[6] There was little doubt he intended to end the war.

Kissinger shared Nixon's judgment about the war and on occasion was even more optimistic about the timetable. "Give us six months," he told a visiting group of Quakers, "and if we haven't ended the war by then, you can come back and tear down the White House fence."[7] When Kissinger got down to memoir-writing a few years later, he got a grip on his enthusiasm. A "tolerable outcome" to the war, he wrote, "could be achieved within a year."[8] Whether it was to be six months or a year, Nixon and Kissinger were both positive they had a plan to bring the war to a swift end. "I do not want an American boy to be in Vietnam for one day longer than is necessary for our national interest," Nixon told newsmen.[9] Whereas Nixon's predecessors had defined their commitment to Vietnam as requiring an escalation of the war, Nixon saw his as enabling an orderly withdrawal from the war.

The question has often been asked: Did Nixon really have a plan, a "secret plan," to end the war, as it was often stated during the 1968 campaign? Not really. In January, a few weeks before the New Hampshire primary, Nixon promised "to end the war and win the peace in the Pacific," a phrase crafted by speechwriter William Safire to satisfy the public's desire for an end to the war without saying specifically how it would happen. Michigan governor George Romney, also running for the GOP presidential nomination, repeatedly challenged Nixon. "Where is your secret plan?" he asked. For political reasons, Nixon left the impression that he had a plan, whether described as secret or not, to end the war, but he refused to divulge it, saying artfully he did not want to interfere with Johnson's negotiations with the North Vietnamese. UPI reporter Milt Benjamin might have been the first to come up with the phrase "secret plan," wrote Safire, but other reporters also began to quote Nixon as saying, "I have a secret plan to end the war." In his *Political Dictionary,* Safire insisted that Nixon never used the words "secret plan"; but reporters and politicians have often returned to the "secret plan" as an example of a proposal more implied than announced but useful nonetheless.[10] The "secret plan" has become an ineradicable phrase in America's political history.

On January 27, 1969, at Nixon's first news conference, Helen Thomas of United Press International cut to the key question. "Mr. President," she asked, "now that you are president, what is your peace plan for Vietnam?"[11] It was clear from the deliberate vagueness of his answer that if he had a plan, he intended to keep it secret. And if he did not have a plan, he was not going to admit it, especially after running as a candidate who left the impression that he did, indeed, have a plan.

More important to Nixon than a formal "plan," with bullet points and highlighted paragraphs, was a gut approach to ending the war, which he shared with his new national security adviser. Kissinger served as Nixon's cheerleader and confidante and, when appropriate, his negotiator. If, as they thought, the United States was no longer willing to pay the price in time and treasure to fight a guerrilla war in Southeast Asia, then the withdrawal of American forces was inevitable. But if they also thought that this withdrawal would damage American "credibility" and "prestige" throughout the world, which they regarded as potentially devastating to global peace, then they had to find a way of disguising withdrawal so it would have minimal effect on American security.

Their formula was an imaginative if ultimately unsuccessful mix of diplomacy and military power. For a time, though, it seemed to work. In an updated version of Metternich's nineteenth-century "balance of power" concept, they constructed, in their mind's eye, a triangular model of international diplomacy with Washington, Moscow, and Beijing at the three corners. The immediate effect would be to diminish Vietnam's importance as a central player on the world stage, allowing Washington to play Moscow off against Beijing, or Beijing off against Moscow, and, in the process, to persuade both communist capitals that it was much more in their interest to help the United States get out of Vietnam "with honor" than it was to prolong the war and thereby run the risk of a wider war, possibly with nuclear weapons, involving one or both of them. "Linkage" it was called, in which every American move on the global chessboard was seen as having an effect on Moscow and/or Beijing. Nothing in this game of power would be left to chance. In this way, Vietnam would be put into a more realistic perspective: What Kissinger called "a fourth rate power like North Vietnam" would not be allowed by this theoretical triangle of linked interests to determine the fate of the world.

Nixon and Kissinger worked very closely, but from the beginning it was clear that these clever, ambitious men represented a very odd couple: Nixon, the politician who loved to be alone in a darkened room with his yellow lined pad writing instructions to his staff; and Kissinger, the scholarly strategist who valued the manipulation of power and the reputation he had encouraged of being a "secret swinger." "Power," he famously proclaimed, "is the ultimate aphrodisiac." If most diplomats abhorred notoriety, Kissinger loved it when it suited his strategy, enjoying nothing more than a photo of him and a Hollywood star on the front page of a tabloid.

By nature, both Nixon and Kissinger were secretive, paranoid, and deeply suspicious— eager to wall off the conduct of foreign policy from the sprawling Washington bureaucracy, stuffed, as they saw it, with unimaginative cookie pushers at the State Department and all-too-cautious generals at the Pentagon. They trusted no one, and they were "unencumbered by moral scruples," as Kissinger had once described Bismarck. Both were obsessed by leaks, always imagining the vast government bureaucracy filled with political enemies plotting to sabotage their policies. And yet, Kissinger and even occasionally Nixon would leak stories to the media. Having reached the pinnacle of power, they were determined to use it in their own ways to their own ends.

It was into this bizarre universe of intrigue and manipulation that Nixon injected a tactic that only he could have conceived. Nixon deliberately created an image of himself as a "madman," so determined to end the war "with honor" that he would do anything, even, if necessary, use nuclear weapons. He was not mad, of course, but there was enough of the oddball in him to give credibility to the image. French journalist Michel Tatu, with a dash of Gallic wordplay, called it "credible irrationality," meaning Nixon's "madness" had to be seen as real.

This image was cultivated in different ways. Kissinger, in his office, would create an atmosphere of cozy comfort, as if only to this one visiting reporter could he possibly convey the awful truth that his boss, the president, was (lowering his voice at this point) "crazy, out of control." Haldeman would arrange for reporters to get the word that "for God's sake, you know Nixon is obsessed with communism. We can't restrain him when he's angry—and he has his hand on the nuclear button." The message was, Nixon must get his way, or . . . God knows what.[12] On occasion, Nixon himself would angrily tell Soviet ambassador Anatoly Dobrynin that the United States was not going to wait "forever" for Soviet cooperation on Vietnam, that the world was teetering on a precipice, and that if Russia didn't help "soon," he would take action. Nixon didn't specify what action, but he allowed the impression to be created in diplomatic chanceries that he was, on this issue, truly unhinged and was prepared to do . . . anything. Nixon was calculating that Ho Chi-Minh would get the word, that Ho would be "sensible," and that he would join in an arrangement for an "honorable" U.S. departure from Vietnam. Nixon was also calculating that Russia and China would encourage Ho to be "sensible."

That was Nixon's early and flawed vision, shared by Kissinger. It took only a few months for them to realize that Ho might have another vision in mind. For the Vietnamese leader, there was only one, unshakable goal in this long war—that Vietnam achieve "full independence," the same goal he shared with Truman in the mid-1940s. Ho saw his splintered Vietnam as one country with a noble history. If, to retain Vietnam's national identity, he and his countrymen had to fight the Chinese, who were chronic antagonists, or the French, who were imperialists, or the Americans, who had stumbled into a colonial war, then the Vietnamese would fight them; and they were confident they would win, no matter how long it would take, how many lives would be lost, how much treasure would be spent. Ho was prepared to fight to the end. If the United States chose to withdraw from the battlefield on terms that would leave the north and south under his control, then that would obviously be the ideal outcome for him; but if his enemy chose instead to go to extremes and bomb Hanoi or Haiphong, invade North Vietnam, destroy the dike system, use nuclear weapons, kill many more thousands of Vietnamese, then the war would continue. Ho had his own calculation: That one day the Americans, 10,000 miles away from home, would leave, either as a defeated nation or as an exhausted and humiliated one, but they would leave. Nixon did not understand Ho, nor did he appreciate the chasm in history, psychology, and ideology that separated the two sides.

Charles de Gaulle, despite France's tragic history in Indochina, tended to agree with Ho, though he hid his views in long disquisitions on Europe, China, and the Middle East. Nixon and de Gaulle met three times during the president's first visit to Paris in February 1969. According to a Nixon note taker, de Gaulle did not believe the United States should withdraw from Vietnam "with undue haste," but he did feel the United States should and could withdraw. "You Americans can make this kind of settlement," he assured Nixon, "because your power and wealth are so great you can do it with dignity."[13] Expanding on the idea, de Gaulle noted that the United States could negotiate both political and military issues at the same time, while establishing its own timetable for withdrawal. This observation was a source of instant gratification for Nixon—it fit into his early thinking.

At a dinner, de Gaulle turned to Kissinger and asked, "Why don't you get out of Vietnam?"

"Because," Kissinger replied cautiously, not wishing to upset the Nixon-de Gaulle rapport, "a sudden withdrawal might give us a credibility problem."

"Where?" de Gaulle wondered.

"The Middle East," Kissinger responded.

"How very odd," said de Gaulle, turning away. "It is precisely in the Middle East that I thought your enemies had the credibility problem."[14]

This was apparently de Gaulle's way of encouraging Nixon to believe that the United States could withdraw from Indochina without a loss of credibility and without the risk of upsetting the global balance of power.

It was always Nixon's strategy to test the ongoing Paris negotiations before embarking on his "plan" to end the Vietnam War. After replacing Averell Harriman as U.S. negotiator with Henry Cabot Lodge Jr.—Democrat out, Republican in—he laid out a reformulation of the old "two-track approach." This meant that in any negotiation there would be both a political track and a military one. Because de Gaulle had suggested this approach, Nixon took it seriously. Kissinger took it seriously, too. He believed that he could negotiate both tracks separately, but if he wished, he could also negotiate both at the same time. Unfortunately, the communists would not play his game. They believed that the two tracks were inseparable—that no settlement of one was possible without settlement of the other.

Lodge, on Nixon's orders, opened the Paris negotiation by proposing a "mutual withdrawal" of "foreign forces" from South Vietnam. He must have known that in 1966 Johnson had proposed a similar plan—that United States forces would pull out of South Vietnam six months after the North Vietnamese had withdrawn. The communists quickly rejected Nixon's plan just as they had earlier rejected Johnson's. They did not see themselves as "foreign."

What next?

On May 14, Nixon delivered a primetime speech on Vietnam—the first of many on the war. It was noteworthy for two important insights into Nixon's thinking at the time: He thought the North Vietnamese had abandoned all hope of a military victory in South Vietnam, which was dead wrong, and he believed the communists were counting on a "collapse of will in the United States," which was right.[15] The following day, at a White House meeting, Nixon asked CIA director Richard Helms for Hanoi's reaction to his speech. The North Vietnamese believed, Helms said, that "domestic dissent will force the United States to pull out."[16]

Hardly a day passed without Nixon worrying about the same thing—that one day "domestic dissent" would reach such a crescendo that his administration—*any* administration—would be forced to trim its sails and adjust its policies and accept an unhappy outcome in Vietnam. He confided to his advisers:

"If we fail to end the war in a way that will not be an American defeat, and in a way that will deny the aggressor his goal, the hawks in communist nations will push for even more and broader aggression." He continued, putting Vietnam in a broader context: "If a great power fails to meet its aims, it ceases to be a great power. When a great power looks inward, when it fails to live up to its commitments, then the greatness fades away." With General Douglas MacArthur, it was old soldiers fading away; with Nixon, it was U.S. greatness fading away. With Dwight D. Eisenhower, as with John F. Kennedy and Lyndon B. Johnson, and now with Nixon, there was always a strong belief that the United States had to "live up to its commitments."

Sadly, Nixon was learning one of the lessons of presidential leadership in the cold war—that the United States could not use its nuclear power to impose its will on smaller nations, such as Korea and Vietnam, without running the risk of a superpower confrontation out of all proportion to the original reasons for the war. Harry Truman had to settle for a stalemate in Korea, and Nixon had to grapple with the possibility of the United States losing a war, which had never happened before. He had difficulty imagining an American defeat, resulting from "domestic dissent," but in a private corner of his mind he seemed to know such a possibility existed.

Nixon, never one to lack a plan, had an immediate next step in mind, cloaked in his usual need for absolute secrecy. It consisted of two steps: First, he would begin a unilateral withdrawal of American forces, based on the totally unrealistic assumption that the South Vietnamese would be trained and strengthened to assume responsibility for protecting their own country; and second, he would, as he had promised in the 1968 campaign, end the draft, which he thought unfair and untenable, and begin an all-volunteer military force. Both the beginning of the withdrawal and the end of the draft were risky steps, and both needed time for proper preparation, but Nixon was determined to move forward. He was deeply concerned about the effect on American democracy of the widespread protests against the war, the anger and disappointment spreading into the middle class, the college campuses ready to explode, the simmering racial violence in American cities, and the drugs so prevalent in the armed forces. Like many Americans who had seen the antiwar protests at the 1968 Democratic National Convention in Chicago, he feared that the very fabric of American society was unraveling, and Vietnam was, if not the major reason, certainly a major reason for the spreading dissent.

For Nixon, withdrawal was the essential first step; ending the draft would follow his presumed re-election. Unlike other presidents from Truman to

Johnson, who kept adding troops to South Vietnam, Nixon decided to begin the process of pulling them out of Vietnam. "Gettin' out" was the way Johnson would have put it. A phased withdrawal would mollify public outrage against the war, he hoped, and it would buy time for the training of South Vietnamese troops to assume responsibility for protecting their country, as the Americans left. "Vietnamization" was the name given to this program. Defense Secretary Melvin Laird, a former congressman from Wisconsin, strongly supported it. He wanted the United States to get out of Vietnam. He was a very practical hawk. "I wanted to rely on the South Vietnamese to do the fighting," he told us. "We had to leave."[17]

Kissinger opposed Vietnamization, believing it was nothing more than "an elegant bugout," a slow surrender to the communists. "We have to impress Hanoi with our staying power," Kissinger stated, "or we won't have flexibility."

"I knew that time was running out for us, because the public wasn't going to support the war any longer," Laird later explained. "Henry didn't understand this because he wasn't a politician. Instead, all he worried about was that Vietnamization would undercut his diplomacy."[18]

Nixon agreed with Kissinger but, for political reasons, supported Laird. "We need a massive training program," he insisted, "so that the South Vietnamese can be trained to take over the fighting, that they can be phased in as we phase out." How eerily similar to President George W. Bush's mantra during the Iraq War—that as "the Iraqis stand up, we will stand down." And President Barack Obama's during the Afghanistan war—that the United States could withdraw by the end of 2014 because the Afghans would, by that time, be able to prosecute the war without the Americans.

Withdrawal was a risky proposition. Nixon understood there was always the possibility the North Vietnamese would wait until the Americans pulled enough troops out of South Vietnam to tip the battlefield balance unmistakably in their favor, and then they would go on the attack, much more certain of ultimate victory. But Nixon had persuaded himself that Vietnamization would work, somehow.

On June 7, Nixon flew to Honolulu to inform General Abrams that he was going to start the phased withdrawal of American forces from Vietnam. The first slice would be 25,000 troops. Abrams's extreme discomfort, Kissinger wrote, was "painful to see." The general suddenly realized that he was no longer in charge of winning a war but of managing a pullout. Abrams had changed American strategy in Vietnam, and the change was working. No longer was it a war of attrition; now it was a counter-insurgency struggle, with the United States trying to win the "hearts and minds" of the Vietnamese peasant.

On June 8, Nixon flew on to Midway and told President Nguyen Van Thieu about the start of the American withdrawal. Thieu already knew of his decision—it was on the front page of every newspaper. As compensation, Nixon promised him massive economic and military aid, but Thieu smelled a betrayal. To that point, he thought the American goal had been, if not outright victory over the communists, then at least enough of a victory to ensure the continued existence of a free and independent South Vietnam, much as Eisenhower had promised in 1959.

Two weeks later, utterly persuaded that he was pursuing the only sensible policy, Nixon decided to withdraw another 35,000 troops. Kissinger groaned. "The more troops are withdrawn," he wrote, "the more Hanoi will be encouraged."[19]

If the North Vietnamese had decided at this point to stop their offensive operations and watch the American withdrawal, many lives, needlessly lost, would have been saved; and they would have gone on to occupy all of South Vietnam anyway, just as they did a few years later. The United States needed what Kissinger called a "decent interval" of time between an American withdrawal and a communist triumph, but the North Vietnamese stuck rigidly to their game plan, refusing to show any flexibility. They did not trust Nixon, nor did he trust them, and so the war continued—in fact, intensified—in a strange interlocking of military action in South Vietnam and growing antiwar demonstrations in the United States. Nixon was fighting one war on two fronts.

During the summer of 1969, a misleading calm settled over Washington. Was it possible, the White House wondered, that its policy was working? No, wrote Laird, in a letter to Nixon that the president found disturbing. "This may be an illusory phenomenon," Laird thought. "The actual antipathy for the war is, in my judgment, significant and growing." A Nixon aide, John Charles Huston, once a U.S. Army intelligence specialist, anticipated serious trouble on college campuses. In a detailed memo to Nixon, Huston predicted "student disorder in the fall, which will surpass anything we have seen before." Sometime between October 15 and November 15, he said, "student militancy will sweep major campuses and flow into the streets of our major cities," requiring "prompt action" and "repression."

Laird and Huston must have owned remarkably clear crystal balls—or good intelligence. For, on October 15, the Vietnam Moratorium Committee, formed by young activists from Senator Eugene McCarthy's 1968 presidential campaign, organized massive antiwar demonstrations in many cities around the country and the world, attracting more than 4 million people who demanded an end to the Vietnam War. "Historic in its scope," pronounced Walter Cronkite on the CBS Evening News. "Never before had so many demonstrated their hope for peace." Huge crowds assembled in Washington, New York, Boston, Detroit, and Miami to protest against the war. College campuses burst aflame with antiwar fervor. Dormitories were trashed, quads destroyed. Clashes occurred between students and police. Placards with photos of Nixon labeled "WAR CRIMINAL" were carried to the Pentagon. If Nixon thought that the start of troop withdrawals would somehow calm the waters of antiwar sentiment, he was obviously mistaken. He was also deeply disappointed, though, on the surface, he assumed a dismissive attitude towards the demonstrations, saying policy "made in the streets" was nothing more than "anarchy."

For months, Nixon had been secretly planning a new diplomatic/military strategy codenamed "Duck Hook." November 1, the first anniversary of Johnson's decision to stop bombing North Vietnam, was the date selected for the start of a dramatic escalation of the war against North Vietnam—if diplomacy failed. Through a number of diplomatic channels, the president, all of his "mad man" credentials now on vivid and deliberate display, sent word to Ho Chi-minh that "measures of great consequence and force" would befall North Vietnam if there were no meaningful progress in the Paris peace talks by November 1. The French served as Nixon's initial intermediary, but he quickly notified others of his intentions and impatience. Moscow was an obvious back channel, too. Kissinger told Ambassador Dobrynin, a diplomat with an ear trained for subtlety, that Nixon was losing patience with diplomacy and planning a major offensive against North Vietnam.

Like what? Dobrynin asked skeptically.

Like nothing you've ever seen, Kissinger replied.

With other diplomats, Kissinger spoke of "severe, punishing blows" against North Vietnam. Nixon added his own warning to Dobrynin. "You may believe you can break me," he said. "You may believe that the American domestic situation is unmanageable. . . . I can assure you the humiliation of a defeat is absolutely unacceptable to my country. Let me repeat that we will not hold still for being diddled to death in Vietnam."[20]

At a National Security Council meeting in early September, Kissinger outlined plans for bombing Hanoi and other cities, a naval blockade of major ports, the mining of rivers and the bombing of dikes; and if these attacks didn't break Hanoi's stubborn negotiating stance in Paris, then a land invasion of North Vietnam including the possible use of nuclear weapons would follow. "We need a plan to end the war," Kissinger said, "not only to withdraw troops." Nixon, in private meetings, shared the "Duck Hook" strategy with congressional leaders, assuming it would leak. In mid-October, operating on the same assumption, he ordered nuclear bombers of the Strategic Air Command to stand by on full alert. He wanted to stimulate a crisis atmosphere.

Except, a few days after the October 15 demonstrations, the largest antiwar demonstrations in American history, Nixon abruptly changed his mind. He quietly dropped his November 1 deadline—he decided once again to turn to television, as he had done so many times in his career, and talk directly to the American people, going over the heads of the demonstrators and the journalists. He wanted to explain his Vietnam policy and appeal to the people's patriotism during wartime. He believed that "the great silent majority" of the American people supported him, not the demonstrators—and would support him even more if they understood his policy better. He took his yellow lined pad to Camp David and alone, jotting down phrases such as "They can't defeat us militarily. . . . They can't break South Vietnam. . . . They cannot break us," drafted his personal appeal to American patriotism. One draft after another, until he felt he had it right. At 8 a.m. on November 1, he telephoned Haldeman. "The baby's just been born," he purred with pride. Then he spent the rest of the day memorizing the speech, modeling himself after Churchill and de Gaulle. He loved quoting Randolph Churchill, who once told him, "My father spends the best hours of his life writing out his extemporaneous speeches."

On November 3, at 9:30 p.m., speaking from the Oval Office, Nixon looked into the television cameras of the three major networks, ABC, CBS, and NBC, and told the American people that it would have been "popular and easy" on assuming the presidency for him to order "an immediate withdrawal of all American forces" from Vietnam. It was, after all, "Johnson's war." Nixon went on to relate a brief history of presidential decisionmaking from Eisenhower to Kennedy to Johnson. The U.S. "commitment" to South Vietnam, he said, had actually started fifteen years earlier, when Eisenhower sent economic and military aid to South Vietnam; and continued seven years earlier, when Kennedy sent 16,000 "combat advisers"; and finally four years earlier, when Johnson deployed a half million "combat" troops to Indochina. (He could also have mentioned Truman's earlier contribution, but didn't.) By naming his three immediate predecessors, one Republican and two Democrats, Nixon meant to italicize Vietnam as a bipartisan "presidential commitment" dating back decades. Many people, "I among them," considered Johnson's decision to be "wrong." But could the United States simply withdraw and go home? No, Nixon continued, "a precipitate withdrawal" would be a "disaster," leading almost inevitably to a "bloody reign of terror" in South Vietnam, "atrocities," and the "massacre" of millions," including among them Catholic refugees. And it would lead to "the first defeat in our nation's history."

So, he totally rejected an "immediate, precipitate withdrawal of all Americans from Vietnam" and defined his new strategy as "our search for a just peace" through either a negotiated settlement in Paris or through Vietnamization on the battlefield. He assured the many millions watching him that the United States "will withdraw all of our forces from Vietnam on a schedule" determined by his success in the Paris peace talks or in the implementation of his Vietnamization program. He offered no timetable. He wanted the domestic advantages of troop withdrawal, but he still thought he could pursue the war on his terms.

"It is not the easy way," he added, but "it is the right way. It is a plan which will end the war and serve the cause of peace." Then, as he prepared to conclude his speech, he acknowledged that it was not "fashionable to speak of patriotism or national destiny these days." But he proceeded to do just that. "The survival of peace and freedom will be determined by whether the American people have the moral stamina and the courage to meet the challenge of free world leadership. Let historians not record that when America was the most powerful nation in the world, we passed on the other side of the road and allowed the last hopes for peace and freedom of millions of people to be suffocated by the forces of totalitarianism."

Then Nixon, like the conductor of a national symphony orchestra, pulled all of his themes together in a thunderous final crescendo. "To you—the great silent majority of my fellow Americans—I ask for your support," he said, looking sincerely and steadily into the lens. "I pledged in my campaign for the presidency to end the war in a way that we could win the peace. I have initiated a plan of action which will enable me to keep that pledge. The more support I can have from the American people, the sooner that pledge can be redeemed: for the more divided we are at home, the less likely the enemy is to negotiate in Paris. Let us be united for peace. Let us also be united against defeat. Because let us understand: North Vietnam cannot defeat or humiliate the United States. Only Americans can do that."[21]

The president asked for the support of "the great silent majority" of the American people, and he got it. Some of it, he knew, had been orchestrated by the Republican National Committee, but so what? Gallup recorded a 77 percent approval rating for the president's speech and, a few days later, reported an overall approval rating for the president himself of 68 percent, up from 52 percent before the Moratorium demonstration. Congress passed resolutions expressing bipartisan support for the president's policy: 300 out of 435 in the House of Representatives, and 58 out of 100 in the Senate. Fifty-thousand telegrams and 30,000 letters flooded the White House, most of them positive. Nixon said triumphantly, "When the lives of our young men are involved, we are not Democrats, we are not Republicans, we are Americans."

A few days later, his feet up on his Oval Office desk, Nixon observed with satisfaction, "We've got those liberal bastards on the run now."

It was, though, a brief moment of satisfaction. Nixon, always on edge for criticism, imagined or real, asked about television coverage of his November 3 speech. Excellent, his aides responded, except, Dwight Chapin reminded everyone, for Marvin Kalb's commentary on CBS News. At the time, I was the network's chief diplomatic correspondent, and I reported that a number of administration officials had told me that, in their opinion, Ho Chi-minh was actually signaling a desire for serious negotiations rather than, as Nixon said, a rigid rejection of the president's overtures. In his speech, Nixon reported that there had been an exchange of letters between him and Ho, and Ho's had been decidedly negative. (Ho died on September 2, 1969, after the exchange.)

TV reporters had been "briefed" on the president's speech hours earlier by a "senior administration official," as Kissinger was often called, and they had also been given copies. This was routine media management for all presidential addresses. I used the time between the briefing and the speech to check with a number of sources at the White House and the State Department, who had also read the speech. They all told me that Ho's letter, far from being as bleakly negative as Nixon described, actually contained a glimmer of hope that the Paris negotiations might evolve into something meaningful. Obviously, Nixon hated my TV commentary and quickly placed me on his secret "enemies list." He then wiretapped my home telephone (and that of three other reporters) in an action of dubious legality, ransacked my broadcast booth at the State Department, ordered an audit of my income tax returns, and later on had me tailed while I was covering the Paris peace talks. The White House also wanted round-the-clock surveillance, but the FBI's J. Edgar Hoover thought it too expensive and unnecessary.

It didn't stop there. When Nixon learned that I had criticized his speech, he erupted in anger and screamed something like, "Well, what do you expect? He's a 'Romanian agent.'" I don't know to this day how he got this "Romanian agent" nuttiness into his head, but there it was. Kissinger, who knew better, nodded in agreement, perhaps further to ingratiate himself with his boss. I once covered a Nixon visit to Romania, and maybe he did not like my coverage there, either. I know of no other Romania-Nixon-Kalb convergence.

My first reaction when I heard about this whacky "Romanian agent" stuff years later was to laugh. If I had to be seen as a spy, I told friends, I wanted to be seen as a British spy, or an Italian spy, someone in any case far more dignified and debonair than a "Romanian spy." But after a while my laughter stopped, and though I didn't cry, I felt a deep sadness for my country.

This pathetic presidential effort to investigate my personal and professional life was an absolute waste of time and money—nothing improper was ever discovered, nothing improper ever done; but it was an outrageous example of a president's neurosis run amok. Was this an example of his vaunted "credible irrationality"? Not to me.

White House aides knew of the president's neurosis; but rather than soothe it, they fed it. During this anxious time, an aide named Jeb Stuart Magruder drafted a memo for Nixon entitled "The Rifle and the Shotgun." His point was that earlier efforts to corral and contain the media were too scattered—this was the "shotgun" approach. Now what was needed was a carefully aimed "rifle" approach—such as, for example, tasking the Federal Communications Commission to monitor "unfair" news reports or to threaten antitrust suits against the networks. It was in the spirit of the "rifle" approach that speechwriter Pat Buchanan came up with a wild, mischievous caper—why not have Vice President Spiro Agnew, who rarely was engaged in anything of value, launch a major assault on American journalism, first on TV news and then on newspaper coverage? Why not intimidate troublesome TV reporters and anchormen? Better still, why not intimidate the networks themselves? Lately, Buchanan believed, they had forgotten how dependent they were on government contracts, handouts, and licenses. If it was true that most Americans got their ideas and impressions about the Vietnam War from television news, then it was time for the administration to undercut the credibility of television news. Nixon thought it was a great idea.

Buchanan was assigned the task of writing Agnew's speeches. On November 13, two days before the next big antiwar demonstration in Washington, Agnew attacked the three networks, declaring that "a small group of men, numbering perhaps no more than a dozen anchormen, commentators, and executive producers . . . decide what forty or fifty million Americans will learn of the day's events in the nation and in the world." Agnew's aim was to isolate this "small and unelected elite" from the average American, to make "this little group of men" seem foreign, distant, and suspect. "These commentators and producers live and work in the geographical and intellectual confines of Washington, D.C. or New York City. . . . They talk constantly to one another, thereby providing artificial reinforcement to their shared viewpoints." He spoke of Washington, D.C., and New York City as if they were Moscow and Beijing.

If Churchill during World War II had had to "contend with a gaggle of commentators," Agnew implied, he would have lost the war. Further, he went on, Americans who relied on television news got a skewed, twisted, biased picture of reality. Most students were not really "embittered radicals," he said. Most "black Americans" were not angry dissidents who hated their country. Most Americans were not demonstrating in the nation's capital. Was it not time for the networks to change their "liberal" ways? Not time for them to be "more responsive to the views of the nation and more responsible to the people they serve?"

Agnew was scratching an exposed nerve end. Television routinely carried the "bad news" from Vietnam to living rooms around the country; but if television news was slanted, then, he asked, how could the American people get straight reports? Television fed the anger that boiled up on campuses and in cities. To Agnew, television was the culprit. If tamed, intimidated, or controlled more effectively, television would not be able to "distort" the news, and the "silent majority" would be able to hear the "truth" about Vietnam. After all, government had the power, through the Federal Communications Commission, to reject station renewal applications, and that power could be used to cut into television's power and prominence.

Buchanan realized that with Agnew's speech he had hit pay dirt: in the vice president he had created "the spokesman of the Middle American, the Robespierre of the Great Silent Majority." He had also encouraged a government crackdown on networks and reporters, which had the effect of driving a wedge between them and their public and of forcing them to be more "understanding" of administration policy in Vietnam. When more than 500,000 Americans demonstrated in Washington on November 15 against U.S. policy in Vietnam, a huge and obvious story deserving live coverage, especially on an otherwise quiet news day, the TV networks, which had covered Agnew's anti-TV speech live, decided not to cover the demonstration live, a strong indication that

Agnew's speech was already having an effect on network decisions. Live, the demonstration would have had an immediate, nationwide impact. Covered as a normal news story, not live, the demonstration lost much of its impact and helped the administration contain antiwar sentiment.

Nixon, in a feisty mood after his November 3 speech, decided that, with the public behind him, he would press forward with another troop withdrawal from Vietnam. For months, he had had a six-figure goal in mind—withdrawing more than 100,000 troops before the end of his first year in office. He had already cut 60,000 troops—first, 25,000, and then 35,000. Now, after consultation with Laird, who also favored a speedy pullout, Nixon decided to withdraw an additional 55,000 troops, meaning that by January 1, 1970, the United States would have withdrawn 115,000 troops, a sizeable reduction that in his mind should have eased the antiwar furor. But it didn't.

The next presidential announcement about troop withdrawals came in April 1970, a particularly gorgeous month in Washington. The Japanese cherry blossoms should have brightened even the president's mood. On April 20, he announced an unexpectedly large withdrawal of 150,000 troops in the next year, but he first arranged to trick the *New York Times* and the *Washington Post* into believing and reporting that the cuts would be much more modest— somewhere in the range of 40,000 to 50,000 troops. At Nixon's direction, both newspapers had been given the same misleading leak. The president loved to fool reporters. That he was also fooling the American people did not seem to bother him. "We finally have in sight the just peace we are seeking," he said.

There was another reason for this eye-catching announcement, though. It was to camouflage a major escalation and expansion of the war. At the time, Nixon was secretly planning to invade parts of Cambodia, and General Abrams needed all the troops at his command for that job—he could not tolerate further troop cutbacks for at least several months. By dazzling the public with his announcement of a 150,000 troop cut, Nixon did not have to be specific about when the troops would actually leave South Vietnam. The effect was to freeze withdrawals for the period of the Cambodian operation, while trumpeting his plan for another huge withdrawal, which, when finally implemented, would cut U.S. troop strength in South Vietnam from 434,000 to 284,000.

Cambodia was very much on Nixon's mind. "We need a bold move in Cambodia," he told Kissinger.[22] By bold, he meant a decisive military strike that would prove to the American people and the world that the United States was winning in South Vietnam. Up to this time, his negotiating strategy had produced nothing, and he wanted a change. Nixon decided that the United States would attack North Vietnamese bases in two border regions called the Parrot's Beak and the Fishhook. The intelligence from South Vietnam was, for a change, positive, and Nixon decided to "hit 'em hard." ARVN, the Army of Vietnam, was reportedly expanding and improving its combat effectiveness. The United States had poured hundreds of millions into the effort. The communists seemed to be on the defensive, pulling back from cities and villages and avoiding confrontations with both the South Vietnamese and the Americans.

Nixon could have exploited this moment to extricate the United States from the war. But rather than pull an imaginative compromise out of the deadlock at the Paris peace talks, he decided to carry the war into neighboring Cambodia, hoping that with this new show of force the North Vietnamese would finally be persuaded to accept his terms for peace—forgetting yet again that the Vietnamese were fighting for their country, their national pride, their place in the history of Asia. Nixon never seemed able to understand the power of Vietnamese nationalism, and the war continued.

As final preparations swung into high gear, Nixon began to drink heavily. He spent most of the day in his darkened office, a bottle of booze sharing the desk with his yellow lined pad, according to a number of his advisers. He was starting to write yet another television address explaining his war policy to the American people. In telephone calls to Kissinger, his speech sounded slurred. For a few days, he did not sleep at all. He drank and he wrote, and when on occasion he emerged from his self-imposed isolation, he would explode in anger at Haldeman, at Kissinger, at his butler, at anyone who happened to be near him.

On April 30, American and South Vietnamese forces crossed the international border and attacked communist sanctuaries in Cambodia. The South Vietnamese army, in the vanguard, slashed its way into the Parrot's Beak sanctuary, and the U.S. troops moved against the Fishhook sanctuary.

In the evening, Nixon appeared on television to explain and justify his decision to send American troops into another Asian country. Though he stressed that American aims were limited in scope and duration, and the United States had no intention of occupying Cambodia, he nevertheless spoke in apocalyptic terms. "We live in an age of anarchy, both abroad and at home," he declared. Expanding on the central themes of his "silent majority" speech, he spoke of "mindless attacks on all the great institutions which have been created by free civilizations in the last 500 years. If, when the chips are down, the world's most powerful nation, the United States of America, acts like a pitiful, helpless giant, the forces of totalitarianism and anarchy will threaten free nations and free institutions throughout the world." Nixon portrayed himself as the defender of Western civilization, another courageous president who kept his word, who honored America's commitments to South Vietnam, even as he was in the process of betraying those very commitments. He saw himself in a historical pageant, starting with Wilson, FDR, JFK, and going on to the First and Second World Wars and the Cuban missile crisis, and now Vietnam.

The president concluded on a personal note, which even in retrospect sounds hollow. "I would rather be a one-term president and do what I believe is right than to be a two-term president at the cost of seeing America become a second-rate power," Nixon said.[23] Nearly forty years later, Senator John McCain would strike a similar tone during the 2008 presidential campaign. The Arizona Republican repeated time and again that he would rather lose an election than lose a war. McCain at the time was speaking about Iraq, of course.

Backstage, Kissinger tried to be supportive of the president while at the same time conveying the impression to certain reporters that he had serious reservations about the Cambodia attack. Stewart Alsop, an influential columnist for *Newsweek,* kept notes on one conversation with Kissinger. "He feared that if the President moved against Cambodia with U.S. troops," Alsop wrote, "some universities would be burned and the whole academic community would be up in arms." Kissinger said that unless the President moved against the communist sanctuaries, Cambodia and Laos would probably both fall to North Vietnam. He then rationalized that the Cambodian invasion bought time for the United States. "We can get out very fast . . . if," Kissinger added, "we have two years."

Alsop interjected: "Henry, you haven't got two years."

"No," Kissinger replied, "but we have to act as though we had. . . . The trick . . . is to stage a great retreat and emerge at the other end still a great power, reasonably cohesive at home."[24] Kissinger, a great believer in the "decent interval" theory, actually believed that the Cambodian operation would open the door to serious negotiations "by July or August." Time and again, in talks with reporters, he would speak of time frames that were unrealized and negotiations that were to prove unfruitful.

Both Nixon and Kissinger lived in their own worlds, often detached from reality. Both also shaved the truth. They announced that 5,000 U.S. troops were in the Cambodia operation. There were, in fact, more than 31,000 U.S. troops and more than 43,000 South Vietnamese troops. On the first day of combat operations, three U.S. helicopters were shot down, their crews either killed or wounded. The casualty report listed only six Americans wounded.

The following morning, May 1, Nixon went to the Pentagon. "I want to take out all those sanctuaries," he told the generals. "Make whatever plans are necessary, and then just do it. Let's go blow the hell out of them. Knock them all out so that they can't be used against us again. Ever." Nixon's language was embarrassingly earthy, laced with curse words. Laird and Kissinger sat mute, concerned that the president seemed "a little bit out of control." Later, Nixon ripped into all his critics. "They hate us, the country, themselves, their wives, everything they do—these liberals. They are a lost generation. They have no reason to live anymore."[25]

On May 2, Haldeman brought "good numbers" to Nixon. The latest polls showed the president with an approval rating of 65 percent, according to one poll, and 51 percent, according to another. Nixon was still locked in a furious rage against all critics, especially those on Capitol Hill who railed against his Cambodian operation. He barged into a meeting of the Cambodian Action Group, posing like a modern Patton, tough, audacious, brave, and determined. Nixon, whenever the slightest uncertainty crept into his consciousness, watched the movie *Patton*, released earlier in 1970, and derived inspiration from this celluloid portrayal of a courageous general leading his troops into the bloodiest battles of World War II.

"Don't play a soft line—no aid and comfort here," Nixon shouted at spokesman Ron Ziegler, as he adlibbed the public line. "Big game is to pull this off," he said. "Bold move, imaginative, none of this screwing around." Then he expounded on what should be said about his critics on Capitol Hill: "Congressmen, really put it to them, some of them are cowards—sticking the knife in the back of US troops, not supporting the President. . . . 'Giving aid and comfort to the enemy'—use that phrase. Don't worry about divisiveness—having drawn the sword, don't take it out—stick it in hard. . . . Hit them in the gut."

But from the battlefield came news both surprising and discouraging. The North Vietnamese, who had excellent intelligence in Saigon, appeared to have been tipped off about America's plans for Cambodia. When U.S. and South Vietnamese troops entered Cambodia and burst into the sanctuaries, reporters said practically no one was there. The communists had withdrawn deeper into Cambodia, leaving the sanctuaries all but empty. U.S. troops drove twenty miles into Cambodia on the first day. They found large stockpiles of ammunition and equipment in the Fishhook sanctuary, but no enemy troops. The *New York Times* headline read: "ALLIED SEARCH IN CAMBODIA YIELDS FEW SIGNS OF FOES." Nixon expressed a different view. He told congressional leaders that more than 2,000 enemy troops had been killed in fierce combat. Six weeks later, when U.S. and South Vietnamese troops pulled out of Cambodia, the sad thought raced through the White House that the United States had accomplished nothing of consequence. One American war correspondent concluded that the invasion was a disaster. "It laid waste an innocent country. . . . It failed to encourage Vietnamization in South Vietnam and instead heightened disillusion and disgust . . . in the United States."[26]

More than "disillusion and disgust," in fact. The Cambodian invasion reignited congressional doubts about the Vietnam war and triggered mass antiwar demonstrations throughout the country, especially on college campuses, where rampaging students broke windows and occupied ROTC installations. The presidents of thirty-seven of the nation's top universities sent an "urgent" letter to the president, warning of planned demonstrations at more than a hundred other universities. Many were already shut down by student strikes.

On May 1, thousands of angry antiwar students ran through the college town of Kent, Ohio, breaking windows and battling with police. On May 2, they burned the ROTC building to the ground. GOP governor James Rhodes—who was waging a losing battle for the party's Senate nomination in a primary election three days later—ordered National Guardsmen to the Ohio State University campus, proclaiming their duty was to "eradicate the communist element." There was no evidence of communist infiltration of the student movement, but, under fire and seeking to portray himself as tough, Rhodes had no interest in facts. He also ordered more National Guardsmen to Kent State University. He called the students there "Nazi brownshirts, worse than brownshirts."

On May 4, the student anger exploded into bloodshed. Two thousand students demonstrated on the Kent State campus commons. Thousands of others huddled nearby. The guardsmen tried to break up the demonstration. They fired tear gas into the crowd. The students shouted insults and threw some of the hot canisters back at the troops. The soldiers kneeled, raised their rifles, but did not shoot. They were apparently hoping to frighten the students. The students, seemingly unintimidated, moved toward the troops. Within seconds, the troops fired into the advancing crowd of students—a fusillade of sixty-seven shots in thirteen seconds. Four students were killed, nine others wounded.

Just before 3 p.m., Haldeman rushed into the president's office with the news of the Kent State killings. "Is this because of me, of Cambodia?" Nixon asked in a hushed tone. "How do we turn this stuff off?"

For months, the antiwar movement had been comparatively quiescent. Now, after the Cambodian invasion and the killings at Kent State, it again rose in fury and anger. It grabbed the nation's conscience and raised profound questions. The front pages of most newspapers showed photographs of a nation in anguish. National Guardsmen in tear gas masks, their bayonets unsheathed, advancing on student protesters. A student in tears, her arms spread protectively over a dead colleague, her face looking upwards to the sky for an explanation she could understand. Tear gas clouded this campus, and soon many others. A father of one of the dead students told a reporter, "My child was not a bum." Editorial writers and television commentators, also looking for an explanation, sharpened their criticism of the war. The stock market registered its biggest drop since the Kennedy assassination. Economist Paul Samuelson wrote in *Newsweek* that "if Mr. Nixon were to announce defeat in Vietnam . . . the market would jump 50 points." The war was so unpopular that the Defense Department feared Washington was in danger of being overwhelmed by furious protesters. It was an amazing sight, un-American in concept: hundreds of combat-ready troops of the Third Army jumping out of trucks and taking up positions in and around the Executive Office Building; buses forming a protective wall around the White House; 5,000 troops occupying government buildings—all in anticipation of tens of thousands of demonstrators descending upon Washington to express their disgust with the president, the government, and the war.

Washington was a besieged capital. Kissinger, watching from his White House office, later wrote: "There was a shock wave that brought the nation and its leadership close to psychological exhaustion."[27] He went further: "The very fabric of the government was falling apart."

Congress, its finger on the pulse of popular discontent, felt an urgent need to move beyond expressions of disapproval for a war that now seemed without end. In American history, there had been many other examples of serious congressional dissent during wartime, but now Congress reached a new plateau, where for the first time it actually considered and passed legislation restricting a president's capacity to fight a foreign enemy. Cambodia was the tipping point. In the Senate, on May 13, Democrat Frank Church of Idaho and Republican John Sherman Cooper of Kentucky, both moderate critics of the war, proposed an amendment to the Foreign Military Sales bill that would stop the funding of all U.S. military activities in Cambodia after June 30. It would also stop the funding of all U.S. military aid to Cambodia. The administration strongly objected to the amendment.

For the next seven weeks, the Senate was embroiled in an emotional debate on what came to be called the Cooper-Church amendment. Day after day, the White House used all of its pulpits to argue that the amendment would give the communists a free hand in Cambodia and that America's sacrifice in life and treasure would have been in vain. Many senators, however, were listening more closely to their jittery constituents than to the White House. On June 30, the amendment passed by a vote of 58-37, suggesting a bipartisan belief that if the administration would not end the war, Congress would end it.

With this amendment, the Foreign Military Sales bill then went to a House-Senate conference, where it remained bottled up until the end of the year. The House, more hawkish in general and more susceptible to White House pressure, refused to accept the Senate version. House Republicans and conservative "blue dog" Democrats did not want to tie the president's hands in time of war. According to Kissinger, it really didn't matter. "By then," he wrote, "the damage was substantially done . . . the enemy was being told by the Senate that Cambodia was on its own."[28]

Two other Senate critics believed that the Cooper-Church amendment, because it was limited to Cambodia, did not go far enough. They had a more ambitious amendment in mind. Democratic senator George McGovern of South Dakota and Republican senator Mark Hatfield of Oregon, both articulate and persistent critics of the war, proposed an amendment to the Defense Procurement bill that aimed at ending the war in Indochina by the end of 1970. And how could that be accomplished? By simply cutting off all funds for the war, they argued. The amendment, in its original form, also called for a complete withdrawal of American forces from Indochina by June 30, 1971, six months into the next year. Up to that time, no other congressional effort had so blatantly defied executive authority. McGovern and Hatfield optimistically envisaged a Senate-House vote that would reflect the broad antiwar sentiment seen and felt throughout the land. Hoping to gain additional support, the sponsors revised the amendment to push back the withdrawal deadline to the end of 1971.

But when it became clear to McGovern that the amendment would ultimately fail—it did, on September 1, 1970, by a vote of 55-39—he rose to address his colleagues in language so emotional that it left them in stunned silence. "Every senator in this chamber is partly responsible for sending 50,000 young Americans to an early grave," he began. "Every senator here is partly responsible for that human wreckage at Walter Reed and Bethesda Naval [hospitals] and all across our land—young men without legs, or arms, or genitals, or faces or hopes. There are not very many of these blasted and broken boys who think this war is a glorious adventure. Do not talk to them about bugging out, or national honor or courage. It does not take any courage at all for a congressman, or a senator, or a president to wrap himself in the flag and say 'we are staying in Vietnam;' because it is not our blood that is being shed." Here McGovern was referring to a number of conservative senators who spoke of the war as a noble enterprise designed to save Vietnam from communism and to maintain America's honor. "We are responsible for those young men and their lives and their hopes," McGovern continued. "And if we do not end this damnable war, those young men will some day curse us for our pitiful willingness to let the executive carry the burden that the Constitution places on us." Because the Tonkin Gulf resolution was no longer relevant and no declaration of war existed, McGovern believed the president had no legal authority to conduct the war and it was time for Congress to fulfill its constitutional responsibility to end what he considered an illegal war.

When McGovern returned to his seat, "you could have heard a pin drop," recalled John Holum, one of his advisers on Vietnam. When the voting process began, one senator slowly approached McGovern, who was a WW II hero, to say that he was "offended" by McGovern's speech. "That's what I meant to do," McGovern replied.

Nixon and Kissinger saw these Senate debates as a "headlong retreat from responsibility." All Hanoi now had to do was "stall" at the Paris negotiations and then "harvest the results of our domestic dissent."

"Shell-shocked" was the word Kissinger used to describe the psychological state of the administration after Cambodia. Early one morning, Nixon, unable to sleep, went to the Lincoln Memorial, where he had an odd encounter with protesting students. He tried to sound sympathetic, but failed. He engaged in an incoherent monologue about Cambodia, his memories of World War II, the value of travel, China and, after learning that one of the students was from Syracuse University, the Syracuse football team. One student later told a reporter that Nixon's monologue was "absurd." The president was not "really concerned about why we were here." Officials in other branches of the government were also unable to sleep. Fifty State Department officials, usually the most diffident of bureaucrats, signed a public letter opposing the president's war policy. Walter Hickel, a cabinet secretary no less, protested the war in public. Health, Education and Welfare Secretary Robert Finch protested in private (Nixon was a personal friend), and hundreds of officials occupied the department's main auditorium in a gesture of protest.

Kissinger met often with university colleagues and students, using his past association with the academy to attempt to assuage their angry disapproval of his current policy. On one occasion, when he welcomed a group of Harvard scholars to the White House Situation Room ("most of them had been my close colleagues and friends," he later moaned), he ran up against a stone wall of opposition to the war. Kissinger wanted to set the ground rules for a serious exchange of views—namely, that it be off-the-record; but they refused. Mercilessly, they unloaded on him, Nixon, and the war. After they departed, Kissinger decided that he could never again return to university life. He considered their "lack of compassion, the overweening righteousness, the refusal to offer an alternative" to the administration's policy to be unconscionable; he concluded that "we would get no help" from the academic community. Of course, his former colleagues thought that if anyone lacked compassion, if anyone suffered from an overweening righteousness, it was Kissinger. They were convinced that Kissinger was stuck in a policy rut that could only ruin the country.

More disappointing to Kissinger than the disapproval of his Harvard colleagues was the defection of his closest White House aides and analysts. Bill Watts, Tony Lake, Roger Morris, and Larry Lynn had all tolerated the long hours, the temper tantrums, the duplicity of his Vietnam policy, and the wiretapping. But when they were asked to help staff the Cambodian invasion, they rebelled and quit. "I'm against this," Watts said, "and I'm resigning."

Kissinger began uncontrollably to throw books around the room. "Your views represent the cowardice of the eastern establishment," he screamed. Watts decided not to punch Kissinger in the face. Instead, he stormed out of the room.

"What the hell did you say to Henry?" asked Kissinger's deputy, Alexander Haig.

"I'm not handling the Cambodian thing," Watts replied.

"You can't refuse," Haig said. "You've just had an order from your commander-in-chief."

Watts, at wit's end, exclaimed: "Fuck you, Al. I can, and I just quit."[29]

For Kissinger, things got only worse. Another of his favored constituencies, the media, also defected from both his policy and his charm. On June 7, the *Los Angeles Times,* probably inspired by the Senate debate over the McGovern-Hatfield amendment, ran an editorial calling for an immediate withdrawal of American troops from Vietnam. "The time has come for the US to leave Vietnam and to leave it swiftly and without equivocation," it said. "Swiftly" was defined as an eighteen-month time frame, which the editorial believed was "less hazardous than the policy the president is presently pursuing." Copycat journalism being what it was and still is, a month later *Life* magazine ran a special editorial advocating a similar course of action—out within a year and a half.

The White House heard the critics but did not listen to them. Haldeman checked the polls and found that the "silent majority" of Americans were still in Nixon's hip pocket—there was no need to change policy. The White House concocted a "Report To The Nation" entitled "Cambodia Concluded: Now It's Time to Negotiate." Enemy killed-in-action was put at 11,349, and wounded at 2,328. Reporters assumed at the time that the more exact the Pentagon figures, the less credible its presentation. On a bloody battlefield could the United States count everybody? The report mentioned no American or South Vietnamese casualties, although 344 Americans and 818 South Vietnamese died in the Cambodian operation. It was no coincidence that the White House released its Cambodia report on the same day that the Senate voted in favor of the Cooper-Church amendment.

Vietnamization was an increasingly slim reed on which to hang Nixon's hopes for an honorable withdrawal of American forces from the Vietnam War, but it remained the core of his policy, even after the Cambodian operation. He was buying time, a precious commodity in a war that continued to defy the best of administration planning. General Abrams had told Nixon that the Cambodian operation would buy a year of relative calm, perhaps even two years; and, during this time, Vietnamization would continue, and the South Vietnamese army (ARVN) would develop into a reliable fighting force capable of protecting the country against further communist assault—and to do this without the assistance of American troops. And if in a year, or two, or three, the South Vietnamese were still unable to defend themselves without U.S. support, at least the United States would then be able to claim that it had done the honorable thing—it had not "cut and run." To the degree that logic played a role in Nixon's calculations, he could always have stopped or slowed down the American withdrawal, but he suspected that if he stopped the withdrawals, or slowed them down, the antiwar movement would spread and further poison and weaken the fabric of American society. He truly believed that domestic agitation was leading to social disintegration, to the "collapse of our establishment." In addition, his own re-election campaign for 1972, which always lay at the heart of his political and strategic planning, would be adversely affected. No, he persuaded himself, the U.S. troop withdrawals had to continue—in fact, if possible, be accelerated—even if the evidence was unmistakable that the South Vietnamese were still not capable of carrying the fight to their enemy without American help.

So, what to do?

In early 1971, Nixon reached another one of his "Eureka!" moments in Vietnam decisionmaking. In his underwear, having just survived another back manipulation by the New York osteopath, Dr. Kenneth Riland, Nixon walked into a White House meeting of top security officials to announce that he had decided to use South Vietnamese troops to cut the so-called "Ho Chi-minh trails" in Laos. As officials squirmed in embarrassment, looking at the open space between his shorts and his socks, the president laid out his reasoning: What, after all, was the main point of the Cambodian operation? To destroy the sanctuaries, which were home for the communist troops and materiel infiltrated into Cambodia. How did the troops and materiel get into the sanctuaries? By way of the Ho Chi-minh trails running from North Vietnam through Laos into Cambodia. Cut those trails in Laos, before the reinforcements even get into Cambodia, and communist planning for the conquest of South Vietnam would have to be changed.

Intelligence at the time suggested that the Ho Chi-minh trails were a sort of superhighway of North Vietnamese men and supplies into South Vietnam. From 1966 to 1971, the CIA concluded, 630,000 troops rode the highway from north to south. Joining the traffic were 100,000 tons of foodstuffs, 400,000 weapons, and 50,000 tons of ammunition. Cutting the trails made sense in both Saigon and Washington—if, in fact, the trails could be cut.

On January 26, Nixon summoned Kissinger, Haig, and Admiral Thomas Moorer, the chairman of the Joint Chiefs of Staff, to a secret planning session. Nixon was always happiest when he was, at least in his own mind, a great general like Patton, planning huge military operations, striking at the enemy, and then returning from battle to admiring crowds. They discussed the latest intelligence from Saigon. Abrams, usually a skeptic about the advisability of expanding the war, was in this case extraordinarily optimistic about the fighting capacity of the South Vietnamese troops—it would be proof of the success of Vietnamization, he said. "Abrams assured me he could do it," Defense Secretary Laird said. "He told me that, and I assured the president on that basis."[30] Abrams was optimistic, too, about the strategic gains to be derived from the operation. Abrams believed that cutting the trails for even one dry season would "significantly" reduce, and possibly eliminate, Hanoi's ability to launch a major offensive in South Vietnam for the indefinite future. Such optimism from the normally cautious general buoyed Nixon's spirits.

The Laos operation, known as Lam Son 917, was thus a huge gamble from the beginning. It could be proof of the success of Vietnamization, or of its failure. It was clearly a complex operation, requiring time and proper planning, but Nixon foolishly put it on a quick track. According to one senior American officer, "planning was rushed, handicapped by security restrictions, and conducted separately and in isolation by the Vietnamese and the Americans."[31] Abrams did not treat his South Vietnamese colleagues as equals. He rarely shared operational secrets with them. The ARVN was about to launch its most ambitious operation of the war—it was going to invade another country without American ground support—and no one in Washington or Saigon considered the consequences of a poorly planned operation. They were allies in reluctant cooperation. Was ARVN really ready for prime time? Interestingly, Abrams thought yes, and his judgment was never challenged. In Saigon, he was emperor. Was it capable of improvising if something went wrong? Was its intelligence secure? How would Hanoi respond? Everyone looked to "Abe," as he was called, and he professed absolute confidence in ARVN's ability.

It was a dangerous crapshoot.

Officially, Lam Son 917 opened on February 8 and closed on March 25. For the first few days, the South Vietnamese fought well, largely because the North Vietnamese observed their bold intrusion from the sidelines. Quickly, however, ARVN was outmanned and outgunned, and the Americans were not there to help. The North Vietnamese threw almost 40,000 troops into the battle, determined to repel the South Vietnamese attack and win. Nixon, ignoring downbeat reports from the battlefield, told Haldeman: "We must claim victory regardless of the outcome." Abrams attempted to restrict media access to the battle scene, hoping to put a cheerful spin on the South Vietnamese operation. Some reporters managed to get into southern Laos and see for themselves; others were not as fortunate. One helicopter carrying Larry Burrows of *Life*, Henri Huet of the AP, Kent Potter of UPI, and Keizaburo Shimamoto of *Newsweek* was shot down on February 10; there were no survivors. Francois Sully, also of *Newsweek*, was killed a few weeks later.

The story in southern Laos defied official spin. Reporters recorded the grisly scene, not all of it but enough to undercut the Abrams spin and convey the reality of the war. What they reported was nothing short of a bloodbath, the kind of front page news that Nixon was desperately trying to avoid. ARVN troops were being slaughtered. President Thieu, under increasing American pressure, threw thousands more South Vietnamese troops into the battle, increasing ARVN numbers in Laos to more than 30,000, but it was to no avail—they were still being outmanned, still outfought. The North Vietnamese baited a trap, and the South Vietnamese fell into it.

Thieu, soon facing an election, decided that one way to avoid a humiliating defeat was to slip into the strategic Laotian town of Tchepone, declare victory, and then snappily withdraw. Abrams approved of the plan and then dispatched almost 300 helicopters to Laos to help the South Vietnamese enter and leave the town. It proved to be the largest helicopter assault of the Vietnam War. Why Abrams would commit so many helicopters to a battle already lost was another of those American decisions sure to baffle military historians. His decision also baffled Kissinger. "There was no point in risking so much to occupy an abandoned Laotian town for three days," he wrote.[32] Dozens of U.S. choppers were destroyed, hundreds of ARVN soldiers were killed, and the remaining troops—battered and bloodied, very few in disciplined ranks— started their fateful pullout from Laos. The withdrawal took more than three weeks. The North Vietnamese threw their full firepower at the South Vietnamese troops and turned their withdrawal into a rout. Sixty percent of South Vietnam's tanks and half of its armored personnel carriers were blasted to bits. Left behind were fifty-four 105-mm and twenty-eight 155-mm howitzers, which U.S. planes then deliberately destroyed to keep them from getting into enemy hands.[33]

Though for public consumption Nixon painted Lam Son 917 as a success, claiming the Ho Chi-minh supply lines had been disrupted, he knew better. It was, in fact, a disaster. It failed by every measure . Casualties were heavy. South Vietnam suffered 1,529 troops killed, another 5,483 wounded, and 625 missing. The U.S. casualty report: 625 killed, another 1,149 wounded, and 38 missing.

The South Vietnamese fought well in the early days of the battle, but then very quickly many of their units disintegrated. Without a continuing flow of American support, they were helpless, clearly no match for the disciplined North Vietnamese army. The promise of Vietnamization faded. The program obviously needed many more years of steady, costly training, and even then there was no assurance it would succeed.

Thieu, clearly desperate, put out the story that Lam Son 917 was "the biggest victory ever." This was not true, and he knew it, but in Saigon's politics there was never a shortage of lies and deception—often of self-deception.[34] The Ho Chi-minh trails were damaged—that much was obvious—but they still functioned effectively. Saigon intelligence was obviously compromised. ARVN leadership, at least what was left of it, was thoroughly corrupt. Nixon knew about South Vietnam's shortcomings but ignored them.

Apparently the president was so desperate for success he looked the other way on issues such as South Vietnam's political and military capacity. He subjected himself to endless briefings, all of them brimming with boundless Pentagon optimism. Even a president of Nixon's experience hesitated to raise questions in front of so much brass. The generals told Nixon that by the summer of 1971 the number of U.S. combat troops left in South Vietnam would be at dangerously low levels, if he still intended to proceed with Vietnamization and with major operations against the North Vietnamese. Abrams knew that Nixon soon intended to announce another troop cut of 100,000 troops, leaving the planned total by year's end at 184,000.

Not to be distracted by facts, Nixon told the American people on April 7: "Tonight I can report that Vietnamization has succeeded."[35] It was amazing to me then—and still is now—that a president of Nixon's cunning could have allowed himself to lie to the American people so blatantly, knowing he would eventually be caught. Or was he simply engaging again in helpless self-delusion? Anything, it seemed, to remain faithful to the commitment of earlier presidents, to the word of America.

As a direct consequence of the Lam Son 917 battle, the ruling North Vietnamese Communist Party decided to launch a major conventional invasion of South Vietnam in early 1972, which was to be known in the United States as the Easter Offensive. They knew, of course, that Nixon was running for re-election in 1972.[36]

But if Nixon could no longer depend on Vietnamization to produce a timely and "honorable" exit from Vietnam, he still had one other option, which he and Kissinger both favored. It was triangular diplomacy, according to which they envisaged the United States playing China off against Russia, and Russia off against China, and, in cold pursuit of their national interests, both communist giants choosing to drop, or lessen, their support of North Vietnam in order to negotiate a better arrangement with the United States, the unmistakable leader of the capitalist world. It was a long shot, but it played to Nixon's sense of diplomatic drama and Kissinger's faith in the old Metternichean formula of a balance of power as the best guarantor of international stability. And, if their vision translated into reality, it would shed Nixon of the bloody nuisance of Vietnam!

When Nixon was selected in 1972 as *Time* magazine's "Man of the Year," an astonishingly questionable selection given his record of obvious failure in Vietnam, the president explained his policy in words suggesting Kissinger wrote them. "We must remember that the only time in the history of the world that we have had any extended periods of peace is when there has been a balance of power. It is when one nation becomes infinitely more powerful in relation to its potential competitor that the danger of war arises. . . . I think it will be a safer world and a better world if we have a strong, healthy United States, Europe, Soviet Union, China, Japan, each balancing the other, not playing one against the other, an even balance." He still believed, even this late in the Vietnam tragedy, that he was capable, one way or the other, of extricating the United States from Vietnam with "honor." The journey from "commitment" to extrication was bumpy, dangerous, and uncertain.

CHAPTER SEVEN

ONE WAY OR THE OTHER
Getting Out, Finally

"If we are run out of Vietnam, our entire foreign policy would be in jeopardy."
HENRY KISSINGER

"We're playing a Russian game, a Chinese game, and an election game."
RICHARD NIXON

CHINA HAD ALWAYS tantalized Richard Nixon, even before he became president. China, he knew, was more than an ancient civilization shrouded in mystery. It was, at the right time, a card to be played.

In September 1970, Nixon hinted in an interview with *Time* that he would like to visit China one day. Mao Zedong picked up the hint and told journalist Edgar Snow in *Life* that he "would be happy to talk to him, either as a tourist or as president."

Henry Kissinger was skeptical but at the same time fascinated by the prospect of a China card. How exactly would it be played?

White House chief of staff Bob Haldeman injected a time frame: "You know, he actually seriously intends to visit China before the end of his second term."

Kissinger replied: "Fat chance."[1]

But in early 1971 Russia and China began to exchange more than angry rhetoric across their long, uneasy border—they started shooting at each other; and these skirmishes triggered tremors of excitement (and anxiety) at the White House. Kissinger wondered whether this might not be the time to push for an opening to China, which the United States had tried to isolate ever since the communist takeover in 1949. With Nixon's strong support, he got busy playing his favorite, if to this point deferred, game of triangular diplomacy.

Always in Kissinger's mind was his firm belief that if the United States was to play the China card, the White House had to control all the diplomatic levers. He had no faith in the usual channels of diplomacy. The State Department, for example, ought to be kept "working away in ignorance" while he and Nixon made the key decisions. He feared leaks and distrusted loose-lipped diplomats, of which there were actually very few but he imagined numbered in the thousands. Congress? It was to be kept at arm's length, if at all possible.

Kissinger and Nixon looked to Pakistan as their perfect intermediary with China. It had the trappings of a democracy, but it was run by an authoritarian general named Yahya Khan, whom Nixon had befriended during an August 1969 journey around the world. The president confided to Khan that he was interested in a new relationship with China. Might Pakistan help? Khan answered, "of course," but for more than a year nothing happened. In October 1970, during a White House visit, Khan informed Nixon that he was on his way to China. Did Nixon have a message he would like him to convey? Yes, indeed, Nixon responded: Would China entertain a proposal for a high-level American envoy to visit Peking? Khan delivered the message to Premier Zhou Enlai and got a quick written reply, which he carried back to Pakistan and gave to a secret courier to be delivered to the Pakistani ambassador in Washington.

Six weeks later, on the evening of December 8, the ambassador handed the reply to Kissinger. "In order to discuss the subject of the vacation [sic] of Chinese territories called Taiwan," Zhou wrote in awkward prose, "a special envoy of President Nixon's will be most welcome in Peking."

Kissinger quickly drafted a response on plain Xerox paper, cleared it with Nixon, and handed it to the Pakistani ambassador. Though Zhou had narrowed the agenda to Taiwan, Kissinger broadened it. The American envoy would discuss "a broad range of issues," including Taiwan. Then, with subtle delicacy, Kissinger linked Taiwan to the Vietnam War. "The policy of the United States government is to reduce its military presence in the region of East Asia and the Pacific [read Taiwan] as tensions in this region [read Vietnam] diminish," he wrote. Zhou did not need a translation. Help us contain the war in Vietnam so we can manage an honorable exit from that country, Kissinger was saying, and the United States will reduce its military presence on Taiwan, which China needed for its policy of eventual reunification of the two Chinas. The groundwork was laid for a historic deal.

In early April 1971, with the Lam Son 917 calamity behind them and with the prospect of an opening to China before them, Nixon and Kissinger were thrilled to see a ping-pong prelude to their unfolding diplomacy. An American team, fresh from a World Table Tennis Championship game in Tokyo, received a surprise invitation to come and play in Beijing. The team accepted, and suddenly, to everyone's astonishment, both China and America, antagonists for decades, began an unlikely courtship around a ping-pong table—the game and scene magnificently bedecked with crisscrossing American and

Chinese flags. Premier Zhou welcomed the teams to a special reception at the Great Hall of the People, noting with eloquent simplicity: "You have opened a new chapter in the relations of the American and Chinese people."

Barely a week later, on April 27, the Pakistani ambassador delivered another secret communication from Zhou to Nixon. The Chinese premier apologized for his delay in responding to the president's earlier message and then said: "The Chinese Government reaffirms its willingness to receive publicly in Peking a special envoy of the President of the United States (for instance, Mr. Kissinger) or the US Secretary of State or even the President of the United States himself."

Bingo!

There were still problems, of course: China and the United States saw the world in radically different ways, one a communist society with imperial ambitions, the other a capitalist superpower led by a politician with strong conservative credentials, and they had clearly conflicting interests in Vietnam. In addition, smaller hurdles remained to be cleared: the secretary of state, William Rogers, did not even know about the back-and-forth with China; Nixon did not want his "envoy" to be received "publicly"—he wanted the glory for himself; and he did not like the timing—he wanted the breakthrough in 1972, the year of his re-election campaign.

Moreover, Nixon was also engaged in serious negotiations with Moscow on a groundbreaking arms control agreement, which he wanted to conclude at a time of maximum political advantage to him, meaning once again during his re-election campaign. It had the makings of a "tremendous splash," Kissinger assured him.

As they sipped Courvoisier cognac from old snifters in the Lincoln Sitting Room, Nixon and Kissinger reviewed the tricky contours of their secret diplomacy with China and Russia with the greatest satisfaction, as if they were both children riding a magic carpet to the Forbidden City in Beijing. They linked their superpower maneuvering to an "honorable" exit from the Vietnam War. As they saw it, the Chinese were opening the door to the United States because they feared either a Russian attack or a U.S.-Russian condominium that would dominate the world; and the Russians were moving toward a strategic arms limitation agreement with the United States because they worried about a Chinese-American alliance against them. At one point, Kissinger leaned over and whispered: "Mr. President, I have not said this before, but I think if we get this thing working, we will end Vietnam this year. . . . Once this thing gets going—everything is beginning to fit together."[2]

Question No. 1: Who should be the "envoy"? At first Nixon teased Kissinger, wondering aloud, as he watched his national security adviser's itching discomfort, whether it should be David Bruce, the able U.S. ambassador to Paris (he would make the Chinese "uncomfortable," Kissinger commented), or Nelson Rockefeller ("he wouldn't be disciplined enough," Kissinger judged), or George H. W. Bush ("too soft and not sophisticated enough," thought Kissinger), or should it be Kissinger, who, in Kissinger's hardly objective judgment, was "the only one who could really handle this." "Oh hell, I know that," Nixon laughed, and the decision was made. Kissinger would be the "envoy."

Question No. 2: How would Kissinger, Washington's most celebrated "secret swinger," get to Beijing without his mission first being leaked to CBS or the *New York Times?* The president took charge of Kissinger's itinerary, sketching the outlines of a cover story that he was sending his national security adviser on a "fact-finding trip" to France, Vietnam, Thailand, India, and Pakistan. While in Pakistan, he would get "sick" and need a few days of down-time to recover from a stomach virus. He would use the down-time to fly to China on a Pakistani jet, negotiate the details of Nixon's follow-up journey to Beijing in early 1972, and then return to Pakistan where, "recovered," he would resume his "fact-finding trip."

Reporters should have known something was up; Kissinger's ego would never have allowed him to admit he was short of facts. He had never gone on a fact-finding trip before. Also, few noticed at the time that Nixon had decided to relax trade restrictions against China—an odd step for a politician who had spent much of his career imposing restrictions on any dealings with China. Nixon was signaling Zhou that he was "serious" about resuming normal relations with China.

This diplomatic planning, involving the China opening and the strategic arms negotiation with Russia, was designed both to embellish Nixon's political campaign and to create a new, safer balance of power in the world. Under this new arrangement, the Chinese and Russians would agree, among other things, to allow the United States to leave the Vietnam War with "honor," it being in their newly defined interests to do so, and to move Vietnam back to the periphery of global concerns, where it should always have been—a proud though unfortunate relic of an earlier colonial era.

On May 10, Nixon asked the Pakistani ambassador to deliver another message to Zhou, proposing a "strictly secret" Kissinger visit to Beijing for the purpose of arranging a presidential visit in early 1972. On June 2, the ambassador returned with Zhou's response: China was ready to receive Kissinger in July and Nixon in early 1972. Kissinger was "ecstatic." He rushed to the Oval Office, "out of breath" and "beaming," to tell Nixon in wildly exaggerated language that "this is the most important communication that has come to an American president since the end of World War II." He went even further. "We have laid the groundwork for you and Mao to turn a page in history," he proclaimed. "The process we have now started will send enormous shock waves around the world. . . . If we can master this process, we will have made a revolution." Historian Robert Dallek described this "hyperbole" as "partly the product of a hunger for a big foreign policy gain after two and a half years of frustration over Vietnam, unyielding Soviet-American and Middle East tensions, and unmanageable events in Chile."[3]

Nixon gave Kissinger his final instructions in person, cautioning his envoy to stay away from lengthy "philosophical talk" and come "pretty directly to the point." Stressing his own experience negotiating with communists, Nixon said: "I don't fart around . . . I'm very nice to them—then I come right in with cold steel. . . . They're bastards; he [Zhou]'s a bastard." Nixon wanted Kissinger to hit one point again and again—that he, the president, was a very tough customer. "This is the man who did Cambodia; this is the man who did Laos; this is the man who will . . . protect our interests without regard for political considerations."[4]

Cambodia? Laos? Did Nixon really think the Chinese considered these ill-fated missions as success stories? Nixon wanted the Chinese to consider him to be slightly unhinged, a leader close to ordering a massive escalation of the fighting in Vietnam, unless he got his way.

Kissinger arrived in Beijing on July 9, 1971. He was whisked to a lakefront guest house near a secluded park that was once the joy of Chinese nobility. At 4:30 p.m., Zhou arrived for the start of negotiations, a sure sign the Chinese were also serious about improving relations. In protocol terms, Zhou was the prime minister of a country, Kissinger an adviser to a president. Yet Kissinger's presence was proof that the United States recognized and respected China as one of the five great powers in the world. One Chinese official wondered aloud whether, this time, a major American diplomat would shake Zhou's hand, a reference to John Foster Dulles's famous slight during the Geneva Conference of 1954. For the Chinese, "the big issue was national pride and ego," recalled Richard Smyser, a Vietnam expert who was a member of Kissinger's tiny team of advisers.[5] Over the next two days, Kissinger and Zhou not only shook hands but spent more than twenty hours together planning Nixon's visit and exploring the delicate U.S.-Chinese relationship. For Zhou, the key problem was Taiwan. For Kissinger, it was Vietnam.

Kissinger stressed the importance of an "honorable" American exit from the war, adding that any other exit, such as an ignominious American pullout, or an American abandonment of a long string of presidential commitments to the Saigon regime, would not only damage America's word and image, it would also hurt China. On the other hand, if China helped the United States withdraw from Vietnam with "honor," it would be serving China's national interests, and America's. Kissinger's reasoning might have been self-serving, but it did convey his true feelings. Zhou, not yet ready for a considered reply, resorted to standard communist gibberish—"Taiwan was part of China," and "China supported the 'just struggle' of the North Vietnamese." He then urged the United States to withdraw from all of its military bases in Asia.

On July 11, Kissinger returned to Pakistan and resumed his "fact-finding trip." He sent a one-word cable to Nixon. "Eureka!" it read. On July 15, Nixon surprised the world by announcing on television that Kissinger had just returned from China and that he, the president, would be going there in February 1972. Nixon emphasized that the opening to China was "not directed against any other nation." He added this point out of concern that the Soviet Union might become so edgy about the possibility of Chinese-American "collusion" that it would attack its weaker neighbor with nuclear weapons. Fortunately, the Soviet Union was not that edgy, but it did react to the news of the China opening by warming, in principle, to the idea of a Moscow summit meeting in 1972 for the purpose of signing the Strategic Arms Limitation Treaty. Nixon had been pressing for such a summit since becoming president, but the Russians had been playing hard to get. No longer. Foreign Minister Andrei Gromyko, after an uncharacteristically warm meeting with Nixon at the White House, invited Kissinger to visit Moscow. Kissinger replied coyly: "I have given you a way for me to be able to do that," meaning if you helped us on Vietnam, I'd be there in a flash. "Always linkage," Gromyko observed, accurately.[6] Occasionally, the war would send Nixon into fits of frustration. How could it be, he wondered in exasperation, that the president of the United States of America, the most powerful man in the world running the most powerful nation in the world, could not bring this war to an end? Nixon knew that his approach to ending the war, ending it "with honor," conflicted with the opinion of a majority of the American people. According to the latest Gallup poll, 61 percent of the American people now believed the war was a mistake and favored a total withdrawal of American forces by July 1, 1972. But Nixon refused to change his approach to an American withdrawal from Vietnam.

The next round of secret negotiations in Paris was truly important. Kissinger was returning to the talks with a seven-point peace plan, a "final offer," he warned, that could break the impasse because it contained two consequential American concessions. Kissinger promised for the first time that U.S. forces would leave South Vietnam six months after an agreement was signed, but he did not call for the withdrawal of North Vietnamese forces. He then added that South Vietnam's president, Nguyen Van Thieu, would resign thirty days ahead of a plebiscite on the political future of South Vietnam. Up to this point, Kissinger had always insisted on a mutual withdrawal of forces—now, suddenly, only the Americans would leave and, by implication, the North Vietnamese could remain in South Vietnam. Also, he never before had hinted that Thieu's removal from office was negotiable. The South Vietnamese could be forgiven if they thought they were hearing the distant bells of betrayal. The North Vietnamese pocketed Kissinger's concessions, which confirmed their expectations that in time they would win the war, one way or another.

At the end of June, scarcely a month later, as Kissinger was busily preparing to leave for China, he was summoned back to Paris. The North Vietnamese had an intriguing nine-point counter-proposal, containing their version of concessions. If the United States withdrew by year's end, they proposed, American prisoners of war (POWs) would be released at the same time. Under previous proposals from Hanoi, the POWs were to be released only *after* the American withdrawal. In addition, instead of demanding Thieu's removal from office, which had been standard fare in all Hanoi proposals, this time the North Vietnamese asked only that the United States "stop supporting" Thieu. Between the lines was the whiff of a suggestion that Thieu would be allowed to participate in the plebiscite, and if he won, which no one on the planet considered likely, he could remain in power or be part of a new coalition government. Hanoi's counter-concessions were what they were—a good cover story, designed artfully to conform to Kissinger's implicit appeal for a "decent interval." Kissinger, excited by the sudden seriousness of the negotiation, imagined a deal on the near horizon, but, he wondered, would his president agree?

Here was the moment when, with barely noticeable legerdemain and only minor adjustments in language, Nixon could have turned a page and proclaimed from the White House rooftop that an honorable settlement had been arranged and American forces could finally come home. The war that had started four administrations ago would end, the commitments of four presidents having been honored. The United States would not have to abandon Thieu, at least not immediately, and the POWs would be released as American forces left South Vietnam. The American people would have been thrilled, the antiwar riots would probably have stopped, the dissent would have ended, and Vietnam would become a fading nightmare—and all in 1972, the year of his anticipated re-election. What a blinding sequence of extraordinary diplomatic triumphs he could have orchestrated: a historic, door-opening summit in China, an arms limitation treaty agreement at a Moscow summit, and then finally, after shedding so much blood and spending so much treasure, an end to the Vietnam War. Each step would have been choreographed in exquisite detail, captured live and televised to the world, as Nixon pirouetted triumphantly atop the globe, peace and his re-election safely in hand.

This was all Nixon's for the taking, but this strange man, who on entering office had told Kissinger that the war could not be won and the United States could only escape behind the papier-mâché shield of Vietnamization, walked away from this opportunity. At least, for the time being. It appeared that, deep down, he distrusted the North Vietnamese so much that he now wanted their surrender, not just their agreement to his terms for leaving South Vietnam. The president was "always more skeptical than I that any negotiation would succeed until there had been a military showdown," Kissinger wrote in his memoirs.[7] Nixon ignored Hanoi's faintly disguised olive branch.

Instead, he went on one of his emotional rollercoasters, angry at the Russians, the liberals, the *New York Times,* CBS, and of course the North Vietnamese—more determined now than ever to bomb them back to the stone age. "About November of this year, I'm going to take a goddamn hard look at the whole card," he sputtered, occasionally with signs of incoherence. "I'm not talking about bombing passes [or trails]," he yelled at Kissinger and Haldeman, who were used to his outbursts. "We're going to take out the dikes, we're going to take out the power plants, we're going to take out Haiphong, we're going to level that goddamn country." Nixon barely paused for a breath. "The point is we're not going to go out whimpering, and we're not going to go out losing."

Well aware of Nixon's ambivalence about the Paris negotiations, Kissinger added that he was going to see Soviet ambassador Anatoly Dobrynin the next day. "I will lay it into him," he said, trying to sound menacing and at the same time reassuring. "Tell their little yellow friends to stop these games. We're not going down quietly." Their bluster seemed only to disguise their growing realization that as American withdrawals continued, U.S. military strength in South Vietnam declined, and the American negotiating posture in Paris weakened and tumbled, like stocks in free fall during a recession. They were in an increasingly untenable position, even though Hanoi understood Nixon could always order another massive bombing of North Vietnam. But the North Vietnamese seemed not to worry about such threats. Xuan Thuy, a Hanoi negotiator, once told Kissinger: "We are afraid of nothing. We are not afraid of threats. Prolongation of fighting doesn't frighten us. Prolongation of negotiations doesn't frighten us. We are afraid of nothing."[8]

On June 12, Tricia Nixon married Edward Cox in the Rose Garden of the White House, the first outdoor wedding ceremony in the 170-year-history of the presidential mansion. Nixon looked very happy. The following day, June 13, the *New York Times* published a two-column picture of the bride and her father on the front page, a source of understandable pride for any father. But, to the right of the picture, was a three-column headline. "VIETNAM ARCHIVE:" it read, "PENTAGON STUDY TRACES 3 DECADES OF GROWING U.S. INVOLVEMENT," which profoundly disturbed Nixon. Unprintable expletives rushed through his mind, as he read this exclusive story. The *Times* had obtained a copy of a 2.5-million-word "TOP SECRET" history of the American involvement in Vietnam from Eisenhower to Johnson, and it started to publish lengthy excerpts. Reporter Neil Sheehan wrote that the war evolved gradually as the United States "developed a sense of *commitment* to a non-communist Vietnam" (italics added). Though the Pentagon Papers, as the collection of documents came to be known, focused on the decisions of four earlier administrations, Nixon was apoplectic. He blasted the *Times* for "treasonable" action, claiming that it hurt America's delicate negotiations with China and Russia. On June 15, he ordered Attorney General John Mitchell to issue a restraining order against further publication. The case went straight to the Supreme Court, which ruled with unusual speed on June 30 that the *Times* had a constitutional right to publish.

The man who leaked the documents, Daniel Ellsberg, had actually worked for Kissinger in the early days of the Nixon administration, but he quit to join the Rand Corporation and there discovered and read a copy of the Pentagon Papers. There were only fifteen copies, two of them in a Rand safe. Already a passionate antiwar critic, Ellsberg went to Capitol Hill and showed his copy to senators J. William Fulbright, George McGovern, and Charles Goodell, hoping one of them would agree to make it public. No one did. Ellsberg then approached Sheehan, who had covered the war and retained a romantic attachment to Vietnam. For the *Times,* it was more than an editorial decision to publish or not, it was also a legal decision. Could a newspaper wittingly publish a top secret document? The *Times* editors thought the times demanded publication, and they set up a small, secret team of reporters and editors to read the whole report and to begin writing a series of newspaper stories. Actual publication awaited a final decision by publisher Arthur Sulzberger, who flashed the green light in June.

It took Nixon and his top lieutenants all of four days to conclude that Ellsberg was the source of the leak. Kissinger's attack on Ellsberg, a former colleague, was surprisingly savage. "That son-of-a-bitch. I know him well. He is completely nuts. . . . He was always a little unbalanced . . . drugs . . . sex . . . shot at peasants in Vietnam." Kissinger feared Nixon would return to earlier doubts about *his* loyalty, and he wanted to put unmistakable distance between himself and Ellsberg. Turning to the president as both protector and adviser, Kissinger deliberately provoked him, perhaps to underscore his own hatred of leaks and leakers, that is, unless the leaks were his, and he was the leaker. "It shows you're a weakling, Mr. President," he said, goading his boss. "These leaks are slowly and systematically destroying us. . . . It could destroy our ability to conduct foreign policy. If other powers feel we cannot control internal leaks, they will not agree to secret negotiations."[9]

How did Nixon respond? How *could* he respond? Exactly as Kissinger had assumed he would. First, he denounced the bureaucracy: "well-intentioned sons of bitches," as he described his own administration. "We've checked and found that 96 percent of the bureaucracy are against us," he said, laying out no supporting data for this astonishingly precise figure. "They're bastards who are here to screw us." Perhaps even more than his own bureaucracy, Nixon truly despised the *Times*. "Those sons of bitches are killing me," he ranted. "We're up against an enemy, a conspiracy. They're using any means. We are going to use any means." Then, finally, he ordered a government-wide crackdown on leaks and leakers, telling aide Charles Colson to "do whatever has to be done to stop these leaks. . . . This government cannot survive, it cannot function, if anyone can run out and leak." The crackdown played to the worst instincts of the Nixon administration and led eventually to the Watergate scandal, which drove the president to his own historic resignation in August 1974.

The Final Push in Paris

Nixon, still ambivalent about the Paris negotiations, was ready in the summer and fall of 1971 to suspend the secret talks. Before each session, Kissinger wrote, there was usually "a protracted internal debate"—Nixon uneasy about the obvious need to compromise, and his negotiator eager to make "one last attempt." The July 12 talks, though, proved to be a "real negotiating session." For the first time, both sides realized there were actually overlapping points of agreement in their negotiating positions. "We took the individual points of both documents, laying them side-by-side," Kissinger observed. An agreement finally seemed possible. "My colleagues and I were intoxicated," Kissinger said, realizing at the time that after negotiating with the North Vietnamese, he would still have to negotiate with his President.[10]

Kissinger persuaded Nixon to allow him to offer one final "final proposal" to Hanoi. This "final proposal" was interesting because it foreshadowed the shape of the final agreement, which was signed in January 1973. "Fourteen months later," Kissinger wrote, "we were to meet and settle essentially on the terms I had presented in 1971."[11] The proposal promised elections within six months after the agreement was signed. The elections would be open to all political parties, including the communists. Thieu would resign one month before the elections. The small American military force still in South Vietnam would be withdrawn unconditionally, meaning the North Vietnamese, at the time numbering about 200,000, would be allowed to remain in South Vietnam, presumably to do as they wished, when they wished. Here was a proposal clearly crafted for an American exit and an eventual communist victory. No gimmick lurked behind a comma. The meaning was obvious. Nixon knew it, Kissinger knew it—at long last, both were prepared to acknowledge in their secret negotiation with North Vietnam that the goal of an independent, noncommunist South Vietnam was no longer on America's agenda. Yet, in their public statements about the war, neither would admit this change in the American position. The fighting continued, and the killing continued.

And if the latest intelligence reaching Kissinger's desk at that time was accurate, the fighting and the killing were likely to rise sharply in early 1972, the year of Nixon's re-election campaign. The intelligence disclosed that the politburo of Hanoi's Lao Dung (Communist) Party had decided to launch a major offensive against South Vietnam within a matter of a few months. After arguing for three years about whether to continue the Chinese model of low-intensity guerrilla warfare or switch over to the Soviet model of large-scale warfare, featuring tanks, artillery, and multidivisional attacks, the politburo decided that this was the right time to gamble on another 1968-style of mass attack—that such an attack might destroy ARVN, shatter Thieu's dwindling support, re-ignite antiwar demonstrations in the United States, and finally force an American withdrawal from the war. "It doesn't matter whether the war is promptly ended or prolonged," an editorial in Hanoi's party journal said. "Both are opportunities to sow the seeds; all we have to do is wait for the time to harvest the crop." They were confident that, one day, they would win. Since 1969, Hanoi had been observing the steady withdrawal of U.S. ground troops, wondering when the military balance in South Vietnam would tip in its favor. The year 1972 was deemed the tipping point. In addition, the politburo decided that it would launch its offensive by surprising everyone, especially the Americans and the South Vietnamese, and smash across the demilitarized zone (DMZ) between north and south, even though such a cross-border operation was specifically barred by the Geneva Convention.

The signs were everywhere: Thousands of troops were being mobilized and positioned for attack, not just north of the DMZ but also in swelling numbers along the Ho Chi-minh trails in Laos and in the Khmer Rouge sanctuaries in Cambodia; strategic sites in and around Hanoi and Haiphong were being fortified against expected American air attack; hundreds of tanks and artillery were being deployed near the northern and western borders of South Vietnam; and Hanoi Radio was beaming nonstop horror stories about American plans for further "aggression" against North Vietnam.

The buildup, the biggest in four years, seized Nixon's attention. If the communist offensive was successful, it could not only disrupt his plans for a summit in China, he thought, it could also cut South Vietnam in two. "I just don't believe you can let them knock the shit out of us," he told Haldeman. By "us," he meant South Vietnam—he never believed North Vietnam, which he often described as "a little shit-ass country," could beat the United States. To convey an impression of strength, Nixon ordered five days of intense air attacks against North Vietnam in December. He was convinced that even without large numbers of American troops on the ground in South Vietnam, the United States could still stifle any communist offensive with its overwhelming air power. Just watch, he seemed to be warning.

From the beginning of his presidency, troop withdrawals lay at the heart of his strategy for getting the United States out of Vietnam. Nixon believed that so long as he continued to withdraw American troops from South Vietnam, casualty rates would drop and the American people would tolerate the occasional upheavals on the battlefield. Proof was in the numbers. In January 1969, when Nixon took office, the number of Americans killed per week in and around South Vietnam was 350, and the nation was boiling with an angry impatience. Three years later, in December 1971, the number had dropped to seven per week, and on January 7, 1972, for the first time in seven years, no American combat death was reported in the preceding week. Only rarely by this time was the public in the streets protesting the war. (Only Congress, behind the curve of public opinion, seemed impatient to end the American involvement in Vietnam.)

In addition, Nixon pushed his staff to come up with a "No Draftees to Vietnam" policy. Here, too, the numbers were compelling. In 1970, more than 8,000 draftees per month were being sent to fight in South Vietnam. By September 1971, the number had dropped to 2,500–5,800 per month. Two months later, in November, it was down to 1,200 per month, and in December, 500 per month. By mid-1972, the White House hoped the number of draftees being sent to Vietnam would be down to zero, and an all-volunteer force, the apple of Nixon's eye, would be started after Congress passed the appropriate legislation.

On February 14, three days before Nixon left the United States for his summit in China, the North Vietnamese sent Kissinger a Valentine greeting. They proposed a resumption of the Paris peace talks on March 11. Kissinger was "ecstatic"—that word again. After months of uncertainty, he was now convinced that the war would be brought to an honorable end by summertime. The president's decision to bomb North Vietnam, his almost certain re-election, and the summitry soon to unfold in televised majesty in China and Russia—these basic facts, unadorned by ideology or national pride, had finally persuaded the North Vietnamese that it was time to conclude the negotiations and end the war. So Kissinger believed. But he was wrong, and Nixon, always the skeptic, was right for two reasons. First, despite the ongoing war, there would be the summit in Beijing, proving that though China supported its communist ally, North Vietnam, in its long and brutal war against the United States, it would still welcome this American enemy into its home in order to satisfy its national interest—namely, diplomatic reconciliation with the United States to give China protection against its ideological foe in the Kremlin. Mao Zedong and Zhou Enlai had learned long ago that the enemy of my enemy was my friend. Second, Nixon believed that no matter what happened during the summit, the North Vietnamese were still planning to attack South Vietnam. Hanoi marched to its own drummer.

The China summit lasted seven days, February 21–28, 1972. It was, Nixon proclaimed triumphantly, "the week that changed the world." Hardly. But it was a week of pomp and circumstance that ended decades of hostility between China and the United States and opened a period of triangular diplomacy that was filled with problems but also with promise. It was a legitimate diplomatic breakthrough. Only the issue of Taiwan remained to be settled during the summit. While Nixon oohed and aahed about the Great Wall of China, Kissinger and Zhou engaged in diplomatic combat before agreeing to state the obvious in a concluding communiqué—that Taiwan was a part of China and not, by implication, an independent nation. Since the Communists and the Nationalists both agreed that Taiwan was a part of China, the phrase offended no one of consequence.

Otherwise, in this summit of summits, the conversation between Mao and Nixon was rather pedestrian, even though Kissinger chose a more exultant description of their first meeting. "Our encounter with history," he called it. Because both leaders preferred to avoid controversy, Nixon suggested they talk about "philosophic problems."

Why? Mao wondered, his curiosity aroused.

"I have read the Chairman's poems and speeches," Nixon replied, "and I knew [you were] a professional philosopher."

Mao objected. "Those writings of mine aren't anything," he said, with false modesty. "There is nothing instructive in what I wrote."

Nixon, playing to Mao's ego, insisted: "The Chairman's writings moved a nation and have changed the world." Mao chose not to argue the point.

The lighthearted banter continued. "I voted for you during your last election," Mao declared.

Nixon laughed. "You voted for the lesser of two evils," he replied.

Mao enjoyed the topic. "I like rightists," he said with a smile. "I am comparatively happy when these people on the right come into power."

Nixon turned serious for a moment. "At least at this time, those on the right can do what those on the left can only talk about." Nixon, a rightist, could go to China and derive a bonanza of political credit for re-opening relations; the Democrats, if they had gone, would probably have been criticized by Nixon and other "rightists" in the Republican Party. Nixon could act, the Democrats could only talk. He wanted Mao to regard him as a man of action.[12] Even at the China summit, when Nixon appeared on television as an American Samson, Kissinger would see him in the privacy of his traveling office as "a lonely, tortured and insecure man," begging for "confirmation and reassurance." When Nixon returned to the United States, he was greeted as a conquering hero by both supporters and critics, and he enjoyed the praise. ABC's Howard K. Smith, reflecting public opinion, said on television: "Mr. Nixon deserves credit for a master stroke both opportune and statesmanlike."

"Last Throw of the Dice"

The president's enjoyment was mixed with worry about intelligence reports about another North Vietnamese offensive. It finally got under way on March 30. "They have launched multidivision offensives across the DMZ, across the Cambodian border toward Saigon and across the Laotian Border into the Highlands," Kissinger told Nixon. It's "Hanoi's last throw of the dice," according to Kissinger.[13]

Supported by more than 200 new Soviet T-54 tanks and many 130-mm recoilless artillery, three North Vietnamese divisions, numbering 30,000 troops, smashed through rickety South Vietnamese and American defenses along the DMZ and moved into Quang Tri Province. Forty thousand South Korean troops, usually ferocious fighters, were based in the province, but most refused to put their lives on the line. Why should they fight when most of the Americans had already been withdrawn? Further south, other North Vietnamese divisions broke out of their Cambodian sanctuaries, crossed the South Vietnamese border, and headed toward Saigon. Laos was also the victim of renewed warfare, as thousands of North Vietnamese troops left their home bases and moved south along the Ho Chi-minh trails. Their destination appeared to be the Central Highlands, always regarded as the most vulnerable part of South Vietnam, because, if seized and held, the country could effectively be cut in two.

Although the United States and South Vietnam were both aware of an imminent attack, when it finally occurred, they seemed for a moment like two deer caught in blinding headlights—they froze. For a time, it looked as if the North Vietnamese could simply sweep through the entire country. The press, covering this blitzkrieg attack, spoke alarmingly of a "rout," of "disarray," of the ARVN suffering a "crushing" blow in this "first real baptism under fire for Vietnamization."

"If this offensive succeeds," Nixon told congressional leaders, "you will have a more dangerous world. . . . If the US fails at this . . . no president can go to Moscow, except crawling." He imagined his détente policy going up in smoke. Kissinger painted an even bleaker picture. "If we [are] run out of Vietnam," he warned, "our entire foreign policy would be in jeopardy."

Later, in the Oval Office, Kissinger asked what would happen if the ARVN collapsed. Nixon snapped, "A lot of things will collapse around here. . . . We're playing a Russian game, a Chinese game, and an election game." At which point Kissinger, sounding more like a general than a national security adviser, said: "That's why we've got to blast the living bejeezus out of North Vietnam."[14] Nixon wasted little time: He ordered a massive air attack against communist troops and installations in South and North Vietnam. "The bastards have never been bombed the way they are going to be bombed this time," he told Haldeman. He was determined to beat back the North Vietnamese offensive, to deny them a military victory, even if the cost was a Soviet decision to cancel the upcoming Moscow summit. In his diary, Nixon noted: "No negotiation in Moscow is possible unless we come out all right in Vietnam." "All right" was the subject of many interpretations; Nixon's was that the United States did not lose on his shift.

On March 30, when the communists launched their offensive, forty-five combat-ready B-52s were within striking distance of North Vietnam. Two weeks later, 130 B-52s were ready for action. Twenty U.S. warships had cruised off North Vietnam; now there were forty, including two aircraft carriers. The Navy had had 150 fighter-bombers ready for combat in the war zone; the number now jumped to 275. The Air Force had had 445 land-based, combat-ready attack bombers in South Vietnam; now another 250 were added to the force.

On April 6, as the weather cleared over both parts of Vietnam, this mighty armada of ships and planes went into battle, targeting hundreds of North Vietnamese surface-to-air missile installations along the DMZ and communist troop concentrations further south. Twenty thousand North Vietnamese troops were only sixty miles from Saigon. They had to be stopped. Other North Vietnamese troops were on the outskirts of the capital of Quang Tri Province. On the weekend of April 15–16, for the first time since the spring of 1968, wave after wave of U.S. fighter bombers attacked the port city of Haiphong, which was formerly off-limits because of the presence of foreign ships. During these raids, four Soviet ships were hit—they were not targeted but they were hit, and the Moscow summit was now clearly in jeopardy. Dozens of Navy F-4 fighter-bombers strafed and bombed the capital city of Hanoi, hitting docks, warehouses, and oil depots. Collateral damage was unavoidable and widespread.

North and south, the battle raged—the climactic battle Nixon had always considered a preamble to any eventual settlement. Nixon was especially gratified by the severity of the air attacks against North Vietnam. "Well, we really left them our calling card this weekend," he told Haldeman.[15] Kissinger, with a degree of glee, sidled up to the president to say, "they dropped a million pounds of bombs." Nixon, pleased, replied: "Goddamn, that must have been a good strike." Then, Nixon recalled Johnson's less than satisfying experience bombing North Vietnam. "Johnson bombed them for years, and it didn't do any good." A reassuring Kissinger said: "But, Mr. President, Johnson never had a strategy. He was sort of picking away at them. He would go in with 50 planes, 20 planes. I bet you we will have had more planes over there in one day than Johnson had in a month."[16]

Nixon wanted these thunderous explosions to be heard in Moscow—he hoped the Russians would balance the cost of continuing support for their stubborn allies in Hanoi against the potential advantages of a superpower accommodation with the United States, including a nuclear arms limitation agreement. Nixon seemed almost to enjoy this risky diplomacy. The Russians could cancel the upcoming summit. True. The Chinese could freeze their new, promising relationship with the United States. Also true. Détente could suffer, and even his re-election, once considered a sure thing, might lose a bit of its political luster. But, at this moment of high drama, the gambler in Nixon was prepared to go all out. He would rather lose the summit than the war, he repeatedly told his aides, though deep down he did not expect to lose either. Hadn't the Chinese received him with open arms, despite his attacks against North Vietnam? What about the Russians? They continued to prepare for the May summit. In Washington, Ambassador Dobrynin met with Kissinger on April 3, 6, 9, and 12, assuring him on each occasion that the Kremlin wanted good relations with the United States, despite the escalating war in Southeast Asia. In fact, they spent more time on the Middle East and bilateral trade than they did on Vietnam. During the April 12 meeting, Dobrynin even urged Kissinger to go to Moscow and discuss Vietnam with Kremlin leaders. It would be worthwhile, the ambassador assured him. Kissinger, a passionate supporter of summitry, would have left for Moscow that evening if it were not for Nixon's deep distrust of both Hanoi and Moscow. He had to wait for the green light, and Nixon was in no hurry to flash it.

This was not an ideal time for the Nixon-Kissinger disagreement to break into the open, but it did and quickly became the stuff of Washington's dinner-time gossip. Rarely did a day go by without a "scoop" about policy differences at the top of the Nixon administration. For diplomatic correspondents, these were the days of paradise on earth. Senior officials at the State Department told me (and presumably other reporters) that "Nixon has gone mad." They genuinely feared that the promise of the Moscow summit was being shattered by his Vietnam strategy. "No one can control him any more—he's nuts," said one national security adviser. Kissinger deliberately leaked stories about Nixon's "strange flirtation with macho diplomacy." Even a number of Pentagon officials joined in criticizing their commander-in-chief, less because Nixon might lose his Moscow summit than because the ARVN might fall apart under relentless communist attack and the Pentagon would be blamed for its defeat. Intelligence analysts told me that Hanoi was, in fact, under Soviet pressure to strike a deal—but refused. Hanoi was in no mood to cave in to Russian or American pressure. Nixon, fortified by booze, also refused to budge. It was a tricky time.

On April 15, Nixon surprised Kissinger, not for the first time. Changing his position, Nixon told his national security adviser to accept Dobrynin's invitation to fly to Moscow on April 20. On this secret mission, Kissinger was to be on an extraordinarily tight leash. He was to relay Nixon's desire for a summit, for better relations with the Russians, but, he was to stress, not at the cost of a defeat in Vietnam. Though Nixon was personally eager for a Moscow summit—he wanted to be the first president to visit the Soviet capital—he felt strongly that America's prestige, its word and commitment, was on the line in Vietnam. He wanted the Russians to arrange for their ally, the Hanoi regime, to accept a reasonable compromise in Paris. Nixon was ready to accept a cease-fire in place, an immediate return of the American POWs, and a withdrawal of all American forces after an agreement was signed. Kissinger thought Nixon's terms were extremely generous. A cease-fire in place meant the invading North Vietnamese army could remain in South Vietnam. Didn't the Russians understand his message?

In Moscow, Kissinger negotiated with Soviet leader Leonid Brezhnev and Foreign Minister Andrei Gromyko for two days, but he was unable to extract a Soviet promise to deliver Hanoi. Hanging in the balance was the fate of the Moscow summit. Would the Russians cancel the summit? Kissinger thought the Russians wanted the summit so badly they would tolerate continuing American attacks against North Vietnam. Nixon thought the Russians were "in direct collusion with Hanoi." The president was, according to deputy national security adviser Alexander Haig, "starchy" and "increasingly restless," and he ordered Kissinger to break off his talks in Moscow and come home. No, Kissinger argued, almost in direct defiance of his president, "we are approaching the successful culmination of our policies: must we blow it in our eagerness to bomb targets. . . .?"[17] Nixon's response: "All that bullshit . . . all that crap."

When Kissinger returned to Washington on April 25, he immediately took to pleading with Nixon for permission to pursue two interrelated approaches to ending the Vietnam war: first, to continue summit preparations with the Russians and, second, to meet once again with Hanoi's negotiator, Le Duc

Tho (known to the Americans as "Ducky") in Paris on May 2. Kissinger felt the summit would eventually compel the North Vietnamese to agree to a compromise solution. Nixon, distrusting everyone, wondered: Had Kissinger been "taken in" by the wily Brezhnev? More important, was the Soviet leader's real goal to "humiliate" him by canceling the summit at the last minute and undercutting his re-election?

The Nixon-Kissinger negotiation was often as dicey as the Kissinger-Brezhnev negotiation, and at this delicate time both negotiations were taking place against the backdrop of another North Vietnamese offensive in South Vietnam.

On April 24, just as Kissinger and Tho were agreeing to meet again on May 2, the North Vietnamese sent thousands of fresh troops into the Central Highlands. Tanks and artillery led the way, as the troops moved against the provincial capitals of Kontum and Pleiku, in the process destroying half of the ARVN's 22nd Division. The southern half of South Vietnam was on the brink of a military collapse. In Quang Tri Province, thousands of North Vietnamese troops encircled the provincial capital while decimating the ARVN's Third Division. Other ARVN units in the area panicked. Deserted by their officers, with no possibility of an orderly retreat, many ARVN troops joined tens of thousands of civilians fleeing Quang Tri along a major highway heading to Hue. It was soon to be called "the highway of death."

John Gunther Dean, the State Department's top official in the province, and Frederick Z. Brown, a young consul based in Danang, boarded an Air America (CIA) helicopter bound for Quang Tri in an effort to help evacuate Americans and advise the South Vietnamese about refugee facilities in Danang. It was, on reflection, a rather risky decision on their part, considering the intensity of the fighting. As they approached Quang Tri, they ran into enemy ground fire—their helicopter was hit, it began to leak fuel, but luckily it limped safely into a nearby American firebase. Within minutes, they were airlifted out by a U.S. military helicopter, which whisked them to a point south of Quang Tri, where they could observe tens of thousands of refugees who had just survived a bloodbath on the highway between Quang Tri and Hue. Neither Dean nor Brown could get into Quang Tri, but they heard about what had happened on the highway. "Thousands of Vietnamese refugees, dependents, women and children, were trying to get out of Quang Tri," Brown remembered. "They headed south toward Danang. A tank in front of the column, a tank behind, the people in between. First, the North Vietnamese took out the tanks, front and back, and then, from flanking positions on both sides of the highway, they opened fire on the people. It was a slaughter, a massacre. Thousands and thousands were killed."[18] Kissinger estimated the number at 20,000, "a large percentage of them civilians." A small measure of the danger was that, on their way back to Danang later in the day, the Dean/Brown helicopter was again hit by enemy ground fire.

Brown was in the area long enough to appreciate the crucial role of the B-52 during the Easter offensive in South Vietnam. Were it not for the tactical use of these strategic bombers, their "Arc Light strikes" against enemy forces, he felt "the North Vietnamese would likely have rushed forward to Hue" and then threatened the rest of South Vietnam. It was, Brown said, a "very perilous" moment in the war.

On May 1, the day before Kissinger was to resume his secret talks with Tho in Paris, Quang Tri fell to the North Vietnamese army after a vicious battle. ARVN marines fought gallantly and suffered heavy losses, but they could not hold off the North Vietnamese. The imperial capital of Hue, filled with tens of thousands of frightened refugees, was only fifteen miles to the south. The country trembled. If the North Vietnamese thought at the time that they were on their final victory lap, they were not far off in their judgment. Nixon, sobered by the news, instructed his Paris-bound negotiator: "They'll be riding high because of all this, so you'll have to bring them down by your manner. No nonsense. No niceness. No accommodations." Later, in a memo to Kissinger, he added: "Now is the best time to hit them. We have crossed the Rubicon, and we must win. . . . The President has had enough, and now you have only one message to give them—-Settle or else!"[19] Under urgent consideration at the White House, as Kissinger left for Paris, was more bombing of Hanoi and Haiphong, the mining of Haiphong and other harbors, and, if necessary, scrapping the Moscow summit and invading North Vietnam.

Sadly, the May 2 negotiation produced nothing. It was an exchange of insults and platitudes. A discouraged Kissinger quickly returned to Washington, resigned to a further escalation of the Vietnam War but still determined to keep the Moscow summit on track. Nixon could not detach Vietnam from his global calculations: "The summit isn't worth a damn if the price for it is losing in Vietnam," he told Kissinger. "My instinct tells me that the country can take losing the summit but it can't take losing the war." Nixon could not imagine toasting Soviet leaders in the Kremlin while Soviet-supplied tanks formed a vanguard for victorious North Vietnamese troops entering Saigon. No, he said, dismissively, that was "ludicrous," "unthinkable."[20]

Nixon was engaged, in fact, in a historic gamble—that with B-52s pound-ing the DMZ and North Vietnamese troop concentrations throughout South Vietnam, producing large numbers of North Vietnamese casualties, the ARVN would be able to hold off a communist victory and produce a military stale-mate of sufficient durability to allow Nixon to proceed with his triangular diplomacy and eventually win an honorable exit from the Vietnam War. It was a gamble fraught with complexity, intrigue, and uncertainty. At any moment, the ARVN could collapse, Thieu could be assassinated, and the United States could lose not only a war but an opportunity for a major advance in its rela-tions with Russia and China.

On May 8, Nixon was back on television, announcing that the United States had to take another major step in the war against North Vietnam—he had decided to interdict the flow of arms and munitions into North Vietnam. He still favored better relations with the Soviet Union, including a summit meet-ing in Moscow, but, at the time, more important to Nixon was an "honorable" end to the war. "All harbors will be mined," he said, and all rail, road and other communications will be interdicted "to the maximum extent possible." He added, as a sweetener for his domestic critics, that as soon as American POWs were released and an "internationally supervised ceasefire" was installed, U.S. troops would be withdrawn from South Vietnam—all of them. Again, he made no mention of allowing North Vietnamese forces to remain in South Vietnam—his key concession at the Paris talks.[21]

As Nixon spoke, 200 Navy planes began dropping mines in the harbors of Haiphong and six other smaller North Vietnamese ports. The mines were set to be activated in fifty-seven hours, more than enough time for Soviet and other cargo ships to leave the ports. It was one of the odd anomalies of the war that Nixon could, when he wished, walk up and down the ladder of escalation at the same time.

"They spit in our eye in Paris," Nixon later exploded. "We have brought home half a million men, and they spit in our eye. What else can we do?" The following day, in a memo to Kissinger, Nixon answered his own rhetori-cal question: "I am determined that we should go for broke. . . . Now that I have made this tough watershed decision, I intend to stop at nothing to bring the enemy to his knees." He put himself in line with Patton, MacArthur, and Churchill as an example of courage under fire. "We have the power," Nixon wrote. "The only question is whether we have the will to use that power. What distinguishes me from Johnson is that I have the will in spades."[22]

In other respects, the reaction to Nixon's mining decision was predictable. The Democratic caucus in the Senate voted 29-14 to condemn the escalation. The *New York Times* called for a cutoff of war funding "to save the president from himself and the nation from disaster," and the *Washington Post* declared that Nixon "has lost touch with the real world." On the streets, antiwar demonstrations popped up again in different cities around the country, but protesters numbered only in the hundreds or low thousands in each location. John Dean, one of Nixon's White House aides, wrote a note to the president saying that the expected antiwar demonstrations "this past weekend fell dramatically short of what had been promised by many antiwar activists." The big, boisterous antiwar demonstrations of 1969 and 1970 had long ago ebbed, as fewer young men were being drafted and sent to Vietnam and fewer casualties were being reported. In this sense, Nixon's domestic strategy was working. Antiwar sentiment had essentially left the streets to become largely a congressional movement to legislate an end to the war.

How would the Russians respond to the mining of Haiphong and the bombing of Hanoi? And the Chinese? Exactly as Nixon, the cynic, had assumed they would. As each day passed without a Soviet cancellation of the summit, and with a continuation of Kissinger-Dobrynin preparations, the working assumption was that the Russians had swallowed their ideological pride and put the promise of better relations with the United States ahead of their alliance with North Vietnam. They had, as Kissinger later wrote, "cut loose from [their] obstreperous small ally on the other side of the globe." Not really. The Russians were again misinterpreting Hanoi's long-term strategy.

On May 9, the Soviet news agency TASS summarized the president's speech, highlighting his assurance that the mining of Haiphong was not directed against any other country. On the same day, the Chinese news agency Xinhua protested U.S. attacks on Chinese shipping but in language considered amazingly mild. On May 10, Dobrynin handed Kissinger a note of protest and then asked whether the president would receive the visiting Soviet trade minister, suggesting that the Russians were, like the United States, willing to continue a business-as-usual relationship despite the mining.

Kissinger was elated—for more than a month he had assumed, even was willing to bet, that the Russians would at least postpone the summit if not cancel it. On May 11, Nixon and Soviet trade minister Nikolai Patolichev met—"warm" and "friendly" were the adjectives officially used to describe the meeting. Afterward, a TV reporter asked Patolichev whether the summit was still on. "We never had any doubts," he replied. On May 12, Kissinger and Dobrynin discussed summit protocol. Which gifts would be exchanged? for example. Dobrynin suggested a hydrofoil for Nixon and a Cadillac for Brezhnev. There was quick agreement. "We have passed the crisis," Kissinger reported to Nixon. "I think we are going to be able to have our mining and bombing and have our summit, too."

Summitry in Moscow, Bombing in Hanoi

On May 22, as Air Force One headed for a headline-catching summit in Moscow, perfect for Nixon's re-election campaign, Kissinger happily bounded into the president's private cabin. "This has got to be one of the great diplomatic coups of all time," he proclaimed with pride. "Three weeks ago, everyone predicted it would be called off, and today we're on our way."[23] Indeed they were: the president with a stubborn determination to end the war in Vietnam in such a way that, from beginning to end, it could be described as honorable—that he had kept America's commitment; and his national security adviser who bought into Nixon's war policy and gave it an academic shine.

Nixon and Kissinger reviewed the key elements of the upcoming summit: an arms control agreement, a significant trade agreement, and a protocol outlining the "Basic Principles of U.S.-Soviet Relations," which, though filled with the platitudes of detente, thrilled the Russians. They also spent time talking about Brezhnev, the man and the leader. He was, Kissinger briefed Nixon, who needed no briefing, "a tough and shrewd union boss, conscious of his position and his interests, alert to slights." Brezhnev abhorred war—he was forever making references to Russia's terrible losses during World War II. He also was truly a Russian nationalist who disliked the Chinese as only someone with strong racist opinions could, describing Americans and Russians as "Europeans," who were noble and civilized, and the Chinese, by comparison, as "Orientals," who were backward and savage. Kissinger was perfectly prepared—indeed, happy—to exploit Brezhnev's racist tendencies at the summit: If the Russian leader distrusted the Chinese, he might then be much more accommodating with Nixon. It was a perfect billiard shot in the game of triangular diplomacy. "Brezhnev has important business to do with you now," Kissinger said, completing his thought by reaching back into history. "Moscow has to get a grip on the Teutonic past so it can deal with a Mongolian future."[24]

Nixon arrived in the Soviet capital at exactly 4 p.m., fulfilling his campaign wish to be the first American president to set foot in the Soviet Union. As vice president, the peripatetic Nixon had been to the Soviet Union in July

1959, while preparing for his presidential run the following year. On both occasions, in 1959 and again in 1972, he felt a properly publicized visit to the homeland of Soviet communism could prove to the American people that he, better than any other candidate, knew how to best the enemy. In July 1959, he engaged in a famous "kitchen debate" with Soviet leader Nikita Khrushchev about the relative merits of their competing systems of government; as one of the reporters covering the vice president's visit, I thought Nixon had won. In May 1972, Nixon was back in Moscow looking for another triumph as political as it was diplomatic.

A fifty-car motorcade raced to the Kremlin along deserted boulevards, the Russian people blocked by buses from displaying their genuine enthusiasm. This was an example of Soviet security gone mad. An entire floor of the Grand Palace was reserved for the president, an extravagant show of Soviet hospitality. Within minutes, in a nearby Kremlin office, Nixon and Brezhnev opened their weeklong summit with a two-hour meeting, devoted first to Soviet complaints about American policy in Vietnam, which, once registered, were no longer addressed, and then to U.S.-Soviet relations during World War II, when they were allies against Hitler's Germany. That was Brezhnev's message: It was time to resuscitate the spirit and promise of the old wartime alliance.

On May 23, the summit proceeded in a warm, friendly atmosphere, as Nixon and Brezhnev dotted the i's on a variety of trade deals and discussed limitations on nuclear weapons.

On May 24, Brezhnev "kidnapped" Nixon, to use Kissinger's verb, and whisked him off to a dacha in suburban Moscow. There, a playful Brezhnev took Nixon on a wild, hour-long hydrofoil ride on the Moscow River. When they returned to the dacha, they were joined by Prime Minister Alexei Kosygin and President Nikolai Podgorny. Each one then took a turn to attack Nixon's Vietnam policy, describing it as "Nazi-like," "cruel," "unlawful," and "sheer aggression."

Brezhnev seemed almost to enjoy his diatribe, at one point warning Nixon that one day Hanoi might invite troops "from other nations" to join the struggle. He mentioned that in 1965, for example, China was ready to intervene with troops in Vietnam. It was a recurring Johnson nightmare. "That threat doesn't frighten us a bit," Nixon shot back, "but go ahead and make it." Brezhnev tried another approach: an American withdrawal from Vietnam, he said, would raise U.S. prestige around the world, a policy recommendation similar to de Gaulle's in 1969. Nixon did not respond. Brezhnev then quoted from Kissinger's "decent interval" theory. "Dr. Kissinger told me that if there was a peaceful settlement in Vietnam," he related, "you would be agreeable to the Vietnamese doing whatever they want after a period of time, say 18 months. If that is indeed true," he continued, "and if the Vietnamese knew this, and that it was true, they would be sympathetic on that basis" to a deal. Brezhnev then asked the key question: If you are really ready to allow Saigon to fall to the Communists in eighteen months, then why not end the war now?

Again, Nixon did not respond. He had, for the most part, sat quietly through the Soviet barrage. Then, just as quickly as the Russians had raised the diplomatic temperature, they lowered it, apparently realizing that they now had what they needed: a transcript of their heated blasts at American policy and their stalwart defense of their North Vietnamese ally. No doubt, the transcript would shortly be on its way to Hanoi.[25]

At 11 p.m. on May 26, the last substantive day of the summit, the United States and the Soviet Union finally reached agreement on their nuclear treaty limiting the number of antiballistic missile sites and temporarily freezing the number of short- and long-range missiles. It was a major accomplishment in the history of arms control, and it was deserving of a special Kissinger briefing for the traveling American press corps—a briefing that started at 1 a.m., Saturday, May 27, and took place in The Starry Sky, a night club in the Intourist Hotel, a few hundred yards from Red Square. For the occasion, the nightclub was cleared of customers. The setting was surrealistic. A stained glass skyline of skyscrapers was the barely perceived backdrop for Kissinger, who stood before the reporters, microphone in hand, like a chubby crooner about to sing a love song. The reporters sat around small tables, taking notes on strategic weapons, the Middle East, trade—and also Vietnam. Kissinger described the talks as "long, sometimes difficult and very detailed."[26]

A few hours later, early Saturday morning, as Nixon was leaving for a tourist's stop in Leningrad—the Soviet name for Peter the Great's "window on the west," namely, St. Petersburg—Kissinger resumed his Vietnam dialogue with Gromyko and once again listened to a Soviet leader appeal for a resumption of the Paris talks. "That is not the issue," Kissinger insisted. "What we want is a negotiation that produces a prospect of an early end of the war."

Throughout the summit, Kissinger had kept a check on the worrisome communist offensive in Vietnam, where an ARVN collapse could have shattered the summit by forcing Nixon to return to Washington. But with each day of the summit producing no calamitous news from South Vietnam, Kissinger had reason to believe that maybe, just maybe, the situation might be stabilizing. Whatever the explanation, the North Vietnamese offensive seemed to have stalled. The expected assault on Hue never developed. The provincial capital of Kontum held, as did An Loc, besieged for weeks. Saigon no longer seemed under immediate threat. The tactical use of the B-52, which produced devastatingly high casualties in communist ranks, appeared for the time being to have blunted the communist offensive and given ARVN a chance to regroup and in places go on the attack. So, when Gromyko returned to the usual Soviet proposal for the establishment of a coalition government, Kissinger rejected it with uncommon force. He stressed again that the only basis for a negotiated end to the war was Hanoi's acceptance of a cease-fire in place, U.S. troop withdrawals, and an immediate return of American POWs. Brezhnev, Gromyko, and the others seemed genuinely puzzled about one aspect of Nixon's policy: If the United States was ready to accept a communist victory a year or two after its troop withdrawal from South Vietnam, why not accept the same outcome now and avoid the losses and disruptions caused by a continuation of the war?

Though the concluding communiqué, which Kissinger and Gromyko finalized on that strange Saturday morning of briefings and negotiating, contained much praise for the newly aroused promise in U.S.-Soviet relations, it was also noteworthy for the brief and very restrained expression of Soviet support for Hanoi. It was almost as though the Vietnam War was, for the Russians, an inconvenient truth to be acknowledged in formal communiqués, but in most other respects to be essentially shoved off to one side of the negotiating table and, when possible, ignored.

After stops in Iran and Poland, Nixon returned to Washington on June 1 and went directly to a Joint Session of Congress to report triumphantly on his Moscow summit. "Man's oldest dream," he said, "a world in which all nations can enjoy the blessings of peace" was now a real possibility. The summit marked the beginning of "a new era of mutually agreed restraint and arms limitation between the two principal nuclear powers," he said.[27] In polls, he led the likely Democratic presidential candidate, Senator George McGovern, by 19 points. His re-election seemed ensured. Now it was Nixon's job to end the war, which meant it was Kissinger's job to resume the Paris negotiations, and he approached this responsibility with a fresh burst of optimism. "I think we are going to finish Vietnam this summer," he told Attorney General John Mitchell. Any day now, Kissinger reasoned, the North Vietnamese would accept the U.S. proposal for a cease-fire in place. Surely, there would be a breakthrough.

On July 19, Kissinger met again with Tho, this time for six-and-a-half hours, longer than any of their other meetings. Tho returned to one theme, one question, again and again: If there were an agreement, would the United States respect it? If, after an uncertain period of time, the North Vietnamese took control of South Vietnam, would the United States then decide to return to Indochina? Kissinger assured Tho that once out, the United States would stay out. Washington was acting "in good faith," he insisted. Were the post-summit Russians now leaning on North Vietnam to be more accommodating to a deal? Possibly, Kissinger thought. He told Dobrynin on his return to Washington: "The tone of the North Vietnamese was more acceptable than it had ever been . . . and the discussions left open the possibility that there might be a settlement." Dobrynin smiled, Buddha-like, but said nothing.[28]

Encouraged, Kissinger arranged another meeting with Tho on August 1. This one lasted eight hours, the longest ever, and again the North Vietnamese appeared to be forthcoming. The two sides agreed to see each other again on August 14. While sharp differences remained on how to handle Thieu—to drop him, to include him in a coalition government, or to arrange an elegant retirement—the mood on both sides was good. Perhaps because on the bloody battlefield of South Vietnam, neither belligerent was at this time winning or losing—an odd stalemate had settled over the war, possibly as a result of Moscow's pressure on Hanoi to be more accommodating to a deal. Kissinger felt that North Vietnam must be facing a crucial decision: to settle now, before the U.S. election, and then play the political game until the time ripened for a coup, or wait until after the election when Nixon could bombard North Vietnam to his heart's delight. Kissinger ignored one other possibility, often the fault of a foreigner trying to outfox a Vietnamese nationalist: that the North Vietnamese had long ago decided to fight to the bitter end for the reunification of their country. Nothing else mattered. Kissinger, analyzing Hanoi's strategy from the perspective of a German-born, Harvard professor–turned–government strategist, was absolutely confident that the North Vietnamese would settle before the election. Not so, thought Nixon. "Henry has never been right," Nixon told Haldeman. In his diary, Nixon wrote: "I am inclined to think that the better bargaining time for us would be immediately after the election rather than before."

Planning for his August 14 meeting with Tho, Kissinger decided that he would add a stop in Saigon. Though Thieu had always been at the knotty center of the Paris negotiations, Kissinger never felt the need to brief him on the state of his secret negotiations with Tho, even though it was Thieu's future that was being decided. Ambassador Ellsworth Bunker, in Saigon, got a limited fill-in from Alexander Haig, and he was the one charged with sharing a few of these nuggets with Thieu. But now, as the pace of negotiations quickened and an end was finally on the horizon, possibly even the near horizon, Kissinger reluctantly concluded that Thieu must be brought into the loop. No breakthrough was recorded at the August 14 meeting in Paris, but Kissinger tried to persuade Tho to strike a deal before the election, and he thought he had made an inch of progress. Maybe two inches, because Tho had indicated that North Vietnam might consider a coalition government including Thieu.

As Kissinger headed for Saigon on August 15, he sent an "Exclusively Eyes Only" cable to Nixon, in which he ventured a bold conclusion: "We have gotten closer to a negotiated settlement than ever before. . . . We still have a chance to make an honorable peace." *Have a chance?*—these words did not exactly impress the Boss, who scribbled a few comments on the cable and sent it to Haig, ". . . which means we have no progress in 15 meetings. . . . No progress was made and none can be expected."[29] Actually, Kissinger's point was that progress had been made, and more could be expected.

Up to this time, in Thieu's chance encounters with Kissinger, he had always been polite and pleasant, probably because he had assumed Tho would not agree to any of Kissinger's proposals. But now that Tho seemed more susceptible to the idea of a negotiated end to the war, Thieu decided to oppose a negotiated end; now, he aligned himself with Nixon and said that he, too, preferred a military solution. "There is only one way to force the communists to negotiate and that consists of the total destruction of their economic and war potential," he had told a Saigon audience. In his talks with Kissinger, Thieu was not only negative about the Paris negotiations, he also demanded six more months of intensive bombing.

But Kissinger left Saigon, as he later wrote, "with a false sense of having reached a meeting of the minds." Actually, he had totally misread Thieu. The South Vietnamese leader had no intention of agreeing to North Vietnamese troops remaining in South Vietnam, nor of allowing the communists to be part of the international committee that would supervise elections for a new government. Why Kissinger imagined that Thieu would have accepted these two crucial elements in his negotiation with Tho was beyond comprehension. Nixon, interestingly, had no such problem. He understood immediately that Thieu was determined, with American help, to inflict a military defeat on North Vietnam. He understood, too, that Thieu was a proud nationalist, who did not like being treated as an American puppet.

Years later, Thieu told writer Walter Isaacson: "There was no effort to treat us as an equal, for [Kissinger] was too arrogant for that. We wanted to be part of the negotiation, but he was working behind our back and hardly keeping us informed." Kissinger suddenly found himself battling two Vietnamese antagonists. Was it Tho or Thieu who would prove to be the more formidable foe?

On September 15, with Nixon's presumed re-election now only seven weeks away, Kissinger returned to Paris for another secret meeting with Tho. He was optimistic about concluding a cease-fire agreement, in part because Thieu's marines had just recaptured Quang Tri. The provincial capital, which once housed 35,000 people, was left an empty wasteland after months of brutal communist occupation and heavy American bombing. For the first time since the start of the Easter offensive, the North Vietnamese seemed exhausted. They had suffered heavy casualties, and, stymied by American bombing and mining, they had been unable to claim a single major victory.

In one negotiating session, Tho paused and asked Kissinger: "Do you really want to bring this to an end now?"

"Yes," Kissinger replied, intrigued by the question.

"Okay," the top communist negotiator said. He rose, walked around the table and shook Kissinger's hand. "We have finally agreed on one thing: we will end the war on October 15?"

"That would be fine."[30]

Fine, indeed, for Kissinger, the negotiator, but not necessarily for Nixon, the president, who had always been fearful of an October surprise sprung either by his Democratic rival, McGovern, or by his enemy in Hanoi. Worse would be a surprise arranged by both: the North Vietnamese inviting McGovern to visit Hanoi before the November 7 election and then giving him a splashy political gift, namely, the release of half or more of the American POWs. That, in Nixon's wildly neurotic but calculating mind, could turn the election from a sure thing into one big question mark. No, he decided, nothing was more important than his re-election, and nothing would be allowed to disrupt it. Kissinger could continue to negotiate in Paris (why not?), but the United States would continue to support Thieu, at least until the election. Nixon, who publicly scoffed at political polls, was privately an avid reader of polls, and one by the Harris organization appealed to him especially. It reported that, by a 55–32 percent majority, the American people favored a continuation of the bombing of North Vietnam as a way of reaching an honorable end to the war. Force as a prelude to peace: that had always been Nixon's strategy. Now, translated into the tactics of presidential campaigning, it meant that the bombing and mining of North Vietnam would continue until after the election, and then, at the proper time, assuming no breakthrough in Paris, these attacks would be intensified until North Vietnam finally accepted Nixon's terms for a cease-fire and a return of prisoners.

For the next few weeks, Kissinger was on a non-stop shuttle between Washington and Paris. With each meeting, he saw encouraging signs of Hanoi moving toward acceptance of a cease-fire, but he also saw dangers. Thieu was opposed to a cease-fire that left North Vietnamese troops in his country, and Nixon was reluctant at this time to accept a compromise settlement. After the election, under certain conditions—yes, but not now.

On October 8, Tho sounded uncharacteristically upbeat, a negotiator with a draft agreement in his hip pocket. A few details yet to be agreed on, but the deal was basically done. "We are at a crucial point," Kissinger cabled Nixon. The next morning, Tho gave Kissinger a copy of the draft agreement. It was, Tho said disingenuously, based on American proposals. Kissinger noticed immediately that North Vietnam was no longer demanding the ouster of the Thieu regime as a prerequisite for a cease-fire. He was "ecstatic" but hoped he did not show it. Outside, when they were alone, Kissinger and Winston Lord, his chief assistant, shook hands. "We've done it," they both whispered. That night, Kissinger cabled Haldeman: "Tell the president that there has been some definite progress at today's first session and that he can harbor some confidence the outcome will be positive." For the next three days, Kissinger and Tho wrestled with the details. Again, definite progress. The mood was sunny. Tho assumed Kissinger had Nixon's approval and Thieu, considered a mindless vassal, would quickly be made to comply with the master's wishes. For a time, Kissinger considered flying directly from Paris to Saigon, briefing Thieu, hopefully winning his assent, and then flying to Hanoi to initial the draft. Nixon had a different itinerary in mind. Kissinger was to return to Washington immediately.

On October 12, at 6 p.m., Kissinger happily informed Nixon: "Well, Mr. President, it looks like we've got three out of three," the three being the opening to China, the nurturing of détente with the Russians, and an agreement to end the Vietnam War.

Kissinger discussed the main points of the agreement:

—A cease-fire in place;
—Sixty days later, the complete withdrawal of American forces;
—That, coupled with an exchange of POWs;
—The establishment of a "National Council of Reconciliation and Concord," including Thieu, the Vietcong, and neutral elements, and operating on

the principle of unanimous consent, which meant Thieu had an effective veto on all decisions;

—The United States would provide an unspecified amount of aid to a unified Vietnam.[31]

Nixon was certain that the North Vietnamese would violate the agreement the day after it was signed, but it did provide for an exit from Vietnam he could describe as honorable. So it seemed, anyway. He ordered the White House mess to bring a steak and a bottle of 1957 Lafite-Rothschild wine to his office, proof that Nixon was for the moment pleased. Of course he was playing games, encouraging his relieved negotiator to believe he had accepted the deal while still banking on Thieu to veto it. Then the fault for failure could not be placed on him. At the heart of all of his calculations, domestic and foreign, was his re-election.

On October 13, Kissinger sent a cable to Lord, who had remained in Paris to help draft the final agreement. It read: "The President accepts the basic draft of 'An Agreement on Ending the War and Restoring Peace in Vietnam' except for some technical issues to be discussed between Minister Xuan Thuy (Tho's deputy) and Dr. Kissinger on October 17." The message was given to Tho, who might by this time have received word from Hanoi that American bombing of North Vietnam had been sharply reduced. Since May 8, the United States had dropped 150,000 tons of bombs on North Vietnam. Nixon wanted to signal his satisfaction with the Paris draft in a way sure to be noticed in Hanoi. He even went so far as to orchestrate the same peace scenario Kissinger had envisioned. Kissinger would go to Saigon, brief Thieu, and then initial the agreement in Hanoi. On October 26, Nixon in Washington and Prime Minister Pham Van Dong in Hanoi would simultaneously announce the end of the war, and on October 31, in Paris, the agreement would be signed by the United States, North Vietnam, the Thieu government, and the Vietcong.

On October 17, Kissinger was back at the negotiating table in Paris. He and Tho agreed on almost every detail in the draft document. He sent an optimistic report to Nixon, who wanted first to make sure Thieu would accept it. Haig warned Kissinger: "Our leader is adamant about the next leg (Hanoi) . . . not taking place unless a firm agreement with full support by Thieu is assured." And that was a big question mark.

On October 19, Kissinger arrived in Saigon, fearing the worst and yet believing he could somehow persuade Thieu to accept the draft agreement. He had clear instructions from Nixon. "Your mission should in no way be construed by him (Thieu) as arm-twisting." If the war was to be concluded before the election, Thieu and his generals had to be "equal partners." This was sophistry at a disarming level. Nixon believed Thieu would object to the deal; he also believed the war could not be ended by negotiation unless and until North Vietnam had first been brought to its knees in a new and pitiless blitzkrieg. Therefore, by allowing Kissinger to play the prince of peace, traveling to Paris and then Saigon, Nixon was really playing a duplicitous game, misleading everyone, including the American people, into believing that peace was just around the corner.

At 10 a.m., Kissinger arrived at the presidential palace. Thieu had always been punctual. This time, he was fifteen minutes late, a sign of uncharacteristic impoliteness. Kissinger handed Thieu a letter from Nixon, filled with praise for Thieu, the ARVN, and South Vietnam but also with the stark reality that the United States had reached "essential agreement" with Hanoi on a peace agreement. "I believe," Nixon asserted, "we have no reasonable alternative but to accept this agreement."[32] Kissinger outlined the terms of the agreement and handed Thieu a copy in English. Later Thieu told an aide: "I wanted to punch him in the mouth." Thieu was angry. Ever since the start of Vietnamization in 1969, he had feared a betrayal. Now he had his proof in the form of a draft agreement between the United States and his mortal enemy, North Vietnam.

On October 20, a meeting between Kissinger and Thieu was scheduled to start at 9 a.m., but it was postponed at the last minute until 2 p.m., again a deliberate snub. And then, in violation of diplomatic protocol, postponed again until 5 p.m., when, without apology or explanation, it was proposed they meet the following morning at 8 a.m. To an impatient Kissinger, this was a "misjustice" of "monumental" dimension. "No ally had a right," he later wrote, "to treat an emissary of the President of the United States this way."[33]

At 9 p.m., a clearly frazzled Thieu telephoned Ambassador Bunker and in a "hysterical" tone of voice accused the United States of trying to organize a coup against him. He provided no evidence then and none has since been uncovered. The spark for Thieu's charge might have been a sentence in the Nixon letter about an earlier fiasco in U.S.-Vietnamese relations. "I would urge you to take every measure," Nixon wrote, "to avoid the development of an atmosphere which could lead to events similar to those which we abhorred in 1963." Was Nixon indirectly threatening Thieu by recalling the horrific coup and assassination of President Ngo Dinh Diem? Thieu had been one of the coup plotters—he did not pull the trigger, but he was in on the planning, and he knew the coup had been instigated by the U.S. government. Bunker flatly denied the charge, but it came from a South Vietnamese leader who was clearly panicking at the nightmarish prospect of confronting North Vietnam without the direct, on-the-ground support of the United States. He had always had America's backing. Now it was ending. "It was not Thieu's fault," Kissinger explained, "that we had simply come to the end of our road."[34]

When they did meet the following morning, Thieu advanced twenty-three specific objections to the draft agreement. He also asked for "a few points of clarification." What, for example, "are these *three* 'Indochinese states'?" The wording appeared three times in the English text. It meant Laos, Cambodia, and one Vietnam. But if there was to be one Vietnam, then what happened to South Vietnam? Kissinger promptly dissembled. "Ah, that must be a typographical error," he said. Thieu pressed his case. After checking the English text against the Vietnamese text, he explained to Kissinger that the English words "committee" and "council" could be translated as "governmental structure" in Vietnamese. In the negotiation, "governmental structure" could end up meaning a "coalition government," which Thieu totally opposed. In other words, in English the words carried little political significance; in Vietnamese, however, they acquired genuine political meaning. One explanation for the language problems, which only deepened Thieu's apprehension, was that in Paris Kissinger had relied almost exclusively on North Vietnamese translators and interpreters. He distrusted American translators, believing they might leak the agreement to reporters. Now he was paying the price.

If Thieu needed another reason for obstructing an agreement, it was provided by *Newsweek* columnist Arnaud de Borchgrave, who had been invited to Hanoi to do an interview with Prime Minister Pham Van Dong. The invitation surprised him, because he was "a well known hawk on the war," as he described himself, and Hanoi had been inviting only "well known peaceniks." For that reason, he had not applied for a visa, nor requested an interview. But Hanoi wanted to convey an important message and figured a prominent critic such as de Borchgrave would be the perfect pigeon. He had already been to Hanoi three times—in 1952, 1953, and 1954. Kissinger, when informed of Hanoi's invitation, told de Borchgrave: "They want to extract some propaganda value by getting someone with your views on the war to write about bomb damage to dikes and other targets they call civilian."

Now, within a few hours after his arrival, de Borchgrave was informed that the interview would take place the next morning in an unimpressive office he remembered only as "sparse" and "rundown." The interview lasted two hours, and it was a "major scoop" in substance and, as it turned out, in timing, too.

For when it was published in *Newsweek,* making a splash around the world, Kissinger was in Saigon trying to persuade Thieu to accept the draft agreement. The interview was an instant best-seller in Saigon. Pham Van Dong's reading of the draft agreement seemed deliberately designed to offend Thieu, describing him as a relic "overtaken by events" and emphasizing, among other things, the establishment of "a three-sided coalition of transition." The North Vietnamese leader, reflecting accurately the true essence of the draft agreement, also spoke of "two armies and two administrations" that would remain in South Vietnam after the agreement was signed. The "two armies and the two administrations" were, for Thieu, red flags—rhetorical expression of the American betrayal he had feared for years, proof in his mind of a perfidious deal struck behind his back by Kissinger and Tho that would leave anywhere from 140,000 to 300,000—depending on the estimate—North Vietnamese soldiers in South Vietnam and that would create a new coalition government. Unintentionally, de Borchgrave's interview with Pham Van Dong became a player in a diplomatic game.[35]

On October 22, crunch day on everyone's calendar, Kissinger received new and puzzling instructions from Nixon. He was now to push Thieu, but only to a "limit without causing a blowup." Sure, Kissinger thought, but how? He was reminded of an apocryphal story from World War II. How did one solve the problem of enemy submarines? Easy, an admiral said. "Let's heat up the ocean and boil them all to the surface." An officer then asked: "But how do we do that, sir?" The admiral dismissed the question: "I've given you the idea, the technical implementation is up to you." Kissinger was also to deliver a new Nixon letter to Thieu, which, despite his instructions to Kissinger, could only be described as arm-twisting. "It is my judgment," Nixon wrote, "that your decision would have the most serious effects upon my ability to provide support for you and for the Government of South Vietnam." This was tough talk. If Thieu was to reject the agreement, he had to be reminded of the consequences. Between the lines Kissinger read a Nixon decision to defer the final agreement until after election day and, somehow, in the meantime keep both Vietnamese belligerents in a relatively quiescent state.

Surprisingly, Thieu arrived for the morning meeting in a comparatively good mood. He restated his opposition to the agreement, focusing especially on the continued presence of North Vietnamese troops, but he restated it in almost philosophical tones. The problem for you, he said, was ending your participation in a war and then going home, but the problem for us [Thieu and his cohorts] was one of life and death. He wanted to confer with his top generals and with the National Assembly. Let's meet again, he suggested, at 5 p.m. Kissinger again misread Thieu. "I think we finally made a breakthrough," Kissinger reported to Nixon. Bunker shared Kissinger's momentary spark of optimism, cabling the State Department that "we both left the meeting more encouraged that Thieu will be trying to find a way through his problems."[36]

At 5 p.m., Thieu received Kissinger and Bunker. This time, he was in a foul mood. He accused Kissinger of "conniving" with Russia and China to betray his country. "I do not appreciate the fact," he said, "that your people are going around town telling everybody that I signed. I have not signed anything. I do not object to peace, but I have not gotten any satisfactory answers from you and I am not going to sign."

Kissinger was shocked by Thieu's blunt rejection. "We have fought for four years, have mortgaged our whole foreign policy to the defense of one country," he replied. "You're the last obstacle to peace. If you do not sign, we're going to go on our own." Nixon had feared the "blowup" that was now developing in Saigon.

Kissinger added, gratuitously: "I am not going to come back to South Vietnam."

Thieu shot back: "Why? Are you rushing to get the Noble Prize?"

Bunker asked in his cool and proper manner: "Is that your final position, not to sign, Mr. President?"

"Yes, that is my final position," Thieu answered brusquely. "I will not sign and I would like you to convey my position to Mr. Nixon."[37]

Kissinger, back at the U.S. Embassy, cabled Nixon the bad news. "Thieu has just rejected the entire plan or any modification of it. He insists that any settlement must contain absolute guarantees of the DMZ, total withdrawal of all North Vietnamese troops, and total self-determination of South Vietnam. . . . It is hard to exaggerate the toughness of Thieu's position. . . . His demands verge on insanity."

Nevertheless, on October 23, the day of his departure, Kissinger asked for another meeting with Thieu, in part to convey the impression to reporters that the two allies remained in close consultation. Thieu agreed. Five minutes, no more, he said. Kissinger spoke with a heavy sadness: "If we continue our confrontation, you will win victories, but we will both lose in the end. It is a fact that in the United States all the press, the media, and the intellectuals have a vested interest in our defeat. If I have seemed impatient in the last days, it is because I saw opportunity slipping away. This is why I leave with such a sense of tragedy." He added that if the war continued for another six months, Congress would surely cut off funding, and South Vietnam would be the victim. A despondent Thieu replied: "If necessary, we will fight alone. . . . This is not a good agreement. If I were to sign it, there would be bloodshed in Vietnam in six months." At this point he turned his back on Kissinger to look at maps on the wall, and then, turning around again and choosing his words carefully, continued: "We had better fight for six more months, out of our remaining resources, and die—than sign this agreement and die now."[38]

At the airport, as Kissinger was boarding his plane, a reporter shouted: "Was it a productive trip?" "Yes," Kissinger replied. "It always is when I come here."

On the flight to Washington, Kissinger looked back upon a "dramatic and exhausting week" that started with high hope and ended with bitter disappointment. Both sides, he later thought, were "doomed to collision." Thieu was driven by a desperate nationalism that obliged him to block an agreement and go for total victory; by his lights, he had no other choice. Nixon was driven as much by electoral politics as by a weary realization that, for the United States at least, the war was over, except for the end.

On October 25, the *New York Times* reported that "a ceasefire could come very soon." Washington bureau chief Max Frankel wrote that "only a supreme act of folly in Saigon or Hanoi" could stop it. Frankel had been briefed by Kissinger. From Paris came another front page story. Flora Lewis quoted French sources detailing the terms of the agreement. Late that afternoon, Hanoi Radio, interrupting its regular programming, announced that "an important statement" would soon be broadcast. At 1:46 the following morning, Hanoi Radio began to broadcast a 2,500-word official statement revealing not only the text of the draft agreement but also the details of the secret negotiations that led up to it.[39] With this broadcast, the North Vietnamese pulled a trick out of Nixon's own repertoire. In January 1972, the president had broken a pledge of secrecy by disclosing Kissinger's secret meetings in Paris with Le Duc Tho. Now, for its own reasons, Hanoi Radio broadcast the terms of the agreement and demanded that it be signed, as agreed to by Tho and Kissinger, on October 31. Hanoi, usually so secretive, had gone public.

Nixon, his mind on his re-election, now only a week away, realized he had a huge public relations problem on his hands. He knew no agreement was possible by election day, but he still wanted to look like a merchant of peace, election or no election. He instructed his spokesman, Ron Ziegler, to sound optimistic about an agreement but to give no details. It was a "mission impossible." The White House press corps became increasingly belligerent, as reporters all over the world seemed to have the story but they had only

Ziegler, who did not know much about the story in any case. They applied heavy pressure on the White House to disclose its version of the negotiation. Finally Nixon caved, and in doing so, broke one of his own unbreakable rules: Kissinger had never been allowed to appear on television, because he spoke English with a German accent, and Nixon's White House was always supposed to project an all-American sound. But in this case who else but Kissinger could explain Kissinger's negotiation? (Kissinger had done dozens of background briefings, but until now he had never been heard or seen—he was only identified as a "senior White House official.")

On October 26, at 10 a.m., Kissinger brought his accent and his reputation to the White House lectern to explain what had happened in Paris and in Saigon. "The purpose of my press conference," he later explained, "was to rescue from Vietnamese hatreds a fragile agreement that would end a decade of agony."[40] He wanted both Hanoi and Saigon to understand that the United States was still committed to the agreement. He said: "We have now heard from both Vietnams, and it is obvious that a war that has been raging for ten years is drawing to a conclusion, and that this is a traumatic experience for all the participants."

He then used an expression that he was later to regret. "We believe that peace is at hand. We believe that an agreement is within sight. . . . It is inevitable that in a war of such complexity . . . there should be occasional difficulties in reaching a final solution, but we believe that by far the longest part of the road has been traversed and what stands in the way of an agreement now are issues that are relatively less important than those that have already been settled."[41]

He ended with a warning to both Hanoi and Saigon. To Hanoi: "We will not be stampeded into an agreement until its provisions are right." To Saigon: "We will not be deflected from an agreement when its provisions are right."

Later, in his memoirs, Kissinger acknowledged that the phrase "peace is at hand" became "a handy symbol of governmental duplicity" in the continuing debate over the war. "It was a pithy message—too optimistic, as it turned out," but it did have an "electric effect" on a nation tired of war. "It was for me," Kissinger wrote, "a moment of unusual pride not leavened by humility." The phrase itself had not been cleared with Nixon, and "if I had to do it over, I would choose a less dramatic phrase." But, Kissinger insisted, "the statement was essentially true." Peace *was* at hand. It required only a few more steps, the most meaningful of which was getting Hanoi back to the negotiating table in Paris.

On October 28, Saigon again registered its strong objection to the agreement, denouncing, among other things, the setting up of a "disguised coalition government." Sometimes directly and sometimes by implication, Thieu was spreading stories of American betrayal and hypocrisy throughout Asia. This rankled the president, who sent another personal letter to Thieu, saying first that Kissinger's October 26 news conference accurately reflected his own views and then, in language unusually harsh for presidential correspondence, he directed an unmistakably blunt threat at Thieu. "If the evident drift towards disagreement between the two of us continues," he warned, "the essential base for US support for you and your government will be destroyed." He cited disturbing comments by South Vietnam's Foreign Minister Tran Van Lam that the United States was "negotiating a surrender." Not true, Nixon insisted, adding that the comments were "damaging," "unfair," and "improper."[42]

On October 30, a break appeared in the gloomy diplomatic clouds. North Vietnam assured Kissinger that an official reply to his call for a resumption of the Paris talks was on its way. Kissinger assumed it would be positive.

On November 4, three days before the election, Hanoi accepted the U.S. offer to resume negotiations and suggested November 14 or "another date which may be proposed by the U.S. side." Kissinger proposed November 15. Tho asked for November 20. Agreed, Kissinger said, pleased that negotiations were again on track.

For Nixon, November 7 might have been the most gratifying day of his long political career. He won re-election to a second term as president with 60.7 percent of the popular vote—that was 47,169,841 votes to McGovern's 29,172,767 votes, this margin greater than any other in American history. He carried forty-nine out of the fifty states, losing only in Massachusetts. He even won 35 percent of Democratic voters. NBC's John Chancellor summed up the result. "This is the most spectacular landslide election in the history of United States politics," he said. Nixon watched the returns on television until 4 a.m. and was back at his desk at 8 a.m.; but rather than bask in the sunshine of his extraordinary victory, he turned to Haldeman and demanded a "pro forma letter of resignation" from his entire cabinet and his senior White House staff. "We need new blood, fresh ideas," he explained. And if the Republican Party complained that its candidates did not do as well as the president, Nixon told Haldeman to "cut that off. Make sure that we start pissing on the Party before they begin pissing on me."

CHAPTER EIGHT

"HONORABLE EXIT" OR
"DECENT INTERVAL"

"We bombed them into accepting our concessions."
JOHN NEGROPONTE

"VIETNAM PEACE PACTS SIGNED, AMERICA'S LONGEST WAR HALTS"
New York Times headline

WITH THE ELECTION now behind him, Nixon again focused on the unfin-
ished business of Vietnam. He did not want to start a second term with the war
still unresolved. Yet, in a number of different ways, he found himself at a dead
end in Vietnam. For one thing, he was certain that by February 1973, Congress
would begin to cut off all funding for the war. Meaning, no matter what he,
as the newly re-elected president, wanted to do, or what he had pledged to
Nguyen Van Thieu that he would do, he would be unable to carry out his policy or be true to his word. He would be denied the funds. Nixon believed that
Henry Kissinger's "peace is at hand" news conference had drastically reduced
his options. Melvin Laird agreed with Nixon. After conferring with his old
buddies on Capital Hill, the defense secretary reached the unhappy conclusion
that it had become impossible to "keep that thing going right now"—"that
thing" being the whole Vietnam enterprise.

Moreover, in the war itself, the South Vietnamese were not winning. They
were also not losing. The Easter offensive had slowly sputtered to another
fragile stalemate. The ARVN, the South Vietnamese army, though still riddled with corruption, had held its own through the summer and into the fall,
largely because U.S. air power had inflicted heavy casualties on the North
Vietnamese army. The communists, bloodied and exhausted, decided that, for
the time being, they would emerge from their tunnels and sanctuaries only to
go after targets of opportunity, a village to be attacked or a convoy of troops to
be ambushed, but they would stay away from costly, large-scale engagements.
The upshot was that, as the possibility of a cease-fire neared, the battlefield
became essentially quiet, except for those times when both sides could not

resist launching a land-grabbing operation. U.S. intelligence believed that the North Vietnamese were hurting and, as a result, shifting their strategy from the battlefield to the negotiating table.

At the Paris peace talks, the biggest stumbling block continued to be Thieu's refusal to accept the presence of North Vietnamese troops in South Vietnam. There were dozens of other objections, but none as significant, as deal-breaking, as this one. Alexander Haig, the deputy national security adviser, on November 13 recalled for Nixon and Kissinger what Thieu had once told him. "You, General Haig, are a general, and I am a general," he had said. "Have you ever seen any peace accord in the history of the world in which the invaders had been permitted to stay in the territories they had invaded? Would you permit Russian troops to stay in the United States and say that you had reached a peace accord with Russia?" There was the problem in a nutshell: The North Vietnamese did not consider themselves to be invaders of, or foreigners in, South Vietnam. They saw North and South Vietnam as one country, and they intended to run it. Thieu saw it as two countries, and with full justification pointed to the countless times one American president after another had "committed" the United States to that view—that is, up until the time Nixon changed American policy and, in the course of the Paris negotiation, conceded this pivotal point to the North Vietnamese. Once the Americans recognized that the North Vietnamese could remain in South Vietnam, they were not only granting the communists a huge advantage in the war that was sure to continue in one form or another after an agreement was signed, they were also accepting the communist view that there was one Vietnam.

On November 20, Kissinger ran into two walls, one in the person of the intelligent and patient Le Duc Tho, and the other in the form of a magazine interview, which severely damaged his already fragile relations with Nixon. Let us deal first with the interview. Shortly after his October 26 news conference, which rocketed Kissinger's ego into a stratospheric arc, he sat down twice with Italian journalist Oriana Fallaci and rhapsodized about his accomplishments—"the single most disastrous conversation I ever had with a journalist," he later wrote. The interview was published in *The New Republic*. Most memorable was this quote, which sent Nixon into a fury. "I've always acted alone," Kissinger said. "Americans admire that enormously. Americans admire the cowboy leading the caravan alone astride his horse, the cowboy entering the village or city alone on his horse. . . . This romantic, surprising character suits me, because being alone has always been part of my style."

It might have suited Kissinger, but it infuriated Nixon. White House chief of staff Bob Haldeman checked with Haig: Isn't it time for Henry to be dumped? he asked. Haig said Kissinger was "completely paranoid." He told Haldeman, who told Nixon, that Kissinger "really screwed things up with the North Vietnamese and the South Vietnamese . . . and needs a very good, long vacation." Haig apparently felt no hesitation criticizing Kissinger, his boss, behind his back. Nixon's ego was brittle in any case. For Kissinger to convey the impression that he alone, "astride his horse," was responsible for the progress in Paris was a huge blunder, which Nixon never forgave and which narrowed Kissinger's room for negotiating an end to the war.

Whether Tho was aware of the interview, and whether the interview played any role in his subsequent approach to the negotiations, was unknown. He never raised it in the opening six-hour session, during which Tho praised North Vietnam's good will and blasted American duplicity. Kissinger, who was in less than perfect form that day, perhaps because of the Fallaci interview, responded by raising many of Thieu's objections to the agreement—a "major tactical mistake," Kissinger later acknowledged. He had no intention of defending Thieu's objections; so why raise them? He knew immediately that he had spoiled the negotiating atmosphere. Tho, always the unflappable diplomat, replied softly that if Kissinger was serious about the Thieu objections, the war would go on for another four years, perhaps longer.[1]

It was clear on the next day, November 21, during a relatively short meeting, that the road ahead was going to be rocky. Tho dismissed most of Thieu's objections and began to raise new objections of his own. On November 22, during their three-and-a-half-hour session, Kissinger tried to put some distance between the United States and South Vietnam. Tho played his usual cat-and-mouse game, offering one small concession and then advancing a larger demand. Nixon, on learning about the setbacks in Paris, blamed Kissinger. He then had Haldeman send an "Eyes Only" cable to him, saying "the P" was "very disappointed" and warning of a break in the negotiations and a resumption of "military activity."

On November 23, Thanksgiving Day, Tho and Kissinger met for six hours. Kissinger tried to strengthen a provision about the demilitarized zone (DMZ), with minimal success, and Tho tried to adjust language about troop withdrawals, also with minimal success.

The bottom line was that the draft agreement, which had seemed so close to completion in October, was being pulled apart, first in one direction and then in another, undercutting mutual confidence between the two sides. That night, Kissinger cabled Nixon and said that in his judgment the president now had only two options: to cut off the talks and resume heavy bombing, or to accept an imperfect document, knowing in advance that Thieu would likely sabotage the deal.[2] It was clear from the tone of their communications that their personal relationship had become "wary and strained," as Kissinger later described it.[3]

On November 24, Kissinger and Tho met for only an hour and a half. They decided to discuss their differences in philosophical terms, but even in their retreat to vagueness, they got nowhere. Kissinger, frustrated and increasingly uneasy about the negotiation, cabled Nixon and suggested a recess for one week—time enough, he hoped, to persuade Saigon to come on board and to show Hanoi that the United States was steadfast in its negotiating position. Why he thought Saigon would change its mind in this week was another of those fanciful Kissinger notions. And why Nixon accepted it is also a mystery.

On November 25, the negotiators met again for two hours. Kissinger recommended a recess. Tho agreed. Both negotiators needed a break. They would reconvene on December 4.

On his flight back to Washington, Kissinger reviewed his six days of meetings with Tho and concluded that the North Vietnamese were pulling back from the October agreement. "All the signs were contrary," Kissinger later wrote. "They kept the goal of a settlement always tantalizingly out of reach. . . . Worse was yet to come."

As it turned out, the "worse" was to come in many forms. Kissinger sensed almost immediately on his return that Nixon was restive and unhappy and his White House aides, always jealous of Kissinger's access to the president and his prominence with the public, were ready to pounce on the apparent Paris failure. "The prospect of imminent disaster always activates the network of gossip, leak and innuendo . . . and failure in Washington requires a sacrificial offering." Kissinger came to the inevitable conclusion: "I was the logical candidate." Savvy reporters waited for action on the question of the day: would Nixon fire Kissinger?

That, in fact, did not happen, probably because Nixon concluded that he needed Kissinger more than he envied or hated him, but what did happen was illuminating and pernicious. From Hanoi came word from Western diplomats that North Vietnam now felt that time was on its side: why make any other concessions in Paris? From Saigon came word from the U.S. Embassy that Thieu was actually enjoying the stories about the widening split between

Nixon and Kissinger. Thieu decided to exploit it by establishing a personal link to Nixon and in this way isolate Kissinger further.

Thieu sent one of his closest advisers, Nguyen Phu Duc, to Washington. If Duc, who served as Thieu's national security adviser, expected a warm welcome from the president, he was to be disappointed. Nixon rejected Duc's many appeals for understanding and urged Duc to persuade Thieu to accept the draft agreement. He emphasized his strong belief that Congress would cut off economic and military aid to South Vietnam, probably by February 1973, unless Thieu bought into the draft agreement. Duc offered no response that was even remotely encouraging.[4]

Thus, with a congressional cutoff of funding now widely predicted, with two Vietnamese antagonists outdueling each other in hatred and distrust, and with Nixon clearly irritated and dissatisfied with the course of the negotiation, a weakened Kissinger returned to Paris on December 4 with no realistic expectation of a breakthrough; and he got none. Indeed, the diplomatic atmosphere was downright chilly. Tho opened the session with a fiery denunciation of American policy and actions and finished with another epic rendition of Hanoi's toughness in the face of foreign aggression. Kissinger, disappointed but equally obstinate, responded by saying it would be "an historical tragedy, an historical absurdity" if they could not conclude the agreement and end the war. He assured Tho of American sincerity, promised a "maximum effort" at the negotiating table, and added that "we have two plans, one for war and one for peace." The one for war was reasonably well known; the one for peace was less a roadmap for settling the remaining issues than it was a schedule of meetings, actions, and travel designed to persuade Tho that the United States was still determined to reach an agreement. First, over the next two days, no longer, Tho and Kissinger would roll up their sleeves and devote themselves to solving all outstanding questions. Second, General Haig, accompanied by Vice President Spiro Agnew, regarded as sympathetic to Thieu, would fly to Saigon with the draft agreement and persuade Thieu to accept it. Third, all bombing of North Vietnam would stop. Finally, the agreement would be signed no later than December 22. Tho listened to Kissinger's presentation with such studied immobility that, for a moment, he looked like a statue, his face betraying no emotion, either of approval or disapproval. North Vietnam had already gone the extra mile, he told Kissinger; it was now time for the United States to make "great efforts." They parted for lunch. When the meeting resumed in the late afternoon, Tho wasted no time in diplomatic niceties—he launched into another fiery denunciation of American policy and actions, and he rejected almost all of Kissinger's proposals.

Nixon, writing in his diary that night, did not disguise his disappointment with Kissinger. "Henry went back to Paris," he wrote, "firmly convinced that he would quickly, within a matter of two days, reach agreement. . . . The North Vietnamese surprised him by slapping him in the face with a wet fish. . . . Expectations have been built so high now that our failing to bring the war to an end would have a terribly depressing effect on this country." Nixon was saying, in effect, that Kissinger, by boldly proclaiming "peace is at hand," when in fact it was not, had badly misled the American people. A breakdown in the negotiations now seemed imminent.

In his nightly report to the White House, Kissinger stated that in his view North Vietnam was "playing for a clearcut victory," based on "our split with Saigon" and "our domestic collapse."[5] The tone of his report was "stiff" and formal: He assumed full responsibility for pushing too hard in October and for failing in December, in effect providing Nixon with the chance to act on this Kissingerian mea culpa. Nixon could now fire Kissinger: He had the justification in a string of misjudgments and mistakes in Kissinger's management of the peace talks. For a few days, Nixon refused even to talk to Kissinger. He would have Haldeman take Kissinger's calls from Paris; he would even have Haldeman cable negotiating instructions to Kissinger, which deeply offended and angered the president's negotiator. Indeed, the president's relationship with Kissinger had become so sour that Nixon asked Haldeman to prepare an extensive memorandum on Kissinger's "mental processes" and "suicidal tendencies." Occasionally, Nixon would threaten to "fire the son-of-a-bitch."

On December 5, Kissinger asked Tho for a twenty-four-hour postponement. Clearly nothing was happening at the negotiating table. Could he have overlooked a promising detail? With his senior associates, including Haig, Kissinger pored over the records and transcripts of the meetings, "seeking to distill some ray of hope from some arcane formulation." But, he concluded, "We could not find any."

Deadlocked in Paris, Kissinger again turned to Moscow and Beijing, hoping they could induce Hanoi to be more flexible and accommodating. The Chinese basically ignored Kissinger's appeal, resorting to boilerplate rhetoric about American aggression. The Russians privately counseled Kissinger to have more patience, assuring him that Hanoi still wanted an agreement based more or less on the October draft.

The December 6 meeting was again a sterile exchange of old positions. After hours of pointless insults, Kissinger proposed with as much seriousness as he could muster that both sides return to the negotiating table the next day with their absolutely final, final, final position. Tho nodded, apparently not because he was thinking of tinkering with Hanoi's draft but because he did not want to be the one to break off the negotiation. Kissinger later cabled Nixon that the negotiation had become "a very high risk operation." The Vietnamese hated each other a little more than they hated the United States; and even if there were an agreement, which he now considered unlikely, Kissinger projected that "it could well break down," because it would lack "the foundation of minimum trust."[6] Not for the first time, Kissinger urged Nixon to go on television, as he had done so many times in the past, and bring the American people up-to-date on the collapsing reality of the Vietnam negotiation; and not for the first time Nixon ignored Kissinger's advice. "K is trying to cover his own mistakes," Nixon explained to Haldeman. "He can't bear to come back and face the press, because he knows they'll attack this time. . . . It's clear that he wants the P out as the blocking back to clear the way." Nixon wanted the "historical record" to show that it was the North Vietnamese, not the Americans, who were responsible for the breakdown of the talks. He instructed Kissinger to keep talking, no matter the provocation, so that when the talks collapsed, it would be Kissinger, not Nixon, who would have to explain what happened between October 26, when "peace [was] at hand" and early December, when peace seemed only a flickering hope.

Years later, Kissinger would write that the four-hour meeting on December 7 "marked the beginning of the real deadlock." Hanoi was deliberately procrastinating, believing that time was now its ally and that "we were hopelessly cornered" by Saigon's maddening intransigence and Congress's growing impatience to end the war. "A bullying tone crept into his presentations, indicating that he thought Hanoi was gaining the upper hand psychologically."[7] Tho would give a little, then take a little, leaving the United States "tantalizingly close enough to an agreement to keep us going [in Paris] and prevent us from using military force." Once again, in his nightly report to Nixon, Kissinger sounded pessimistic, but this time not only about the lack of progress in the negotiation but also about the value of the peace agreement itself. "We can anticipate no lasting peace in the wake of a consummated agreement, but merely a shift in Hanoi's modus operandi."[8] In other words, Kissinger now thought the agreement was essentially meaningless because Hanoi would never abandon its ultimate goal of unifying Vietnam under communist rule. The negotiations were a kind of fig leaf of diplomatic respectability for Hanoi and, as it turned out, for the United States. The only difference was that Hanoi was determined to win the war, one way or the other, and the United States was desperate to abandon the war—with "honor," as it was put. Kissinger felt that the agreement would survive only so long as the communists chose not to break it. That was why he always insisted that the United States needed a "decent interval" between the signing of the agreement and its almost certain collapse, an interval of time long enough for the United States to claim victory and escape political retribution at home before seeing the situation either wither away because of American inaction and indifference or be snatched away in one overwhelming military swoop to victory by the North Vietnamese.

December 8 saw Tho give and take with infuriating consistency. He would make a major concession and then almost immediately raise a new objection to an old problem. For example, he finally agreed to drop his earlier insistence on a "governmental structure," which Thieu had properly translated as a "coalition government," but then he insisted on reworking the DMZ language so that it was deliberately left open to differing interpretations. Tho did not want the DMZ to be seen as a firm, legal dividing line between two independent countries, which was exactly what Thieu and Kissinger wanted. Tho wanted the DMZ language to be wrapped in diplomatic gauze and therefore open to both legal ambiguity and continued exploitation as a route for the infiltration of troops and supplies.[9]

Still, what were Kissinger's options? He could not really adjourn the negotiation, because he knew Nixon wanted it to continue. He could not really assume a good faith effort on Tho's part to settle the outstanding issues, because by his action and rhetoric Tho demonstrated that he was stalling. But, deep down, for reasons utterly inexplicable, based on a questionable optimism about his negotiating skills, Kissinger truly believed that one good and productive meeting with Tho could crack the two remaining obstacles: language for the DMZ and language for American civilian advisers to help the ARVN. But, once again, he had misread his opponent. He had sent Haig back to Washington on the mistaken assumption that Tho shared his desire for a quick breakthrough on December 9, which would have allowed Haig to join up with Agnew for the trip to Saigon to get Thieu's assent.

While Kissinger and Tho were wrestling in Paris with the frustrating task of finding acceptably evasive language for ending the war, Nixon was meeting at Camp David with Admiral Thomas Moorer, chairman of the Joint Chiefs of Staff, to freshen up plans for another massive air assault against North Vietnam. Nixon was learning that it was much more difficult to end the war on his terms than it was to fight it. Congress was moving resolutely toward cutting off funding for the war, perhaps as early as February 1973; and the American people, judging by many polls, were turning decisively against the war. They had had enough of the negotiating deadlocks and the military stalemates. No one seemed able any longer to justify the death of one more American soldier. Again, Nixon could have had his negotiated exit from Vietnam by simply authorizing Kissinger to initial the October draft. He could then have had a celebratory signing ceremony in Paris; he could have proclaimed on network television the myth of peace with honor—and who at that time would really have objected, other than Thieu? Nixon could have explained the subtle twists and turns of the Paris negotiation to a field of skeptical journalists and given an exclusive or two to sympathetic journalists; and with a tweak here and there, he could have emerged from Vietnam as a great president who had kept his word—and America's. Though many of his critics would still have grumbled, most of the world would have cheered his decision finally to bring the American war in Vietnam to an end.

But that was not Nixon's way. He had to leave Vietnam like the goliath who has crushed his enemy, both guns blazing as he backed out of the swinging doors of a saloon in a Hollywood Western. Therefore, his instructions to Kissinger continued to be: make "some" (any?) concession (never defined) and just keep talking.

December 9 came and went. Kissinger proposed a compromise on the DMZ, essentially the addition of a sentence recommending that both North and South Vietnam discuss "the authorization of civil movement" across the DMZ. Then, unexpectedly, Tho interrupted the negotiation to complain of a headache and high blood pressure and suggested he needed a day or longer to recover. Was Tho really ill? Kissinger was skeptical, but he could not object.

On December 11, Tho returned, apparently in good health, and raised questions that had already been resolved. To settle them, Tho declared disingenuously that Hanoi needed more time. It was becoming painfully clear to Kissinger that Hanoi did not want an agreement, at least not during this round of negotiations. He thought Tho's behavior was "irritating" and "doubly insulting." In his report that night, he described it as "cock-sure insolence." What was up Tho's sleeve?[10]

When the negotiators reconvened, Tho announced that he had to return to Hanoi and would leave Paris on December 14, ending this round on an inconclusive note. He suggested, without being explicit, that there would be no agreement unless and until he had time for face-to-face talks with skeptics on the politburo who opposed the deal. Kissinger was disappointed but not entirely surprised. Earlier in the day, in another example of the split between

Washington and Saigon, Thieu had addressed his National Assembly and announced that he would never sign an agreement that left North Vietnamese troops in South Vietnam.

On December 13, Tho discussed old issues that had been settled days, weeks, or months before, as if they were new to the negotiation. He dusted off old critiques of American aggression. He praised his country's fortitude and courage and its honest and logical pursuit of its national interests. Even a diplomatic novice could see that Tho did not want an agreement, at least not then. On reflection, Kissinger wrote years later that "there was no intractable substantive issue separating the two sides, but rather an apparent North Vietnamese determination *not to allow the agreement to be completed*" (Kissinger's italics).

When Kissinger had arrived in Paris on December 4, he had instructions to reach a deal, and he thought he could do so within two days. On December 13, when he left Paris, he knew that Hanoi had decided to pause—finalizing an agreement could wait. Hanoi had its reasons: perhaps differences in the politburo that froze the negotiation, but certainly the evident split between Washington and Saigon, the embarrassing divisions within the U.S. administration, and the imminent return of a Congress committed to ending the war. Nixon had his own reason for the breakdown in Paris, and it was Kissinger. "The South Vietnamese think Henry is weak now because of his press conference statements," Nixon told Haldeman and John Ehrlichman, another senior aide. Referring again to Kissinger's October 26 news conference, he exploded, "That damn 'peace is at hand'! The North Vietnamese have sized him up; they know he has to either get a deal or lose face. That's why they've shifted to a harder position."[11] Haldeman reported, without clarification, that Kissinger has been "under care . . . and doing some strange things." For Kissinger, who felt "isolated" and "devastated," it was a long and "somber trip home," during which he returned again and again to an old theme—that Vietnam, in his view, seemed "destined to break American hearts."[12]

On returning to Washington, Kissinger went directly to the White House. Using language he knew Nixon would not find objectionable, he told the president, "They're just a bunch of shits. Tawdry, filthy shits." He compared the North Vietnamese to their communist allies. "They make the Russians look good, compared to the way the Russians make the Chinese look good when it comes to negotiating in a responsible decent way!" But, what to do? In Kissinger's view, the North Vietnamese had become "greedy" and as a result made a "cardinal error"—they had "cornered" Nixon, and he was "never more dangerous" than when he felt he had run out of options.

Uppermost in Nixon's mind at the time was ending the war, "our national trauma," before the start of his second term. He turned again to his military option, only this time he decided he would hold nothing back, short of the use of nuclear weapons. Once or twice he had vented his frustration about the war by raising the option of nuclear weapons, but no one took him seriously. In April 1972, when he resumed the bombing of North Vietnam, he had held back on using the big, strategic B-52 bomber against Hanoi and Haiphong. Now, on the morning of December 14, he lifted all restrictions: He ordered Moorer and the Joint Chiefs to reseed the mines left in Vietnamese ports and to prepare the B-52s for strikes against Hanoi and Haiphong. This was to be, Kissinger later wrote, "*his* last roll of the dice." Laird opposed a resumption of the air war, which angered Nixon; and when Moorer raised a question about it, Nixon exploded. "I don't want any more of this crap about the fact that we couldn't hit this target or that one," he shouted. "This is your chance to use military power effectively to win this war, and if you don't, I'll consider you responsible."[13] In addition, Nixon sent an urgent cable to Hanoi, warning that "serious negotiations" would have to be resumed within 72 hours—or else; and he drafted a different kind of warning to Thieu—sign on or see aid cut off. Finally, with a sort of impish if perverted pleasure, he told Kissinger to hold another news conference explaining why, after first projecting that "peace [was] at hand," it was now barely in sight.

Kissinger appeared behind the White House lectern on the morning of December 16, and his tone was deadly serious. He realized that his job was on the line—Nixon firing Kissinger was certainly a topic of hot speculation among the president's closest aides. On October 26, Kissinger had mentioned Nixon three times. Now, under strict orders to underline Nixon's "consistency, unflappability, firmness, patience and farsightedness," Kissinger dutifully mentioned the president fourteen times and predictably blamed Hanoi for the stalemated negotiation. "Peace can be near," Kissinger said, choosing "a more careful formulation," but the United States would not be "blackmailed . . . stampeded . . . [or] charmed into an agreement until its conditions are right." Kissinger did not mention Nixon's decision to resume the bombing.[14]

Nixon never expected Hanoi to accept or even answer his three-day ultimatum, and on December 17, for the first time, he ordered B-52s to attack Hanoi and Haiphong. In the early morning hours of December 18, the first wave of B-52s—129 of them in all—and hundreds of F-111s and A-6 fighter bombers began to attack airfields, power plants, rail yards, and communication centers in and around North Vietnam's capital and major port—the "most heavily defended anti-aircraft area in the world," according to the Pentagon. The B-52s flew in formations of three, dropping their payloads in a rectangular pattern about a mile long and a half mile wide. Each plane carried two dozen 500-pound bombs and 4,750-pound bombs. Nixon, briefed frequently on this operation code-named Linebacker II, was in a strange state of anxiety, anticipation, and delight. "One of the beauties of doing it now," he told Kissinger, "we don't have the problem of having to consult with Congress," which had adjourned for the Christmas/New Year holidays.[15]

Unspoken was the deadline of January 3, when Congress was scheduled to return. Like a coach cheerleading his team, he turned to Haig: "Move on it right now, move, move, move—get the damn thing going." A hundred B-52s, Kissinger reminded Nixon, were "like a 4,000 plane raid in World War II. It's going to break every window in Hanoi."[16]

It broke much more than that. Dubbed the "Christmas bombing," the air attacks continued for twelve days with a thirty-six-hour break, ironically, to celebrate Christmas, and it was greeted by a thunderclap of criticism, disgust, and bewilderment, made worse by the fact that neither Nixon, nor Kissinger, nor any senior official explained the operation while it was under way. A bizarre and frightening silence fell over the administration, but not over the media, not over Congress, and not over the rest of the world. The *Washington Post* described it as "the most savage and senseless act of war ever visited . . . by one sovereign people over another." "TERROR BOMBING IN THE NAME OF PEACE" read one typical headline.

Premier Olaf Palme of Sweden broke diplomatic protocol by blasting Nixon for a "form of torture and an outrage similar to those linked to names like Guernica, Lidice, Babi Yar, Sharpeville, and Treblinka." Soviet leader Leonid Brezhnev went beyond eloquent denunciations. He considered delaying his scheduled visit to the United States, and he charged that the United States bore "grave responsibility" for these "barbaric acts." Premier Zhou Enlai warned that Chinese-American relations were "imperiled" by the air raids. Pope Paul VI said the "unforeseen worsening of events has intensified bitterness and anxiety in world opinion." French and Swedish diplomats and journalists reported that residential neighborhoods in Hanoi were being targeted and reduced to rubble. Collateral damage was said to be very high. Kissinger found a sympathetic scholar who wrote that only 1,300 to 1,600 people were killed and that such numbers were "surely not indicative of terror bombing."

"That was an extraordinary period," Kissinger told me, shaking his head. "Simply extraordinary."

While Hanoi was being bombarded by B-52s, Saigon was being bombarded by a Nixon ultimatum that had the diplomatic, political, and economic force of a B-52. On December 19, Haig was given a letter for Thieu that Kissinger drafted and Nixon hardened "to the point of brutality." It was to be handed to the Saigon leader at 11 a.m. on December 20. Haig was on time, but once again Thieu deliberately kept a presidential envoy waiting without explanation. Finally, at 3:30 p.m., he arrived and was handed the letter. It contained Nixon's "final" and "irrevocable" decision to strike a deal with Hanoi if the communists met "the requirements for a settlement which I have set." It was, without doubt, an ultimatum.

"I have asked General Haig," Nixon wrote, "to obtain your answer to this absolutely final offer on my part for us to work together in seeking a settlement along the lines I have approved or to go our separate ways. Let me emphasize . . . that General Haig is not coming to Saigon for the purpose of negotiating with you. The time has come for us to present a united front in negotiating with our enemies, and you must decide now whether you desire to continue our alliance or whether you want me to seek a settlement with the enemy which serves U.S. interests alone."[17]

Thieu, who was no fool, remembered what had happened to President Ngo Dinh Diem: assassinated, with U.S. complicity, nearly ten years earlier. He read the Nixon letter for what it was—an ultimatum and an implied threat. In responding, he was patient and polite and, using extremely careful diplomatic language, told Haig that he could not "accept" the continued presence of North Vietnamese troops in South Vietnam, but he did not say that he would not sign the agreement, if one were reached. He predicted that Hanoi would resume the tactic of guerrilla warfare but keep it at a level low enough not to invite American retaliation. Thieu conveyed the impression that if he had to succumb to American pressure, he would ultimately do so; but, in Saigon, he wanted it noted that the decision to sign a flawed agreement would be Nixon's, not Thieu's.[18]

When Haig, upon returning to Washington, reported Thieu's reaction to Nixon and Kissinger, he expressed a degree of sympathy for Thieu and recommended that Nixon continue the bombing of North Vietnam until Hanoi agreed to withdraw all of its forces from South Vietnam. Otherwise, Hanoi would be given a huge advantage in the political and military skirmishing sure to follow a cease-fire. Nixon shook off the recommendation. No, by this time, the president had made up his mind: If he could obtain an acceptable deal with Hanoi, he would take it, with or without Thieu. Kissinger agreed with Nixon. Thieu "seems to leave us little alternative except to move toward a bilateral arrangement," he said. Kissinger blasted Thieu as "a complete SOB" and the South Vietnamese as "maniacs."

The question now was whether Hanoi would decide to return to the bargaining table, a decision that was to be made under a bombing barrage not seen since World War II. On and off for eight years, the United States had been bombing communist targets in South and North Vietnam, in that time dropping more tonnage on Vietnam than it had dropped in all theaters during World War II. Though the tonnage severely damaged the North Vietnamese infrastructure and killed tens of thousands of Vietnamese, Ho Chi-minh's communists continued their stubborn struggle for national unification under communist rule, using both military and diplomatic weapons. Now, Hanoi decided, it was again time to switch gears, which meant Tho would return to Paris and conclude an agreement that still left open the handy option of major military operations against South Vietnam, whenever desirable.

Hanoi's response came slowly and sometimes indirectly. On December 20, at the technical talks continuing in Paris, the North Vietnamese vice foreign minister, Nguyen Co Thach, "protested" the bombing but in language that was, by Hanoi's standards, comparatively mild, and then he proposed a recess until December 23. He did not break off the talks. In Washington, Kissinger was intrigued. On a hunch, he sent a secret cable to Hanoi offering his negotiating partner, Tho, a choice: Either we continue to slide deeper into a worse conflict, or we make "a serious final effort to reach a settlement at a time when agreement is so near." Later, after checking with Nixon, Kissinger proposed that if Hanoi agreed to resume talking, the U.S. bombing would stop on December 31 and the Kissinger-Tho talks would resume on January 3. In Paris, Minister Thach showed up on December 23, as he had promised, and though little was accomplished at the meeting, at least both sides met. On December 26, the day after the thirty-six-hour Christmas bombing pause, the United States launched a particularly heavy air assault against Hanoi and Haiphong. Interestingly, on that same day, North Vietnam responded directly to Kissinger's offer in a tone that was amazingly nonpolemical. It stated that Tho could return to Paris not on January 3 but on January 8 "to settle the remaining questions with the U.S. side." Health was cited as the reason for the slippage. Noteworthy, Hanoi placed special emphasis upon "its constantly serious negotiating position."

With Nixon's approval, Kissinger replied swiftly to Hanoi's new and positive-sounding response. He proposed a resumption of the technical talks on January 2, and he accepted the January 8 date for the resumption of his talks with Tho but insisted that they last no longer than three or four days. Meantime, he added, the bombing would continue.

On December 27, Hanoi answered Kissinger. Never before in this long negotiation had the North Vietnamese demonstrated such speed and such apparent eagerness to reach a settlement. OK on January 8, and OK on January 2, Hanoi said, but the bombing would have to stop as soon as the talks began.

On December 28, Kissinger cabled Hanoi that Nixon accepted the proposed dates and promised to end the bombing at the same time as the announcement was made on the resumption of the peace talks. Late the same day, again setting a record for speed, Hanoi agreed.

On December 29, consistent with the new, optimistic rhythm of the Kissinger-Tho exchanges, Nixon stopped the bombing. He informed Hanoi of his decision and added sternly that the United States was making "one final major effort" to reach a "rapid settlement." Kissinger, he stressed, would spend "no more than four days" in Paris. That afternoon, as Nixon prepared to leave for a Camp David celebration of the New Year, he summoned Charles Colson, a fiercely loyal aide, to his office. "I have something to tell you," he said, "but not another person in this building can know. The North Vietnamese have agreed to go back to the negotiating table on our terms. They can't take the bombing anymore."

Nixon might have believed that the Christmas bombing brought the North Vietnamese back to the negotiating table. Certainly Kissinger thought so. "We had won our gamble," he wrote in his memoirs, "the next round of negotiations [will] succeed." Many diplomats and journalists disagreed, accusing the twin architects of American policy of self-serving hypocrisy. To have persuaded themselves that the bombing broke Hanoi's will to fight or hastened its return to the negotiating table was to have ignored the power of Vietnamese nationalism and the resilience of the Vietnamese people. Diplomat John Negroponte quipped: "We bombed them into accepting our concessions." The CIA said privately at the time that "the October draft agreement was not changed by the bombing."[19] North Vietnam was hurting, clearly, and it was ready for a time-out; but there was no reason to believe that the North Vietnamese saw a negotiated agreement as anything more than an agreed-upon truce. The real end of the war, in their judgment, would come with the final conquest of South Vietnam.

Nixon had his own slant on this concluding phase of the war. He had always said that hostilities would cease after a climactic battle, from which the

United States would emerge looking like a Roman centurion standing atop his crushed enemy; and in his mind so the United States looked after wreaking horrific damage on the North Vietnamese and moving them to accept the peace agreement as drafted in October. Closer to reality was the tenacious North Vietnamese determination to kick the Americans out of Indochina, one way or the other, just as they had the French twenty years earlier.

In different ways, what Hanoi and Nixon both knew was that the United States had lost its appetite to pursue the fight in Indochina. Proof, if any more were needed? On January 2, 1973, the day before the technical talks were to resume in Paris, the House Democratic caucus voted 154-75 in favor of cutting off all funds for military operations in, over, or around Vietnam, so long as Americans troops and all POWs were permitted to leave Vietnam and return home safely. Two days later, the Senate Democratic caucus, by a vote of 36-12, passed essentially the same resolution.

These were the latest in a series of congressional resolutions, dating back to 1970, designed to do more than express popular opposition to the war— they also limited funding for the prosecution of the war, and, toward the end of 1973, in the ground-breaking War Powers Resolution, Congress spelled out and attempted to limit the war-making powers of the president for the first time in American history. Nixon vetoed many earlier attempts to curtail the president's powers, but, on November 7, 1973, both houses of Congress finally overrode his veto in a joint resolution, which had the same status as a bill. It became the law of the land. No longer would a president be able to conduct a war, such as the ones in Korea and Vietnam, without specific congressional approval. Henceforth, a president would have to inform Congress within forty-eight hours after committing troops to battle and then end their involvement in combat within sixty days (or up to ninety days in exceptional circumstances), unless authorized by Congress to continue fighting.

On January 3, in a "deeply somber" mood, the technical talks reopened in Paris. The North Vietnamese quickly took advantage of the moment to denounce the Christmas-time bombing, but they did that once and never referred to it again. Both delegations quickly got down to business and within a few days reached agreement on four of the eight outstanding issues.

On January 5, Nixon fired off another letter to Thieu, pointing to the two congressional resolutions as proof that the "survival of South Vietnam . . . [was] gravely jeopardized." He urged Thieu to support the negotiation and assured him that if the North Vietnamese violated the agreement, "we will respond with full force." He did not have to mention the Christmas bombing—that was obvious to everyone. In his reply, Thieu did not endorse the negotiation, and he repeated his major objections, but once again he did not say that he would not sign the agreement. Kissinger found only small comfort in the omission.

On January 6, as the White House continued to trumpet the president's strength, patience, and determination, Nixon quietly instructed Kissinger "to settle on whatever terms were available."[20] His image-creators had constructed a public Nixon, an American giant standing astride the globe, China under one foot, Russia under the other. The real Nixon had secretly told his negotiator to wrap up the war on any terms "available." He was so desperate to end America's role in the war before the start of his second term that he could tolerate just about anything, even a shrill shriek of betrayal from Thieu. What was indisputable was the fact that as a result of the agreement, the Americans would leave South Vietnam and the North Vietnamese would remain there.

On January 8, Kissinger and Tho returned to their negotiating site in Gif-sur-Yvette on the outskirts of Paris. Much to Kissinger's disappointment, they got nowhere. Was Tho again stonewalling, as he had in December? Or, was he planning to spring another surprise? In his report to Nixon that night, he speculated that maybe, so soon after the bombing, Tho could not immediately assume an accommodating demeanor.

But, on the following day, one Kissinger was later to describe as "breakthrough day," Tho started with a helpful suggestion: that the diplomats in the technical talks work "full-time" to complete the remaining four unresolved issues. Then, in a very welcome switch in tone and tactics, he said to Kissinger: "We should adequately take into account each other's attitude. Naturally, there should be mutual concession, and there should be reciprocity. If one keeps one's own stand, then no settlement is possible. Do you agree with me on these lines?"

Kissinger nodded, but cautiously. He decided on the spot to test the new Tho by advancing compromise language on the DMZ, one of the two major obstacles now blocking an agreement. Tho, without argument, accepted the compromise. The other obstacle concerned the signing ceremony. How would the four parties—the United States, North Vietnam, South Vietnam, and the Vietcong—actually sign the final document, if two of the four parties—South Vietnam and the Vietcong—refused to acknowledge each other's existence? When the negotiations began in 1968, the big roadblock was the shape of the table; now, five years later, the roadblock was of a similar madness: who would sign the document, in what order, on one sheet of paper or two? Saigon would not sign a document that was also to be signed by the Vietcong—that was the heart of the problem. It took Kissinger and Tho several days to break this deadlock. They arranged to have North Vietnam and the Vietcong sign one copy of the document, and the United States and South Vietnam sign an identical copy, each copy to be considered the original document.

Coincidentally, January 9 was Nixon's sixtieth birthday, and in his nightly report to the president, Kissinger had a very special birthday greeting. "We celebrated the president's birthday today by making a major breakthrough in the negotiation," Kissinger began. "In sum, we settled all of the outstanding questions in the text of the agreement, made major progress on the method of signing the agreement, and made a constructive beginning on the associated understandings." Then, remembering the long, rocky road of his negotiations with Tho, Kissinger added: "The Vietnamese have broken our heart several times before, and we just cannot assume success until everything is pinned down, but the mood and the businesslike approach was as close to October as we have seen since October."[21]

By January 13, everything was in fact pinned down. For the first time, both delegations broke bread together, and Kissinger and Tho raised a glass to the prospect of a Vietnam spared the daily drumbeat of war. They had their agreement. At the airport, as Kissinger was leaving Paris, he chose his words carefully and reserved a special place of honor for Nixon. "Special Adviser Le Duc Tho and I have just completed very useful negotiations," he said. Reporters who had followed the negotiations for years picked up on the significance of the verb "*completed.*" Kissinger added: "I shall be returning to report to the president. The president will then decide what next steps should be taken to achieve a peace of justice and of reconciliation."

Kissinger flew to Key Biscayne, stopping in Washington to pick up Haig. Nixon, enjoying the Florida sun, received Kissinger with elation and an "odd tenderness." "We spoke to each other in nearly affectionate terms," Kissinger recalled, "like veterans of bitter battles at a last reunion."[22] Before them was one last hurdle—somehow, to win Thieu's approval. After Kissinger's ugly encounter with Thieu in October, the Saigon file was entrusted to Haig. On January 14, briefed by both Nixon and Kissinger, he left for Saigon, carrying another blistering ultimatum. It stated, among other things, that the bombing of all of North Vietnam would stop on January 15, Kissinger would return to Paris on January 23 to "complete the agreement," meaning to initial it, and Nixon would then go on television to announce and explain the agreement to the whole world. In his message to Thieu, Nixon concluded, in stark terms,

"I have therefore irrevocably decided to proceed. . . . I will do so, if necessary, alone." If Thieu did not go along with the deal, Nixon would declare that "your government obstructs peace." What would follow would be the "inevitable and immediate termination of U.S. economic and military assistance."[23] The ultimatum was, to use Kissinger's word, "scorching."

Still, Thieu held his ground. On January 17, he asked Nixon to renegotiate the protocols of the agreement. No, Nixon replied, and he demanded Thieu's final acceptance by January 20, inauguration day. If Thieu again refused, he would have to assume full responsibility for the "consequences."[24] At White House instigation, Senators John Stennis and Barry Goldwater, a Democrat and a Republican, both staunch supporters of the Saigon government, publicly warned Thieu that relations between the United States and South Vietnam would be seriously damaged if he did not join the signing ceremony. On January 20, right up against the deadline, Thieu "relented with dignity," as Kissinger put it, and accepted the agreement, requesting only a statement from the United States recognizing Saigon as the only legitimate government in South Vietnam.[25] He explained to an aide: "The Americans really left me with no choice—either sign, or they will cut off aid. On the other hand, we have obtained an absolute guarantee from Nixon to defend the country. I am going to agree to sign and hold him to his word." The aide asked: "Can you really trust Nixon?" Out of options, Thieu replied: "He is a man of honor. I am going to trust him."[26] Here was proof of the power of a presidential pledge. Nixon had given his word, and Thieu responded on the assumption that the president's word was America's word, and he accepted it. What else could he do?

Thieu sent his foreign minister to Paris to join in the signing of the agreement. On January 23, Kissinger joined him there to "complete" the negotiation by initialing the draft agreement, and on January 27, Secretary of State William Rogers—who had effectively been cut out of the negotiation, much to his displeasure—participated in two concluding ceremonies and signed the agreement, protocol, and all other attendant documents sixty-two times. His right hand must have hurt after so many signatures, but his damaged ego was soothed.

The following morning, the Paris signings earned a banner headline in the *New York Times:* two rows of inch-tall letters reading: "VIETNAM PEACE PACTS SIGNED; AMERICA'S LONGEST WAR HALTS." Flora Lewis, reporting from Paris, noted the "eerie silence," "the cold, almost gloomy atmosphere" that marked the ceremonies ending "the longest, most divisive foreign war in America's history." No minister spoke. The "Agreement on Ending the

War and Restoring Peace in Vietnam," the formal name of the accords, was "as ambiguous as the conflict" itself, Lewis reported. But though the name spoke of "ending the war" and "restoring peace," the reality spoke of continuing conflict among the Vietnamese, now without the participation of the Americans. Another front page story—this one by Fox Butterfield from Saigon—focused not on an end to the war but on a "ceasefire" that was supposed to have gone into effect at 8 a.m. on January 28 but that was violated by both sides from the beginning. An unarmed helicopter carrying Vietcong diplomats was shot down, Tan Son Nhut airfield was rocketed by communist forces, and Saigon's military command told reporters that North Vietnamese and Vietcong troops had initiated 334 "incidents" throughout the country in the preceding twenty-four hours, the highest number ever recorded since the start of the war.[27] Also sharing the front page was a photograph of President Nixon, his wife, and one daughter, their heads lowered in prayer, their eyes closed, as they honored the twenty-four-hour "day of prayer," which Nixon had proclaimed in Key Biscayne as Rogers affixed his signature to the documents in Paris. If the world needed additional assurance that the United States was definitely, definitively out of the war, Nixon added that he was withdrawing an additional 23,000 American troops from Vietnam, leaving behind only 2,500, and they would be withdrawn within two months. For him, the Vietnam War was over, but already nipping at his heels was the Watergate scandal, which was soon to overwhelm him and his administration and destroy his ability to help South Vietnam, if and when such help was needed.

But, in this moment of what he called "prayer and thanksgiving," Nixon could derive a large measure of satisfaction from one other accomplishment, which, from the beginning of his presidency, had always been an integral part of his "war strategy": first, an end to America's military involvement in the Vietnam War, and second, an end to the draft. In Nixon's strategy, the two were related and one would mesh with the other. By reducing the number of soldiers being drafted into the U.S. Army and, at the same time, by withdrawing soldiers from Vietnam and thus lowering American casualties, he could create just enough tranquility at home to negotiate an honorable exit from the war. Timed for optimum positive publicity, Nixon arranged for Defense Secretary Laird to announce an end to the military draft on the very day Nixon announced an end to the war. For the first time since 1940, on the eve of World War II, no American would be conscripted into military service. "With the signing of the peace agreement in Paris today," Laird said, ". . . I wish to inform you that the armed forces henceforth will depend exclusively on volunteer soldiers, sailors, airmen, and marines. The use of the draft has ended." And the volunteer army was born.

When Nixon was inaugurated as president in January 1969, about 40 percent of the U.S. Army was composed of draftees. Eligible men between the ages of nineteen and twenty-six were being drafted, more each month as the U.S. military engagement in Vietnam widened and deepened and casualty rates climbed to alarming levels in 1967–69.[28] Nixon immediately urged Congress and Laird to reform the draft. On November 19, 1969, Congress obliged and authorized the "draft lottery," which dramatically changed eligibility rules. Now, only those nineteen years of age would be drafted under a lottery system, no longer all those between nineteen and twenty-six, and on April 1, 1971, this system of selective service was extended for another two years. By this time, almost 50 percent of U.S. Army personnel in Vietnam were draftees, and antiwar demonstrations spread across the United States, at one point worrying Nixon so much he feared for the cohesiveness of basic national institutions. But with the United States now "honorably" extracted from the war, Laird's spokesman was able to assure young Americans, "we will draft nobody."

Thus, Nixon's first term ended with "peace in Vietnam." His second began with the death of the draft. He had made and honored these two pledges, but at a terrible cost in lives, treasure, and reputation, forever raising questions about the reliability of presidential commitments before and during the war.

One question galloped over the horizon within weeks after the signing the Paris accords. Thieu had warned Nixon that the communists would not abide by the accords, and Nixon had assured Thieu that he would again clobber North Vietnam, as he had done at Christmas time, if it violated the agreement. But only a few weeks into his second term, it was already clear that the accords were not only being violated, they were being shredded. The CIA had what it considered reliable intelligence that the North Vietnamese were sending one brigade after another of fresh troops into South Vietnam, perhaps as many as 35,000 troops. This was sobering intelligence, especially in light of the devastating U.S. bombing assaults against North Vietnam conducted in late December, only a few months before. Obviously, North Vietnam was still capable of rising from the ashes and mustering the will and determination to send more troops to the battlefield. And not just troops. North Vietnam also sent more than 30,000 tons of military equipment, 400 tanks, and 300 pieces of heavy artillery—proof for Kissinger that "the ceasefire was merely a tactic . . . a barely disguised cover . . . a way station toward their objective of taking over the whole of Indochina by force."[29] For North Vietnam, the war clearly was not over.

Kissinger and the Joint Chiefs of Staff strongly recommended to Nixon that the United States bomb the Ho Chi-minh trails, which were again crowded with trucks, troops, and supplies heading toward South Vietnam. During the worst days of the war, the North Vietnamese regularly used the trails at night to avoid American air attack. Now, Kissinger told Nixon, "they are operating in daylight and the traffic is so heavy as to be congested." Year after year, the United States had bombed the trails but had never stopped the infiltration. Why renewed bombing would have succeeded in 1973, when it consistently failed earlier, Kissinger never explained. Nixon, at first, did not want to bomb—not, he insisted, until many more American POWs were released. At the end of March, when more were released, he considered approving a roughly month-long bombing campaign against North Vietnam but oddly never gave the final order. He temporized, he dawdled, he dithered. He knew that by April, the North Vietnamese had increased their combat personnel and equipment in or near South Vietnam to a higher level than a year earlier, just before they launched the Easter offensive; but he did nothing. He seemed, Kissinger recalled, "unable to concentrate his energies and mind on Vietnam." Thieu squirmed and screamed, but his complaints seemed to fall into a dark, deaf pit. Nixon was not listening.. Kissinger tried gamely to engage Nixon's attention to the new dangers in Indochina but found that his mind had drifted elsewhere. "He approached the problem . . . in a curiously desultory fashion," Kissinger later wrote.[30] "He did not home in on the decision in the single-minded, almost possessed, manner that was his hallmark." Nixon was, by this time, already so absorbed with the unfolding cover-up of the Watergate scandal that he could not focus on Vietnam, nor, it seemed, on any other major issue. He spent hours discussing political strategy with Ehrlichman and Haldeman, listening to secret Oval Office tapes, or sitting alone in his darkened office in the Old Executive Office Building, wondering how he could have allowed himself to get into this position and whether he could still save his presidency. Vietnam was no longer his burning concern.

On April 14, Kissinger learned for the first time that the Watergate scandal might touch Nixon himself. One White House attorney, Leonard Garment, told him that Nixon was probably involved in the cover-up, meaning he might be guilty of "obstruction of justice." "I was," Kissinger wrote, "appalled by the knowledge, seeing, for the first time clearly, how the Watergate challenges could reach to the heart of the Presidency and destroy all authority." Without presidential authority, another U.S. bombing campaign against North Vietnam would fail. A weakened Nixon could not lead a divided administration and a dispirited nation, which just a few months before had been told that the war was over. "Our strategy for Vietnam was in tatters," Kissinger admitted.

In time, Kissinger would come to the self-serving conclusion that Watergate, more than any other issue, destroyed American policy and undermined the prospect of the United States saving South Vietnam from ultimate communist subjugation. In his 1,521-page memoir about Nixon's first term, a hefty and impressive work, one would have expected that he would have devoted a full chapter, at least, to this central issue, but in a strange example of rhetorical asymmetry, he touched on Watergate's role in the Vietnam tragedy in a single footnote on page 986. He and Nixon had foreseen, he wrote, just about every eventuality in fighting the war and negotiating its end except "the debacle of Watergate." "It was that which finally sealed the fate of South Vietnam," he continued, "by the erosion of executive authority, strangulation of South Vietnam by wholesale reductions of aid, and legislated prohibitions against enforcing the peace agreement in the face of unprovoked North Vietnamese violations."[31]

The fate of South Vietnam was sealed by many other factors, which Kissinger, despite his meticulous scholarship, never seemed able to acknowledge:

—The pervasive corruption of the Saigon establishment, which was spoiled by American power and money;
—Thieu's ineffective, self-centered leadership;
—The selfishness and provincialism of his military commanders;
—The overbearing presence of an American military and political establishment that haughtily thought it knew everything, but actually knew pathetically little, about Vietnam;
—Only late in the day did the United States launch the Vietnamization program and begin the training of the South Vietnamese to organize a modern army capable, for example, of flying a combat helicopter;
—Presidential blinders that blocked out alternative strategies and presidential stubbornness that saw victory, or a form of it, as the only acceptable outcome to a cold war struggle;
—The tenacity of North Vietnamese nationalism, which was never fully understood or appreciated by U.S. military commanders in Vietnam or senior diplomats in Washington;
—The continuing flow of Russian and Chinese arms to North Vietnam after Congress cut off the flow of American arms to South Vietnam;
—An arrogant attitude of disdain and annoyance toward the Vietcong, those "little men in black pajamas;"

—A willingness of these "little men" to stand up to any hardship in pursuit of their goal of a unified Vietnam under communist control; and

—Their fundamental distrust of Western colonialism, which meant, in the final analysis, that the Paris peace accords were not worth the paper which they were written on.

No, it was not just "the collapse of executive authority as a result of Watergate," as Kissinger put it at the very end of Chapter XXXIII. It was much more, and it was all to be played out in different ways until April 30, 1975, when the North Vietnamese, seeing their historic opportunity, blasted their way into Saigon, seized control of the government, and reunified their country. Along the way they might have paused for a moment on August 9, 1974, to tip their hats to a formidable foe. For it was on that day that Nixon quit the White House, the only president in American history to resign in disgrace.

If, before his shameful exit, Nixon had had the time to read National Intelligence Estimates (NIE's) about the post-war war in Vietnam, he would have learned that on October 12, 1973, the CIA believed that North Vietnam was gearing up for a "major offensive." The "final decision" on timing had apparently not yet been made, but North Vietnam had the capability to kick it off in "less than a month," should it choose to do so. The CIA believed "the odds favoring a major communist offensive will increase significantly" in the 1974 dry season. And if not then, the CIA estimate continued, then surely in 1975, which was when it happened. Another NIE dated May 23, 1974, was less certain about the date of the anticipated offensive but seemed even more certain that it would happen "with little warning." "At some point," the NIE said, "Hanoi will shift back to major warfare." As, in fact, it did.[32]

A succession of American presidents had made commitments to support an independent, noncommunist South Vietnam. Many of the commitments were honored. Proof stares at the skeptic from the austere, low-slung Vietnam War Memorial in Washington, D.C., where more than 58,000 names have been carved into the granite walls. But their ultimate commitment was betrayed. When South Vietnam needed American help to keep it from collapsing to communism, it was not there. For many reasons, ranging from national exhaustion to Watergate, it was not there.

CHAPTER NINE

THE ISRAEL MODEL

Unprecedented and Unpredictable

"Israel will not be alone unless it decides to go it alone."
LYNDON B. JOHNSON, 1967

IF THE U.S. relationship with South Korea has been based on a mutual defense treaty, buttressed by the presence of 28,500 troops and backed until 1991 by nuclear weapons, and if the U.S. relationship with South Vietnam was based on a string of solemn presidential commitments and a joint resolution of Congress, then one might imagine that the U.S. relationship with Israel, so central to American foreign policy in the Middle East, would be based on at least a mutual defense treaty, joint resolutions of Congress, and perhaps even the stationing of large numbers of American troops in or around Israel. But that is not the case.

The U.S.-Israeli relationship is based primarily on private presidential letters to Israeli prime ministers, containing commitments that are often honored but sometimes betrayed. There are other factors, too, including strong, overlapping political, religious, and cultural ties. Indeed, as journalist Peter Grose observed, "Americans and Israelis are bonded together like no two other sovereign peoples."[1]

But, when it comes to matters of national security—when Israel's fate may hang in the balance, or America's interests may be directly threatened—neither country can turn to a binding mutual defense treaty, or a joint resolution of Congress, to find sanctioned reassurance of what each can expect from the other. For example, no matter how often the United States and Israel have conferred about Iran's nuclear program, Washington can never be certain about Israel's next step: will Israel go out on its own and strike Iran, immediately affecting America's national interest? Unlikely, but possible. Nor can Israel rest comfortably in the belief that the United States will definitely live up to its word about never allowing Iran to develop nuclear weapons. A president can always change his mind. And, deepening this uncertainty is the personal chemistry between an American president and an Israeli prime minister. Is there genuine trust between the two leaders, especially important when both must depend in the final analysis on their private correspondence? Between President Barack Obama and Prime Minister Benjamin Netanyahu, trust has been a commodity in short supply. They both depend on an exchange of private and personal letters, a truly unique relationship. Is that enough?

One Specific Example of a Presidential Commitment

On the night of September 1, 1975, a remarkable day in the history of U.S.-Israeli-Egyptian relations, a private letter from President Gerald Ford to Yitzhak Rabin was delivered late at night to the prime minister's office in Jerusalem. It spelled out a number of secret American commitments to Israel's security, without which Rabin would not have initialed the second Disengagement Agreement between Israel and Egypt earlier in the day. The letter seemed to have the power and authenticity of a formal bilateral defense treaty.[2]

Secretary of State Henry Kissinger bought Rabin's agreement with unprecedented promises of American aid, arms, and assurances of diplomatic support. He negotiated as the president's personal agent, both believing that the agreement served America's national interest. Congress was not consulted, though Kissinger assumed Congress, if asked, would have accepted the deal. With Israel, then as now, many of the most sensitive agreements between the two countries have been based on similar presidential commitments. It has been a unique experience for American presidents and Israeli prime ministers, since both operate in democracies where domestic politics plays a key role in fashioning public policy.

Rabin, Begin, and the Ford Letter

No two personalities could have been more different. On the morning after the Ford letter reached Rabin, the prime minister invited Menachem Begin, the head of the opposition Likud party, to his office. Rabin was hoping for his support. The prime minister, once a general, was exhausted from the long negotiation, somewhat disheveled, a cigarette dangling from his lips. Begin, as always, was meticulous in dress and manner. Characteristically, he wore a dark suit, white shirt with a blue tie, and his shoes sparkled from a recent shine. A bespectacled, deeply conservative lawyer, Begin was from the beginning highly suspicious of Rabin's negotiations with Kissinger. He considered Rabin soft. "All one has to do is exert pressure," Begin taunted the prime minister, "and we shall change our minds." Also, Begin thought Rabin was bending excessively to Washington's will. Both understood the importance of the United States to Israel's security, but, unlike Begin, Rabin believed that "wherever possible, we have to synchronize our best interests with those of America. And I believe that to advance peace, America must keep us militarily strong. This new agreement cements our ties with Washington in both senses. It places the US-Israel relationship on an entirely new footing."[3]

Begin did not share Rabin's upbeat judgment. He remained skeptical. He was not the only Israeli leader who felt uncomfortable, almost claustrophobic, in America's strategic embrace. Like most proud Zionists, he cherished Israel's independence, its absolute freedom to act, even to attack, if necessary, to protect their country. It was their firmly held conviction that, in the final analysis, only Israel could protect Israel. The United States was a close and valuable ally, Israel's only true friend in the world, proven time and time again, but, in Begin's view, Israel could not latch its security too closely to any other nation, even a friendly nation such as the United States, and no Israeli prime minister should fully trust an American president.

The differences between the two nations were profound: Israel was small and Jewish, living in a large, generally hostile Arab neighborhood, and America was a superpower living confidently an ocean away. What Israelis might consider an existential threat Americans might judge to be only a serious problem.

Rabin, sensing no give in Begin's position, pulled a rabbit out of his hat, or thought he had. It was the Ford letter. As a courtesy, Rabin had sent Begin the draft agreement, but not the letter, which he considered special—it was a private "Mr. Prime Minister" letter, and it contained the core of a new U.S.-Israeli understanding. Rabin figured that if he as prime minister could not persuade his political opponent to support the agreement, perhaps an American president could. Begin, adjusting his glasses, read of Ford's "resolve to continue to maintain Israel's defensive strength through the supply of advanced types of equipment," including F-16 planes and Pershing ground-to-ground missiles, then to ask Congress "for military and economic assistance in order to help meet Israel's economic and military needs," and finally, on the sensitive diplomatic front, to remove, once and for all, Rabin thought, the chronic Israeli fear of a solution imposed by the "Great Powers." "Should the U.S. desire in the future to put forward proposals of its own," Ford promised, "it will make every effort to coordinate with Israel its proposals with a view to refraining from putting forth proposals that Israel would find unsatisfactory."[4] Fascinating, Begin thought, truly fascinating. But what specifically did the president have in mind? Ford responded in his next paragraph, almost as though he had anticipated Begin's question. "The U.S. has not developed a final position on the borders. Should it do so, it will give great weight to Israel's position that any peace agreement with Syria must be predicated on Israel remaining on the Golan Heights." Here was Ford pledging America's backing for the Israeli position on the Golan, one of the most delicate issues in the Mideast negotiation. It was, according to Dennis Ross, for years one of America's top Mideast negotiators, "one example of commitment through presidential correspondence."[5]

"Well, that *is* interesting," Begin acknowledged. No American president had ever come down so solidly on the Israeli side of a border dispute. But, not to be misunderstood—he still opposed the agreement with Egypt—he added a lawyer-like reservation. "It's hardly a binding commitment to support our retention of the Golan Heights," he told Rabin, "but it's important nevertheless." He went no further, but, before leaving, he turned to Rabin and said: "You understand, Mr. Prime Minister, that I shall be voicing my opposition to your so-called interim agreement from the rostrum of the Knesset [Israel's parliament] and from every other position I can find." Rabin replied, with a slight smile of resignation, "I expect nothing less, Mr. Begin. Are you not in the habit of saying that the job of the opposition is to oppose? Well, feel free—oppose, and I shall answer."

Ford's letter, one of many from U.S. presidents to Israeli prime ministers, contained a number of specific American commitments to Israeli security. Over the years, these letters have become, in President Obama's words, an "ironclad commitment to Israeli security," but they do not add up to a treaty, nor do they represent a congressional resolution. In this sense, Israel is not, as diplomat John Negroponte put it, a "legal ally," even though, in the Defense Authorization Act of 1987, as one way of reassuring Israel of America's backing, Israel was named a "major non-NATO ally." I am convinced that presidents, when making a commitment, have Israel's interests at heart, but conditions change. A commitment made today might be altered tomorrow.

Another president, three or four administrations down the line, might simply, for good political or diplomatic reasons at the time, disagree with Ford's promise about the Golan Heights. As incumbent, he would have the power to renege on that promise. Israel could complain, of course. Israel could remind the incumbent of the former president's promise, showing him a signed letter. Israel could leak its acute dissatisfaction to the media, a tactic almost certain to ignite a storm of protest from many in the American Jewish community, from pro-Israel lobbyists, from American evangelicals (who feel a powerful religious connection to the holy land), and from congressional friends who control the purse strings. The U.S.-Israeli relationship has always been fraught with controversy and uncertainty. It is truly unique. A letter signed by a president has power. His words have consequence, but they no longer, if they ever did, roar from the top of the mountain.

When Obama, a craftsman of words, discusses his administration's policy toward Israel, he almost always uses his favorite adjective—"ironclad"—to describe it. (On December 16, 2011, the president's spokesman, Jay Carney, added a few of his own: "absolute," "resolute," "unshakable," and "unprecedented.") Obama could use other adjectives, too. Robert Satloff, executive director of the Washington Institute for Near East Policy, suggests "unbreakable," used 92 times in a presidential context, "unshakable," used 226 times, or "unwavering," used 312 times.[6] But, Satloff asked, should Israel take comfort from Obama's "ironclad" commitments? "Not really," he answered, noting that though Lyndon Johnson often spoke of America's "unwavering" commitment to South Vietnam, Congress pulled the plug on providing additional financial support and ultimately the United States lost the war.

When I put a similar question to the highly experienced Martin Indyk, a former U.S. ambassador to Israel and now vice president and director of foreign policy at Brookings, he replied: "They [the Israelis] will always doubt the commitments of the US." In his many conversations with Israeli leaders, I wondered, did they talk about the reliability of America's commitments? "Oh yes," Indyk replied, "it's hard to get them off the topic." The conversations would apparently begin and end "with them saying, 'We can only depend on ourselves,'" a refrain of the old Zionist credo of self-reliance.[7]

During Obama's time in office, an interesting irony emerged in the U.S.-Israeli relationship, which in some respects had become closer than ever before, particularly in matters of national security and intelligence-sharing. The closer the two nations became, the more Israel depended on the United States, the more fearful it became that one day it would lose what former prime minister Ehud Barak called "Israel's independence of action." Israel cherishes the vital importance of American support, but not quite as much as it values its "independence of action." Always, in the mind of any Israeli prime minister, there is the discomforting question: If I trust the president too much, will I be betrayed? Again? Will Israel be betrayed?

Betrayal

This question of possible betrayal dates back to the Johnson administration, when the president felt he could not honor an earlier commitment to Israel by Dwight D. Eisenhower, because he was absorbed with other, more pressing, business, such as his beloved Great Society program and his nightmare war in Vietnam. Ever since, Israeli prime ministers have welcomed presidential commitments while at the same time, in a corner of their minds, doubting their reliability.

These Israeli doubts originated in the way the Eisenhower administration responded to the Suez Crisis of 1956, which had been brewing for some time. Ever since the Tripartite Agreement of 1950, which pledged U.S.-French-and-British support for the existing Arab-Israeli armistice lines arranged in the late 1940s, Israel had been objecting to repeated Arab violations of its borders, but no one seemed to be listening. When Egypt, in September 1955, became the beneficiary of a huge arms deal with the Soviet Union, though the weapons were funneled through Czechoslovakia, Israeli leaders scrambled to find a sympathetic arms dealer. "We made desperate efforts to acquire the minimum armaments supplies required to deter the enemy," Prime Minister David Ben-Gurion later reported to the Knesset. "We were completely unsuccessful." The balance of power seemed suddenly to shift in the Arabs' favor. "They could now choose the time to wipe out Israel," Ben-Gurion lamented. "The enemy's sword was not only hanging over our head but directed straight at our heart."[8]

Ben-Gurion was describing how Israel's generals, glancing nervously across the Sinai, began considering a pre-emptive war. Rabin, at the time a general, said then what he was in essence to repeat ten years later, just before the start of another war, the "Six-Day War," in June 1967. "It is now a question of our national survival, of to be or not to be."[9] In a comparatively short period of time in 1956, Rabin would see the arrival of Soviet ship after Soviet ship, weighted down with 250 tanks, 500 long-range guns, 150 Mig fighter planes, and 50 Ilyushin bombers. Submarines were also part of the deal. It was, up to this point, the biggest infusion of foreign armaments into the Middle East, Moscow's dramatic way of telling the United States and the rest of the world that it was now a player. The Middle East was no longer to be solely a play-ground for Western ambition, a source of oil and power. Israeli ambassador

Michael Oren, a historian by trade, described the Soviet arms deliveries as "an existential threat to Israel." Ben-Gurion and Defense Minister Moshe Dayan thought Egypt could "absorb this weaponry in about six months," meaning that in this limited time the Egyptians would be able to "learn how to fly the planes and run the tanks."[10] When the Israeli cabinet met, the ministers debated only one question: should Israel launch a preemptive attack against Egypt—and when?

The Middle East can always be depended on for a surprise, and, on July 23, 1956, Egypt's flamboyant leader, Gamal Abdul Nasser, nationalized the Suez Canal, shocking the United States, France, Britain, and other users of the canal. They met and pondered a response equal to the challenge. The U.S. secretary of state, John Foster Dulles, huffed and puffed about international law and maritime rights, but no one really believed the United States would intervene militarily. France and Britain decided to act on their own, a bit of secret collusion that was quickly to involve Israel. They produced what Oren later described as a "crazy plot, pretty bizarre in retrospect." Codenamed "Operation Musketeer," it was also unprecedented and incredibly dangerous. Israel would act as the provocateur, ready, almost eager, to play the role by joining two Western powers in a preemptive war against Egypt—something it was considering anyway. Israel would send paratroopers into the Mitla Pass in the Sinai peninsula, twenty-five miles from the canal. An act of war, without doubt. The Egyptians would surely react, sending their armies into the Sinai to fight the Israelis. France and Britain, by prearrangement, would then decry the outbreak of hostilities, declare the Suez Canal to be endangered, and send troops to Egypt to protect the canal.

But, of course, little worked according to plan. The British and French botched their end of the operation—they were late in attacking Egypt. The effect: Nasser survived, and the canal remained in his hands. France and Britain succeeded only in infuriating President Eisenhower, who was otherwise absorbed with presidential campaigning (his re-election then only a week away) and who did not like being kept in the dark on matters of war and peace, especially those concerning a vital American interest. To his secretary of state, John Foster Dulles, he exploded: "Foster, you tell 'em, goddamn it, that we're going to apply sanctions, we're going to the United Nations, we're going to do everything that there is so we can stop this thing."[11] Meantime, the Israelis took full advantage of the uproar and confusion to destroy three Egyptian army divisions, capture small mountains of military hardware, and besmirch Nasser's once lofty, firebrand image in the Arab world; but they too ran into the wrath of an angry president. Eisenhower was severely impatient with Israel's nonstop arguments about Nasser's duplicity. He demanded an immediate Israeli withdrawal from the Sinai and Gaza, but Israel dawdled, arguing that it would withdraw, but only after it obtained UN (and possibly U.S.) guarantees for its security.

For the better part of five tumultuous months, Eisenhower and Ben-Gurion engaged in a pitched battle. Letters were exchanged, Eisenhower's with "urgent appeals" and "grave warnings" and Ben-Gurion's with personal pleas for understanding and sympathy. Negotiations took place in the quiet corners of UN corridors. Ben-Gurion had two basic demands: (1) "free passage" in the Straits of Tiran in the Gulf of Aqaba, through which Israel was getting precious shipments of Iranian oil; and (2) an end to Egyptian attacks from Gaza. "In no event and in no manner," Ben-Gurion insisted, "will Israel agree to [the] return of [the] Egyptian invader."[12] Eisenhower, at this time, had one demand: that before Israel's needs could be met, it had to pull its troops out of Arab lands. Ben-Gurion wanted guarantees, Eisenhower wanted compliance. Deadlock.

For Israel, this represented a traumatic moment. Ben-Gurion had always based his security calculations on one overriding consideration: that, if possible, Israel should never act alone, that it should always have a major power on its side. During the Suez Crisis, he thought he had two major powers, France and Britain, but he had misjudged them. They were no longer the giants of World War II. They were now smaller players on the sidelines of the cold war struggle between the United States and the Soviet Union. Once the war started, Ben-Gurion understood, perhaps for the first time, that Israel was essentially on its own. He had a friend in the United States but not a companion in war. Eisenhower was not going to fight Russia or the Arabs for Israel's sake. Moreover, the president believed that if he took Israel's side, he might jeopardize oil deliveries and throw the Arab world into the Soviet orbit.

At the United Nations, many nations pushed for economic sanctions against Israel, and Eisenhower was determined to support them—but, at the last minute, changed his mind. The reasons were compelling. First, his secretary of state opposed the imposition of sanctions, arguing they would amount to Israel's "death sentence." Second, Congress was overwhelmingly on Israel's side. Senate majority leader Lyndon Johnson (D-Texas) warned he would cut off funding for the president's Mideast policy if Eisenhower joined in UN sanctions against Israel. And, finally, the American public supported the Israelis, one newspaper editorial after another increasingly critical of the president's policy. Eisenhower had to come up with a better policy to advance American interests.[13]

On February 20, 1957, a frustrated president went public, attempting to break the deadlock. He appeared on prime time television and blasted Israel for refusing to withdraw its troops from the Straits of Tiran and the Gaza Strip. It was his way of using harsh rhetoric as a cover for his next diplomatic move. "It was a matter of keen disappointment to us," he said, that Israel "still felt unwilling to withdraw." He then strongly implied that if Israel did not withdraw, voluntarily and immediately, the UN, including the United States, would have to take action (unspecified) against Israel. Eisenhower said it would be a "sad day" if the United States had to compare Israel's actions in Egypt with the Soviet Union's actions in Hungary, but that was, in fact, what he was doing. The Russians had just invaded Hungary in an effort to crush an anti-communist uprising. Eisenhower added that no UN member (read Israel) had the right to attack another UN member (read Egypt), and then set conditions for its withdrawal. "I would, I feel, be untrue to the standards of the high office to which you have chosen me," he said, throwing his reputation as president into the argument, if he allowed Israel to "exact conditions for withdrawal."[14] No other American president had ever lambasted Israel on television, and none has since.

Eisenhower added that it was a "fateful moment," and indeed it was. Boldly and bluntly, Eisenhower was warning Israel that if it did not comply with his wishes, Israel would be on its own. Worse, in fact. He was again threatening Ben-Gurion that the United States would join UN sanctions—and actions—against Israel. It was, for U.S.-Israeli relations, a moment of crisis.

In his TV report to the nation, Eisenhower took time, very carefully, to suggest in public what U.S. officials had been promising Ben-Gurion's government in private. In other words, even as the president was scolding Israel in public, he was advancing a secret deal to break the diplomatic deadlock. If Israel pulled its troops out of Gaza and the Straits of Tiran, the president pledged, he would ensure "some participation by the United Nations" in the administration of the Gaza Strip, which was a step toward meeting one of Israel's major demands—that Egypt be prevented from assuming control of Gaza. Eisenhower also "expressed the conviction that the Gulf [the Straits of Tiran] constitutes international waters and that no nation has the right to prevent free and innocent passage in the Gulf." He said the United States was "prepared to exercise this right itself and to join with others to secure general recognition of this right." That was a big step toward meeting Israel's other key demand—that it too have the right of "free and innocent passage" in the Straits of Tiran. In fact, Eisenhower went even further, declaring that if Egypt once again blocked Israel's passage through the Straits, Israel would have the right under Article 51 of the UN Charter to defend itself. Dulles understood that Eisenhower's support for the Israeli plea for the same right as others to "free and innocent passage" was more valuable than "red ribbon and seals on paper treaties."[15] Dulles was, in this period, torn between his professional dedication to protecting American interests and reaching a deal with the Israelis and his personal feelings that American Jews were frustrating his efforts to be fair and judicious on their behalf. Often, he complained about "the pressure of the Jews," creating "a very nasty situation on the Hill;" about "the terrific control the Jews had over the media," causing "very serious trouble" with public opinion; and about how "all we get is a battering from the Jews" and "no support from the Protestant elements of the country."[16]

Ben-Gurion quickly showed his appreciation for Eisenhower's efforts and assurances while at the same time bending to his obvious pressure. On February 24, he authorized his foreign minister, Abba Eban, to tell Dulles that Israel would withdraw from Sharm al-Sheikh, which controls the Straits of Tiran, and Gaza if the United Nations Emergency Force, and not Egypt, moved in and occupied both contested areas, and if the United States and other maritime powers publicly endorsed Israel's right to free passage in the Gulf of Aqaba. For several days, Dulles and Eban fought for every comma while successfully negotiating the details of the agreement. On March 1, the UN General Assembly was officially informed that Israel would withdraw from Sharm al-Sheikh and Gaza in accordance with UN resolutions. Breakthrough!

The results of this secret, highwire negotiation were contained in an exchange of letters between Eisenhower (March 2, 1957) and Ben-Gurion (March 7, 1957) and in secret aide-mémoires negotiated and drafted by Dulles and Eban. The letters were remarkable examples of diplomatic code language; the aide-mémoires were impressively, if ponderously, detailed. Eisenhower assured Ben-Gurion he would "have no cause to regret" his decision to withdraw from Gaza and Sharm al-Sheikh, but he added, for clarity and effect, the withdrawal had to be done "promptly and fully" and "with utmost speed." Israel would be conforming to "the strong sentiment of the world community" (read the Eisenhower White House) and its "hopes and expectations" for peace would "prove not to be [in] vain." Trust me, he was saying. Ben-Gurion assured Eisenhower that though he had strong reservations about withdrawing, he would do so because he indeed trusted Eisenhower as a "noble and moral personality," on "whose word Israel could rely." He added that he was "confident that we shall, in your words, have no cause for regret," and the "statements" (read promises and pledges) of Dulles and the president "will in the very near future become a lasting reality." I trust you, sort of, Ben-Gurion was responding.

The Israeli prime minister might have been reading too much into Eisenhower's assurances, but, always the realist, he thought he had little option. Which other power in the world would be as helpful? Israel was, as usual, occupying a lonely spot on the globe, and it had few tested friends.

When Ben-Gurion personally handed his "Dear Mr. President" letter to American ambassador Edward Lawson on March 7, it was already late in Jerusalem, and the prime minister and the ambassador savored the moment in a brief chat. Ben-Gurion wanted to make it clear to Lawson that he was not entirely content with the agreement, but he had faith in the president to live up to his word. He said, to be specific, that "while there is no clear understanding, still we feel the president gave us assurances." Those "assurances" meant a great deal to Israel's prime minister. Ben-Gurion then recalled that he had met the president "when he was *only* a general," and he was a "man upon whom you can rely."[17]

Ben-Gurion explained to his colleagues that though Eisenhower's plan did not represent an ideal settlement, not in the best of all possible worlds what he and they would have preferred, it did represent an acceptable compromise that did not, in the final analysis, jeopardize Israeli security. Just as important, by accepting it, he stopped the hemorrhaging of good will in the Israeli-U.S. relationship. Ben-Gurion had pushed Eisenhower to the limit but had the wit to stop at the water's edge, believing it was always vital to Israel's national interest to have a superpower friend. And who better than the United States?

Ten years later, Eisenhower's assurances, contained in his compromise plan for ending the U.S.-Israeli deadlock, again occupied center stage, reminding Israeli leaders of what they took to be a set of very special presidential promises to support Israeli security. But instead of easing their anxieties in the tense buildup to yet another Mideast war in early June 1967, the Eisenhower assurances ended up having the opposite effect: Uncertainty about whether they would be honored stoked Israeli fears of an American betrayal.

The story is both fascinating and depressing. It could not have come as a surprise to anyone studying the Middle East that the 1956 war settled nothing. Many Arabs continued to question Israel's right to live in their neighborhood. Not only their newspapers but also their school books were filled with hateful editorials, stories, and cartoons savagely ridiculing Israel and Jews.

They seemed to derive a perverted pleasure in proudly boasting that they were readying themselves for a big war that would obliterate Israel, that would "drive Israel into the sea." There was little in their propaganda and actions to suggest that the Arab world could even imagine a policy of peaceful coexistence with Israel. Equally disturbing, Palestinian extremists, called fedayeen, conducted raids into Israel, disrupting normal life and killing innocent civilians. Israelis demanded security, and their government, if only for political reasons, felt the need to strike back.

In November 1966, shortly after the Palestinians killed three Israeli soldiers in a guerrilla attack, the Israeli government decided enough is enough and sent a small army unit into a Palestinian camp in the village of as-Samu in Jordan, killing fourteen or twenty-one Palestinians (the exact number is still being debated) and wounding another thirty-seven. It was the largest Israeli operation in an Arab country since the 1956 war, and it triggered worldwide condemnation, including a UN Security Council resolution accusing Israel of aggression. Tensions rose throughout the area. By springtime 1967, Arab and Israeli leaders began to act as though another war was just over the near horizon. Army units were mobilized, warnings were shot across borders, and the UN Security Council sounded a hollow bell of alarm.

Syria staged impressive army maneuvers near the Golan Heights, suggesting it would strike Israel at any moment. Israel, not to be outmaneuvered, mobilized army units south of the Golan and staged hit-and-run attacks across the border. Syria roared provocatively, prompting UN secretary-general U Thant on May 11, 1967, to condemn Syria. Usually, his condemnations were reserved for Israel. He denounced Syria's role in the unfolding crisis as "deplorable," "insidious," and a "menace to peace." Days later, apparently to demonstrate his even-handedness, he leveled the same harsh criticism at Israel.

The Soviet Union, Syria's primary sponsor and arms supplier, exploited the crisis by planting a false report in the pliable Arab press of an imminent Israeli invasion of Syria, further inflaming an already combustible situation. Egypt's Nasser, on May 16, pretending he was deeply worried about his ally, Syria, moved a 160,000-man army into the Sinai, supported by almost a thousand Soviet-made tanks. Three days later, without explicit warning, he unceremoniously expelled UN peacekeepers from Gaza and Sharm al-Sheikh, in direct violation of UN agreements reached in 1957. Nasser seemed to be on a war path, declaring his government's "basic objective will be the destruction of Israel." In case anyone missed his message, he added, "the Arab people want to fight." Clearly, Nasser enjoyed the sound of his own voice.

On May 22, Nasser took the decisive step on the road to war. He closed the Straits of Tiran to Israeli shipping, knowing that for Israel that was a casus belli. On March 1, 1967, Israel's Foreign Ministry, working within the framework and spirit of Eisenhower's assurances a decade earlier to Ben-Gurion, had warned Nasser that "interference by armed force" with Israeli shipping in the Gulf "will be regarded by Israel as an attack," entitling Israel to the "inherent right of self-defense under Article 51 of the UN Charter." Openly defying the UN and with a wave of his hand dismissing Israel's "right" to protect its maritime access to the Gulf, Nasser pushed unmistakably toward war. Israeli leaders, led by Prime Minister Levi Eshkol, a cautious politician, knew they would soon be engaged in another fight with Egypt. "There's going to be a war," Eshkol told his deputy defense minister, Zvi Dinstein. "I'm telling you, there's going to be a war."[18] Though cautious, he then doubled the number of Israeli reserves in the south and ordered 300 tanks to move through the Negev toward the Egyptian border.

The prime minister's military advisers favored a preemptive strike against Egypt, as soon as possible, but Eshkol, like Ben-Gurion, was in no rush to go to war. Again, an Israeli prime minister was looking for a superpower ally, and only the United States could fill that role. Comfort, he believed, could be found in Eisenhower's 1957 assurances, clearly pledging America's support for Israel's right to free passage in the Gulf, and, if free passage were denied, Israel's right under Article 51 of the UN Charter to fight for that right. Israel was soon to learn a painful lesson about presidential commitments. Eshkol had assumed, naïvely, that a commitment made by one president would always be honored by subsequent presidents. As historian Oren explained, "because of the way the United States is constituted, where the president has prerogatives in foreign affairs, we have to rely on presidential commitments. And our expectation is that those presidential commitments, commitments made by one president, will be honored by his successors. This has the effect of a treaty. . . . We have to believe that those [commitments] have the effect of sort of a signed treaty."[19] Except that, by 1967, the Eisenhower commitment to Israel ran into the Johnson commitment to South Vietnam, and Johnson's prevailed—not because Johnson would not have wanted to help Israel (he always considered himself "a friend in the true sense of the word") but because he was infuriatingly trapped in his expanding war in South Vietnam. He could not fight a major war in Southeast Asia and take on another in the Middle East and pursue his expensive and controversial Great Society program at home— all at the same time.

When Israelis reminded Johnson of Eisenhower's assurances, he claimed at first that he knew nothing about them. Were there letters? Aide-mémoires? No one at the White House seemed able to find any. Archivists frantically searched White House and State Department files, but to no avail. Finally, national security adviser Walt Rostow had to travel to Gettysburg, Pennsylvania, to get copies of the relevant letters and aide-mémoires from Eisenhower. Israel's ambassador to the United States, Avraham Harman, also traveled to Gettysburg to urge Eisenhower to make public the private pledges he and Dulles had made to Israel in 1957. Eisenhower, then ailing, agreed to help. "I don't believe Israel will be left alone," he assured Harman.[20]

Johnson sincerely wanted to help Israel. But how? Eisenhower had considered organizing an international naval task force to open the Straits of Tiran for everyone, including Israel. It never happened, but Johnson liked its political provenance and thought he would give it another try. In this way, he would be helping Israel and not getting the United States into another war. But even if, like Eisenhower, he would not be able to organize a task force, he would at least be buying time for diplomacy to work its magic, if indeed there was any magic left in the Middle East.

In his conversations with the Israelis, of which there were many, Johnson kept making one point: don't be the first to open hostilities. On May 26, Johnson welcomed Israel's number one diplomat, Abba Eban, to the Oval Office for a meeting, which proved to be momentous. Historian Oren offers the best account. Eban was tasked by his prime minister to get an answer to one question: "Do you [Johnson] have the will and determination to open the Straits? Do we fight alone or are you with us?" Johnson thought he detected a "tormented look" on Eban's face. But while he sympathized with Israel, Johnson still could not commit the United States to a military course of action until he had exhausted all UN options. Why? wondered Eban. How would/could the UN help?

"I am not a king in this country," Johnson stressed, "and I am no good to you or to your prime minister if all I can lead is myself. . . . I know that your blood and lives are at stake. Our blood and lives are at stake in many places [read Vietnam] and maybe in others. . . . I do not have one vote and one dollar for taking action before thrashing this matter out in the UN." Actually, like Eban, Johnson had little confidence in the UN, but, for political reasons, he felt he had to go through the motions. He thought this UN exercise would take two weeks. "I'm not a feeble mouse or a coward and we're going to try," he said. "What we need is a group [of maritime states], five or four or less or if we can't do that, then on our own. What you can tell your Cabinet is that the president, the Congress and the country will support a plan to use any or all measures to open the Straits." One would have thought that such a presidential pledge would have satisfied Eban—"use any and all measures"—but the Israeli diplomat still sensed a problem.

It was Johnson's fear of an Israeli first strike. He told Eban that his intelligence chiefs believed that Egypt was not intending to attack Israel, and even if it did attack, Israel would beat it back and win. "If your Cabinet decides to do that [to attack first], they will have to do it on their own. I am not retreating, not backtracking, and I am not forgetting anything I have said. . . . I think it is a necessity that Israel should never make itself seem responsible in the eyes of America and the world for making war. *Israel will not be alone unless it decides to go it alone*" [italics in the original]. To emphasize his point, Johnson repeated the line three times. Then, he repeated it once more, but in another form. He handed Eban a handwritten note from Secretary of State Dean Rusk. It read: "I must emphasize the necessity for Israel not to make itself responsible for the initiation of hostilities." Speaking for Johnson's cabinet, he added, "We cannot imagine that Israel will take that position." But that was exactly what Rusk feared: that Israel would in fact initiate hostilities, and the United States would be made to look helpless before the Arab world. Johnson stressed: "Our Cabinet knows your *policy*. What they want to know is your *disposition to take action*."

To that specific point, Eban did not reply—how could he? He said time was of the essence and urged Johnson not to get enmeshed in endless UN debates. "I would not be wrong," Eban asked, as he rose to leave, "if I told the prime minister that your disposition is to make every possible effort to assure that the Straits and the Gulf will remain open to free and innocent passage?" Yes, Johnson replied. They shook hands, Eban left, and Johnson dejectedly concluded, "They're going to hit, and there is nothing we can do about it."[21]

Eban, on his way to New York for a meeting with Washington's ambassador to the UN, Arthur Goldberg, was stunned by Johnson's "rhetoric of impotence." He saw Johnson as a "paralyzed president," who spoke in "defeatist terms," even though it was apparent that Johnson was in fact going beyond Eisenhower's 1957 commitment to free passage by pledging to act in the creation of a naval task force, or Regatta, as it was called. But, in the mind of Eban, an astute judge of the symbols and nuances of international diplomacy, the failure of Johnson to suggest the drafting of a joint communiqué, or some written, public pledge of American support for Israel at this critical time, was graphic testimony that although Johnson wanted to help Israel, he had other problems that demanded his immediate attention. Goldberg felt that it was his responsibility to make sure that Eban was returning to Jerusalem with an accurate impression of Johnson's position. "You owe it to your government," Goldberg emphasized, "because lives are going to be lost and your security is involved, to tell your Cabinet that the president's statement means a joint resolution of Congress, and the president can't get such a resolution because of the Vietnam War."[22]

Johnson felt that he could not get the sort of resolution he got in 1964 to fight in Vietnam, ironically because of opposition from Vietnam doves, a number of whom were Jewish. He resented pressure from American Jews who opposed his policy in Vietnam but favored a deeper American commitment to Israel at this critical time. Don't they understand I'm trying to help Israel? he asked. Two members of Johnson's White House staff, Larry Levinson and Ben Wattenberg, urged the president to send a message of support to a "mass meeting of American Jews" in Lafayette Park, arguing that in this way he might be able to "turn around a lot of anti-Vietnam, anti-Johnson feeling." Johnson blew up at both of them. One day, with his fist raised, he screamed in the White House hallway that they were "Zionist dupes. . . . Why can't you see I'm doing all I can for Israel. That's what you should be telling people when they ask for a message from the President for their rally."[23]

Eban left the United States knowing that he had failed to get the answer from Johnson that his prime minister had hoped for—that the United States would be Israel's ally in the event of war. Instead, he got a cool warning not to launch a preemptive attack. He had heard that warning before. It had come from French president Charles de Gaulle, whose policy toward Israel had been, charitably put, less than helpful. Eban had stopped briefly in Paris, hoping the French leader, for reasons of his own, might try to persuade the Soviet Union to use its influence with Nasser to head off war. Before Eban could even make his case, de Gaulle said: "Do not make war. Do not be the first to shoot." Eban, in response, replied that Nasser had taken the first step; Nasser was the one who blocked the Straits, knowing that Israel would regard such an action as an act of war. Besides, Eban continued, France had supported free and open passage through the Straits in the Suez Crisis a decade earlier. "That," de Gaulle snapped, "was 1957. This is 1967." In 1957, France had been Israel's principal provider of military hardware, one of its major diplomatic supporters. No longer. Clearly, in 1967, France was not going to honor its earlier commitments. Now, having also conferred with Johnson, Eban feared that the United States was groping for an acceptable pretext for backing out of its 1957 commitment too.

When Eban returned to Jerusalem and reported to the prime minister, Eshkol was shocked. A "deep unhappiness" settled over his cabinet, recalled Samuel Lewis, later an American ambassador to Israel. The ministers were suddenly overwhelmed by "feelings of betrayal."[24] Israeli military leaders, led by Defense Minister Moshe Dayan and Chief of Staff Yitzhak Rabin, had already been preparing for a preemptive strike, believing they had a small window of opportunity, it was closing, and they had to move. But Eshkol refused to flash the green light. He had kept hoping that Eban would return to Jerusalem with good news, that America would join Israel in its battle against Egypt. When he heard that the American president, on whom he had placed so much hope, was planning to engage the UN in new, peace-salvaging talks, while at the same time trying to set up a naval task force, getting a congressional resolution, similar to the Gulf of Tonkin resolution of 1964, battling with his Vietnam critics, who objected to any American military role in the Middle East, and holding off threatened cuts to his cherished Great Society program, he imagined weeks of unsuccessful haggling when his defense officials were thinking in terms of days, two or three at the most, before they felt they had to move against Egypt.

It was impossible to hold off war, Eshkol concluded, after a painful night of soul-searching. Israel could not depend on the United States, which was otherwise absorbed with its own problems. Israel, facing what it considered an existential threat, could not stifle feelings of American abandonment and betrayal. Eshkol asked how could one president make a commitment to Israel and another president, for whatever reason, renege on that commitment? He asked, wasn't a presidential commitment also a national commitment? Eshkol had naïvely assumed yes. Now, once again, he realized that, in a pinch, Israel could only depend on Israel. War was now inevitable, and Israel would be alone.

It started on June 5, 1967, and ended five days later. Journalists called it the "Six Day War." It was a military triumph for Israel. On the first day, Israel effectively wiped out the Egyptian air force, and, over the next five days, encircled the Egyptian army in the Sinai, captured the Golan Heights from Syria, and moved into all of Jerusalem and the West Bank. In Washington, officials breathed a sigh of relief while also wondering how far Israel would go. One night, during the war, while doing a TV report on the White House lawn, I spotted President Johnson walking from one door to another. When he paused for a moment, I asked him how well he thought Israel was doing. He did not want to do a formal interview, but he did say, with a steady, vigorous nod of his head, "Feisty. A very feisty country!" I had the impression he meant "feisty" as high praise. He seemed pleased that Israel was winning the war, and I suspect he would have been shocked to learn that the Israelis were using the word "betrayal" to describe his lack of support for their position.

Betrayal, Post-1967

The smell of possible betrayal has hung over the U.S.-Israeli relationship ever since the 1967 war. In many conversations with Israeli leaders, including Rabin and Menachem Begin, I heard them express a basic uncertainty about American support of Israel, recalling the deep disappointment they felt in 1967. When I reminded them of the generosity of American support of Israel—military, economic, and diplomatic, especially after the Egyptian-Israeli peace treaty of 1979—they expressed their deepest gratitude. But there was often a "but," implied if not stated. When differences arose between the two countries on matters the Israelis judged to be of fundamental importance to their national security, the Israelis would wonder whether they would soon be facing another 1967 betrayal. No matter how many times American presidents stressed their "ironclad commitment" to Israeli security, Israeli prime ministers and generals were unable to hold off a nagging sense of skepticism, a feeling that in the final analysis Israel would be left on its own. Israel always sought and needed American support, but if it was not forthcoming, if it did not satisfy Israel's judgment of its needs, then Israel would operate on its own and brook no interference from anyone, including the United States.

This was even the case before the Johnson "betrayal." When President Kennedy came to office in January 1961, the outgoing secretary of state, Christian Herter, told him that there were two countries on a clear path toward producing nuclear weapons. One was India, he said, and the other was Israel.[25] This worried the new president, because one of his key planks during his campaign was nuclear nonproliferation.

In May 1961, in a private letter to Ben-Gurion, Kennedy asked about Israel's nuclear program at Dimona, an easy-to-miss town in the Negev desert, but the Israeli leader ducked a direct response. The United States wanted regular inspections of the Dimona nuclear site. Israel, using one excuse after another, consistently refused. On May 18, 1963, an irritated Kennedy demanded access to Dimona, warning that America's commitment to Israel "would be seriously jeopardized" if Israel continued to refuse. According to Yuval Ne'eman, a physicist who advised Ben-Gurion, Kennedy was "writing like a bully. It was brutal." In effect, Kennedy was demanding unconditional access, or else.

A month later, Ben-Gurion resigned, in part because of Kennedy's pressure. On July 5, Kennedy sent another stiff note of warning to the new prime minister, Levi Eshkol, repeating that "this government's commitment to and support of Israel could be seriously jeopardized" unless it was given immediate access to Dimona. Eshkol, like many other Israeli leaders, believed that Israel must develop nuclear weapons for use as a last resort in its national defense. Were it not for Kennedy's assassination in November 1963, U.S.-Israeli relations would likely have ruptured over this issue. Israel was determined, Washington's threats notwithstanding, to develop nuclear weapons.

Johnson had other priorities, and the issue slowly faded from sight. It was not until September 26, 1969, that President Nixon and Israeli prime minister Golda Meir reached a secret agreement that exists to this day—that Israel would keep its nuclear capabilities hidden behind code words such as "opacity" and "nuclear ambiguity," and the United States would not pressure Israel to sign the Non-Proliferation Agreement. This 1969 agreement may resurface in 2013, however, if Iran demands an end to Israel's nuclear program in exchange for Iran abandoning its own program.[26]

Ariel Sharon, once a swashbuckling general and later a conservative prime minister, got into a bitter argument with American Mideast envoy Morris Draper about the Sabra and Shatila massacre of September 16–18, 1982. Israeli troops controlled the Beirut suburb where many Palestinians lived, and they stood by while right-wing Lebanese Phalangist militia murdered hundreds of Palestinian and Lebanese civilians. Draper strongly objected, reminding Sharon, then Israel's defense minister, that the United States had just facilitated the evacuation of the Palestine Liberation Organization (PLO) from Lebanon as a favor to Israel. Sharon saw it differently. He shouted that no one was going to stop Israel from killing "international terrorists." When the issue was an "existential threat" to Israeli security, as the Israelis saw it, then they would do what they felt they had to do. "When it comes to our security," Sharon angrily told the American diplomat, "we have never asked [for permission]. We will never ask. When it comes to existence and security, it is our own responsibility and we will never give it to anybody to decide for us."[27]

That pugnacious attitude had prevailed when Begin read Ford's letter to Rabin in 1975, pledging American support to Israel's negotiating position on the Golan Heights. And so it prevailed in the late 1990s, when the United

States repeatedly assured Israeli leaders, among them General Ehud Barak, who was soon to become prime minister, that the United States would "prevent Pakistan from crossing the nuclear threshold." When Pakistan tested its first nuclear device in 1998, the United States condemned the test but then quickly and quietly adjusted to the new reality in South Asia. "The lesson Barak absorbed," according to journalist Dan Ephron, was that "even ironclad American assurances are never ironclad." Things change.[28] Israelis now joke darkly that President Obama will also adjust to a nuclear Iran, even though they know that Obama has repeatedly pledged he will not permit Iran to go nuclear.

A U.S.-Israeli Mutual Defense Treaty?

Once, late in the administration of Bill Clinton, the United States and Israel actually considered leapfrogging presidential commitments and drafting a mutual defense treaty between the two countries, even though Israel had always maintained that it did not want a written treaty. Israel felt a treaty would limit its "freedom of action." Yet, during the Camp David summit of July 11–24, 2000, it was Ehud Barak, then Israel's prime minister, who surprised everyone by raising the idea with President Clinton. He explained that if he succeeded in negotiating an Israeli-Palestinian peace agreement, he would need the backing of an American defense treaty to sell the Palestinian agreement to the Israeli people. Moreover, Barak and Israeli generals were coming to the conclusion that a defense treaty, ratified by Congress, would be a more reliable guarantor of Israeli security than a presidential commitment, which, while important, would not necessarily survive a change in administrations.

This was not a utopian idea, pulled from a fantasy oasis in the Middle East. Back in the hot summer of 1970, Senator J. William Fulbright (D-Arkansas), often regarded as an uncompromising critic of Israel, rose on the floor of the Senate on August 24 to deliver a controversial speech. Called "Old Myths and New Realities II, The Middle East Bilateral Treaty between the United States and Israel," it proposed that in exchange for an Israeli withdrawal from occupied Arab territories in the West Bank and Gaza, the United States provide firm security guarantees to Israel in the form of a defense treaty.[29] Later, in 1975, he explained that only "by an explicit, binding American treaty guarantee of Israel" would Israel feel enough of a genuine sense of security to be able to pull back.[30]

Fulbright's 1970 proposal made the front page of the *New York Times* but generated only muted excitement in the State Department or the Foreign

Ministry in Jerusalem. Neither country apparently felt it could make the jour-ney from a Senate speech to a ratified treaty. Nevertheless, in the mid-1990s, U.S. ambassador Martin Indyk delicately touched on the idea with Israeli prime minister Yitzhak Rabin. Indyk, a student of Middle East negotiations, was "touring the horizon." He was not advancing a formal overture. Yet, in Israel, where even secret talks quickly become public, his "tour" appeared in the press and then in an American newspaper. When national security adviser Samuel R. Berger read about it, he erupted in bureaucratic anger and scolded Indyk in a 3 a.m. telephone call. A hush fell over the idea of a U.S.-Israeli defense treaty until Barak raised it at Camp David.

Clinton thought it was a good idea, but, unfortunately, Palestine Liber-ation Organization chairman Yasser Arafat refused to accept the proffered terms of an Israeli-Palestinian agreement, which was the essential first step to a U.S.-Israeli mutual defense treaty. So the Barak idea, though eye-catching and inventive at first glance, withered on the vine. Within a few months, the Palestinians, encouraged by Arafat, launched the bloody uprising known as the second Intifada, ending, at least for that time, the possibility of a negoti-ated Israeli-Palestinian peace agreement. The absence of an agreement in turn obviated the possibility of an American-Israeli mutual defense treaty. One was always dependent on the other.

But, for a brief time in the summer of 2000, in the cool mountain breezes of the Camp David summit, Barak's idea for an American-Israeli mutual defense treaty produced a surge of promising diplomatic activity. On the U.S. side were several old hands at Mideast negotiating, among them Martin Indyk, serving for a second time as the U.S. ambassador to Israel, and Bruce Rie-del, the president's special assistant for Near East and South Asian affairs at the National Security Council. They knew that the president wanted to help Barak "sell a controversial and painful series of compromises to the Israeli public."[31] On the Israeli side were Danny Yatom, Barak's chief of staff, and Zvi Shtauber, his foreign policy adviser. The Israelis came ready for action. They had a draft treaty, already loaded with American "commitments" to defend Israel in the event of an Arab attack. They envisaged a NATO-like treaty that would include, according to Riedel, "a nuclear umbrella commitment by the U.S., i.e., an American promise to respond to a nuclear attack on Israel with American nuclear forces."[32]

Not only did Israel introduce the controversial element of American nuclear protection, it also included a new financial commitment, amount-ing to roughly $35 billion over the next few years, to help the Israelis and

Palestinians meet the costly challenges of a peace treaty. Theoretically, the money would come from not only the United States but Europe and Japan as well. In addition, the Israelis requested purchasing rights to the sleek Tomahawk cruise missile and the advanced F-22 fighter jet. For years, American negotiators, in flights of fancy, had imagined a defense treaty with Israel to be expensive, but as they got deeper into the negotiation at Camp David, they were truly shocked at the potential cost.

In addition, Clinton's negotiators knew there would likely be considerable opposition to certain elements of the draft treaty, especially to the technology transfers and to the nuclear commitment. Congress might also balk at the very concept of a mutual defense treaty with Israel, believing it might drag the United States into every Israeli confrontation with its Arab neighbors and in this way jeopardize, among other things, oil shipments to the United States. Equally important, the Israeli Knesset, split into battling parties and factions, might object to the loss of Israel's vaunted "freedom of action," implied in a mutual defense treaty, and reject the treaty.

Still, Camp David was again the site of an extraordinary diplomatic endeavor. On one level, the United States and Israel explored the contours of a mutual defense treaty. They were obviously making progress, because drafts were circulated within the U.S. government and lawyers were summoned to review the language of every proposed American commitment. On another level, the negotiation focused on an Israeli-Palestinian peace agreement, conducted at a summit level, involving Clinton, Barak, and Arafat, and surprisingly they too made progress; but Clinton and Barak soon sensed that Arafat was not ready for a deal. The Palestinian leader, playing the role of odd man out, never proposed anything and rarely raised a question. He attended the summit more as a representative of his people than as their negotiator. Only on the issue of the right of Palestinian refugees to return to their original homeland, now Israel, did Arafat raise a few questions, but he never pursued them.

The details were closely held, reporters kept at a distance. Clinton hoped that the location, famous for the successful negotiation that produced the Egyptian-Israeli peace treaty in 1978, might inspire a positive result. He knew he risked failure but thought, nonetheless, that he could persuade anyone to do anything. Having successfully avoided impeachment for his role in the Monica Lewinsky scandal, he was in those days on cloud ten, marching to his own drummer. History beckoned, and he thought of himself as a man of destiny. The Middle East, though, has often been the graveyard of ego and ambition, and much else. After two weeks of exceptional effort, Clinton realized that he could not overcome the twin realities of Palestinian opposition and the needs of Israeli security.

Moreover, a U.S.-Israeli defense treaty was always contingent on the success of an Israeli-Palestinian peace agreement. Without a peace agreement, there could be no treaty; and sadly Arafat would not or could not accept an agreement, perhaps because an agreement would have ended his lifelong struggle for a Palestinian state, standing on its own, occupying all the land of ancient Palestine, sharing none of it with an Israeli neighbor. Apparently Arafat valued the struggle more than an accommodation with Israel. Clinton ran out of time to pursue this promising possibility, in part because he had wasted so much of his second term on the Lewinsky scandal. Barak subsequently lost power in an election to his political rival, Ariel Sharon. By the end of January 2001, the dream of Camp David had died.

"You are a great man," Arafat was supposed to have said to Clinton, as he left Camp David. To which, according to this story, Clinton replied: "I am not a great man. I am a failure, and you made me one."

The Transient Nature of a Presidential Commitment

For any student of the Middle East, one of the most interesting examples of the transient nature of a presidential commitment was President Barack Obama's response shortly after his inauguration to the fascinating exchange of letters in April 2004, between Israeli prime minister Ariel Sharon and President George W. Bush.

With the draft defense treaty between the United States and Israel now a fading memory, both nations reverted to tested formulas in their search for peace. If there was to be any progress in the on-again, off-again talks between the Israelis and the Palestinians, it would be the result of high-level talks between their leaders, always with the United States playing a major role as intermediary.

In the spring of 2004, Sharon was in political hot water, the Israeli media filled with stories of graft and corruption, and he needed a public pat on the back from an American president, one noted for his staunch support of Israel. Bush was the perfect president in this respect. He obligingly invited Sharon to Washington, where the two leaders met and discussed the so-called "roadmap to peace," the latest in a long series of American efforts to start and sustain a viable peace process between the Israelis and the Palestinians. This roadmap broke new ground. It enjoyed Israel's reluctant support, and the Palestinians, though wary, accepted its basic premise. In a June 24, 2002, speech, which set the stage for the "roadmap" concept, Bush had pledged American support for "a vision of two states, a secure State of Israel and a viable, peaceful, democratic Palestine." Here was an American president in open sponsorship of a new state of Palestine, committed to a peaceful relationship with Israel. Sharon trusted Bush so much he raised no objection. A "Quartet" of the United States, Russia, the European Union, and the United Nations was organized to help convert the vision into reality. They thought it could all happen in three years, which was totally unrealistic. The Israelis and the Palestinians laid out conditions that severely complicated their task. None of the conditions should have come as a surprise. The Israelis demanded an end to terrorism, and the Palestinians demanded an end to Israeli settlements on the West Bank and in East Jerusalem.

On April 14, 2004, by pre-arrangement, Bush and Sharon exchanged letters during their heavily covered White House summit. Sharon's letter gushed with praise of Bush, describing his June 24, 2002, speech as "one of the most significant contributions towards ensuring a bright future for the Middle East." Israel, he said, supported the roadmap ("a practical and just formula"), but because "there exists no Palestinian partner" for negotiating a possible deal, Sharon disclosed that Israel, on its own, would initiate a number of actions designed to "reduce friction between Israelis and Palestinians." First, Israel would begin to "relocate military installations" in the Gaza Strip, another way of saying it was pulling out; and, second, would build a "security fence" up and down the spine of Israel designed to protect Israelis from Palestinian terrorists. It would be "temporary" in nature, and its only purpose was security. Sharon promised to "limit" the growth of settlements and to pursue peace with the Palestinians. In closing, Sharon again praised Bush for his "courageous leadership," his "important initiative," and his "personal friendship and profound support for the State of Israel."

Bush, in his letter, restated his June 24, 2002, "vision" of "two states living side-by-side in peace and security" and "welcomed" Sharon's plans for pulling out of Gaza. He then reassured Sharon on three key points: First, that the United States would "prevent any attempt by anyone to impose any other plan," meaning no imposed settlement by outside powers; second, that the United States would maintain its "steadfast commitment to Israel's security, including secure, defensible borders, and to preserve and strengthen Israel's capability to deter and defend itself, by itself, against any threat or possible combination of threats," meaning increased U.S. support for Israel's "qualitative military edge" over its Arab neighbors; and, third, even after Israel withdrew from Gaza and parts of the West Bank, the United States would support continued Israeli control of "airspace, territorial waters and land passages" of the areas just vacated. The Palestinians instantly denounced the U.S. role as an honest broker between the two sides, saying Bush's letter proved that the United States had lost all its credibility, not the first time they had reached that conclusion.

Bush then demonstrated, in a few loaded sentences, why he was considered one of Israel's best friends. He stepped into the delicate turf of unresolved issues between the two sides and, time and again, came down unreservedly on Israel's side. The president stressed America's strong "commitment" to "Israel's security and well-being as a Jewish state." His specific reference to a "Jewish state" was music to the ears of Sharon and his political partners. They firmly believed that a final settlement with the Palestinians had to include their recognition of Israel as a "Jewish state," not one that could in time be overwhelmed by a massive infusion of Palestinian refugees. For many years the Palestinians had held out for the right of Palestinians to return to their former holdings in what had become Israel, and the Israelis had retorted that those Palestinians ought more properly to return to the new state of Palestine, when created. Bush, in his letter, explicitly supported the Israeli position, saying "a solution to the Palestinian refugee issue . . . will need to be found through the establishment of a Palestinian state, and the settling of Palestinian refugees there, rather than in Israel."

Bush also stepped into the equally sensitive issue of Israeli settlements in West Bank lands formerly owned or controlled by Palestinians. Here, too, he fully supported Sharon and infuriated the Palestinians. Bush wrote that in any future agreement Israel had to have "secure and recognized borders." Israel had always sought to fashion its future by establishing "facts on the ground," which would then become the starting point in negotiating any international agreement. Bush used slightly different words, but meant the same thing. "In light of new realities on the ground, including already existing major Israeli population centers," he wrote, choosing his words carefully, "it is unrealistic to expect a full and complete return to the armistice lines of 1949, and all previous efforts to negotiate a two-state solution have reached the same conclusion."

Bush concluded by cautioning Sharon not to think of the "security fence" as anything other than a "security fence" (in other words, not as a border), and once the need for the fence passed, it should be dismantled. Nevertheless, Bush described Sharon's initiatives as "bold and historic" and his decisions as "courageous," and he closed by saying that the United States was Israel's "close friend and ally."[33]

Bush's letter was immediately enshrined in Israeli history as a memorable example of a presidential commitment to support the Israeli positions on settlements and on the Palestinian "right of return"—a commitment that paralleled Israeli policy and would undoubtedly be cited in future Israeli dealings with the United States. Sharon and earlier Israeli prime ministers had been tutored on the history of Eisenhower's pledges to Israel in 1957. They knew about them, but also knew that in 1967 Lyndon Johnson had "betrayed" Israel by being so preoccupied with other, more pressing demands that he could not honor his predecessor's promises. They understood the tricky, transient nature of a presidential commitment—valid one day, possibly abandoned the next. A new president entering the Oval Office had an inherent right to support a prior commitment or, in light of changing circumstance, shelve it.

Obama's new secretary of state, Hillary Rodham Clinton, put a nail in the Bush-Sharon exchange of letters by immediately making it clear that the Obama administration wanted no part of them. The letters, she announced, "did not become part of the official position of the United States government." And that was that.[34]

CHAPTER TEN

WHERE ARE THEY NOW?

"They want to flee from Afghanistan just as they turned tail and
ran from Vietnam. When America faced utter destruction in Vietnam,
they came up with the formula 'declare victory and run' and want to
use the formula of 'transfer security and run' here in Afghanistan."
—TALIBAN STATEMENT, January 2, 2013

SINCE THE END of World War II, the United States has made many "commitments" to defend countries considered vital to its national security interests.
One such commitment was the mutual defense treaty with South Korea in the
early 1950s. Like all treaties, it was ratified by the Senate, and it mushroomed
into a major military obligation, involving the stationing of tens of thousands
of American troops in South Korea. Another kind of commitment—costly in
the extreme in lives, treasure, and national reputation—was to South Vietnam
in the 1950s and 1960s. It grew out of an obsessive cold war fear that if South
Vietnam fell to the communists, all of Southeast Asia, and maybe Japan, would
also fall, like a line of dominos, jeopardizing American interests everywhere.
This commitment was not rooted in a defense treaty, but Congress did pass
a resolution of support. Finally, the U.S. commitment to Israel is, to quote
President Barack Obama, "ironclad," and yet it has no basis in a treaty or an
all-embracing congressional resolution. It grew out of a series of presidential
letters to Israeli prime ministers pledging American military support to Israeli
security needs. The American commitment to Israel is unique.

In each case—whether relating to South Korea, South Vietnam, or Israel—
the American commitment has been different, each one emerging at a special
time from circumstances understood by the president of the United States to
directly affect the national security interests of the United States. In the world
of commitments, the role of the president is vital, infinitely more so than the
words in any document, official or not. If the president considers a commitment to be of current value and importance to the United States, then, by his
statements and actions, it would be recognized as such. But if he considers a

commitment to be dated, no longer of consequence to the United States, then, by his silence or inaction, it would easily be dropped from the official lexicon, in this way losing all of its former relevance. It is always up to the judgment of one man or woman, the president of the United States, who in recent decades has accumulated almost unprecedented power in the arena of national security. Here, the president is the master. Is this a good or a bad thing?

South Korea: The Treaty Commitment

Pactomania, it was called. The United States, in the early 1950s, went on an alliance-building spree everywhere, using NATO, set up in 1949, as its model. Within a few years, the United States succeeded in negotiating bilateral defense agreements with a string of Asian and Pacific states, running from South Korea and Japan in the north to the Philippines further south, near the South China Sea, and then, still further south, to Australia and New Zealand. In 1955, it also sparked the creation of the Southeast Asia Treaty Organization, which banded together nations very distinct in background and location—Thailand, Pakistan, and the United Kingdom, for example—but all of them sharing a commitment to fight against communist expansion, more or less under American direction. They were the junior partners in this alliance, a number fearing a communist takeover (in many places, a distinct possibility) and needing the support and protection of the United States, the most powerful nation in the world. With each treaty, the United States adopted a "commitment" to defend another country, but the wording was often left deliberately loose, open to different interpretations, all of them depending in the final analysis on what the president in power wanted or needed at his moment of decision.

"It has to do with what goes on in the brain of the president," said John Negroponte, a former deputy secretary of state and director of national intelligence, who had worked closely with many presidents. "No amount of history or science can change that. It's how [they] feel when faced with the facts."[1]

With the Korean War still unresolved, the United States signed a "mutual defense treaty" with the Philippines on August 30, 1951; a few days later came a "security treaty" with Australia and New Zealand, called the ANZUS treaty. Then, after the Korean armistice agreement was signed, the United States negotiated a "mutual defense treaty" with South Korea on October 1, 1953, and a "mutual defense assistance agreement" with Japan on March 8, 1954. In all of these treaties, one would have to look long and hard to find language that locked the United States into a firm commitment to come to the defense of the other country, no matter what. For example, with the Philippines, the United States was obliged to "consult together from time to time" and to "recognize that an armed attack in the Pacific Area on either of the parties would be dangerous to its own peace and safety." The treaty continued: Each party "would [then] act to meet the common dangers in accordance with its constitutional processes," which were left undefined and which could mean the parties would take military action, or would not, and with no time frame for action written into the treaty.[2]

Same for the treaties with Australia, New Zealand, Japan, and South Korea. With Australia and New Zealand, for instance, Article Four read: "Each party recognizes that an armed attack in the Pacific on any of the parties would be dangerous to its own peace and safety and declares that it would act to meet the common danger in accordance with its constitutional processes."

With South Korea, Article Three read: "Each party recognizes that an armed attack in the Pacific area on either of the Parties . . . would be dangerous to its own peace and safety and declares that it would act to meet the common danger in accordance with its constitutional processes."

With Japan, the "mutual defense assistance agreement" was far more complex, reflecting the special post–World War II relationship between the two countries. The United States had dropped two atomic bombs on Japan, and American troops were already based in Japan. Therefore, the agreement related not only to "collective self-defense" but also to basing rights and privileges, economic agreements including "an exchange of industrial property rights," tax exemptions and "technical information for defense," and diplomatic protection for each party's personnel. The bottom line, though, was that both nations were pledged to help each other in accordance with their national traditions and "constitutional processes."[3]

While the treaty language was, in this sense, unexceptional, it did contain one diplomatically ambiguous phrase: that the United States would act to protect Japan and "the territories under the administration of Japan." The "territories," as it turned out, included the Senkaku Islands, located north of Taiwan, so small in size and insignificant in appearance that one scholar noted "you can't even find [them] on most maps." The Senkakus consist of five small islands and three rocky outcroppings, a total landmass of seven square kilometers, or three square miles, incapable of supporting human habitation or economic development. Yet sovereignty over the Senkakus would validate a claim to roughly 71,000 square kilometers of the continental shelf, meaning access, according to one calculation, of almost 100 billion barrels of oil and rich fishing grounds.[4] It is not surprising, therefore, that both Japan and China, two neighboring giants, quickly claimed sovereignty over the Senkakus, each mesmerized by exciting visions of economic reward.

In 1945, when Japan surrendered, the United States decided to administer the Senkakus as a stopgap way of avoiding a clash between Japan and China over the question of who owned the islands, which China calls the Diaoyu; but, in word and deed, Washington seemed to favor Japan's claim, and it accepted responsibility for administering the islands until a more formal arrangement could be reached. In 1960, the U. S. position shifted. In the wording of the U.S.-Japan security treaty, the United States assumed a legal obligation to help Japan defend the Senkakus, even though it maintained a "neutral" approach toward sovereignty over the islands. In 1971, the United States took a crucial step forward, saying that, so far as it was concerned, the islands belonged to Japan. This, of course, satisfied the Japanese but infuriated the Chinese.[5] Did that mean that if the Senkakus were threatened or attacked, presumably by the Chinese, the United States would be obligated by the treaty to come to Japan's assistance, militarily if necessary, and defend Japan's claim to the islands? These questions were asked but never quite answered.

In the summer of 2012, Japan and China, not for the first time, found themselves in a spiraling argument over the still troubling question of Senkaku administration, and the United States found itself in the middle of a dangerous controversy. The Chinese were warning the United States to stay out of the argument, while some of the more conservative Japanese politicians seemed eager to use the language of the treaty to test America's commitment to Japan's defense. The United States, of course, tried to cool nationalistic passions in both Japan and China, saying on an almost daily basis that there was no good reason for a confrontation over the Senkakus. Talk but don't fight, was the advice from Washington.

But neither Japan nor China seemed to be listening. Before stepping down as secretary of state in late January 2013, Hillary Rodham Clinton said that the Obama administration would oppose "any unilateral actions that would seek to undermine Japanese administration" of the islands. That seemed only to repeat the American position, but the Chinese angrily denounced Clinton anyway, claiming she "ignores the facts and confuses right and wrong."[6] China and Japan had, in recent months, been escalating their dispute by sending civilian maritime vessels to the Senkakus. On January 10, China had ordered a surveillance plane to the area, provoking Japan to scramble F-15 fighter jets, which then prompted the Chinese to dispatch J-10 fighter jets. Tensions rose, but no shots were fired.

In this environment, experts in Tokyo and Washington found a front page article in the *Chinese People's Liberation Army Daily* to be of special interest. It read in part that China had to dust the cobwebs off its military. "A long period without battle," it noted, "has encouraged the fixed habits of peace in some of the military so that their preparedness for battle is dulled."[7] The same newspaper reported that troops had recently conducted exercises in the Beijing region. In China, an article of this sort is not the result of journalistic discovery. The newspaper is the official newspaper of the Chinese army, and its references to "dullness" and "preparations for battle" and military "exercises" are intended to convey a stern message to Japan and the United States.

During an earlier fracas, in 1996, a State Department spokesman, Glyn Davies, tried soothing hot passions in Tokyo and Beijing. "We urge all the claimants to exercise restraint," he urged. "We're not going to predict what's likely to happen. We're simply going to confine ourselves to calling on both sides to resist the temptation to provoke each other or raise tensions . . . it's not the kind of issue that's worth elevating beyond a war of words."[8] *Time* magazine framed the dilemma in a question that seemed to have an obvious answer: "Will the next Asian war be fought over a few tiny islands?"

Then, as now, on the issue of the Senkakus, another dangerous confrontation between Japan and China could develop, if rising nationalism in both countries is not kept in check. But diplomats wonder what the United States would do if Japan, citing the defense treaty, asked for American help? Would the United States fight for Japan's claim to barely inhabited and inhabitable islands? Unlikely, but given the language of the U.S.-Japan security treaty, that is what the United States is committed to doing.

In the drafting of these pactomania treaties, according to Brookings scholar Richard C. Bush, there has often been a terrible tension between "abandonment" and "entrapment:" a feeling of "abandonment" on the part of the junior partner—that, no matter how binding the treaty language, one day the senior partner would find a way of evading his treaty obligations; and a fear of "entrapment" on the part of the senior partner—that one day the junior partner, using the treaty, would find a way of sucking him into a war or crisis he didn't really want or need.[9] Or, to quote another Brookings scholar, Michael O'Hanlon, it would be a case of "allies behaving in ways that you may not have as much interest in."[10] In other words, defense treaties specify that one nation would help the other in a time of crisis. But, as many observers have cautioned, times change, and the parties to a treaty might not always share identical interests. A commitment pledged one day may be honored or betrayed the next, depending on what the president in power considers vital to American interests.

For example, consider the U.S.–South Korean treaty. Logically, it should have soothed South Korean anxieties about another North Korean assault. After all, it tied the world's most powerful nuclear nation to the defense of South Korea. In addition, tens of thousands of American troops have been based in South Korea, just south of the 38th parallel, since the 1953 armistice, constituting a kind of trip-wire commitment of American forces to South Korea's defense in the event of a North Korean attack. Moreover, as though the trip-wire troop commitment were not enough to ease South Korea's chronic anxieties, the United States also deployed tactical nuclear weapons in South Korea from 1958 until 1991—just in case the Chinese were again thinking of sending hundreds of thousands of troops across the Yalu River, just in case the North Koreans were again getting itchy and plotting another attack across the dividing line. Most people would have thought the United States, by these actions, proved its earnest commitment to the defense of South Korea. Yet, South Korean leaders continued to worry about the uncertainty of "the day after tomorrow." What might the United States do then?

For the South Koreans, one measure of American resolve was the number of American troops stationed in South Korea, even after a very costly war: 54,000 Americans killed, more than 100,000 wounded, and more than $75 billion spent, or roughly 5.6 percent of U.S. aggregate gross national product between 1950 and 1953.[11] According to author Don Oberdorfer, the country was left "devastated": "around 3 million people . . . killed, wounded or missing. . . . Another 5 million became refugees." Property losses were put at $2 billion. It seemed as if there was nothing left between North and South Korea but hatred and distrust.[12]

In the late 1950s, there were 60,000 American troops in South Korea, a rather sizeable trip wire. Ten years later, President Richard Nixon decided to withdraw an army division of 20,000 troops, consistent with his policy of reducing American troop strength in Asia and relying more and more on the growing strength of local allies, such as South Korea. There were still to be 40,000 American troops there, more than enough, according to the Pentagon, to trigger a major American response to any communist attack. Nevertheless, the South Koreans went into a tailspin of anxiety, fearing that the

United States was preparing to abandon them. The upshot was that South Korea began to develop a nuclear arms program of its own, which ran counter to American strategy and plans, and it infuriated the White House. President Jimmy Carter threatened to withdraw all American troops and cut military and financial assistance unless South Korea abandoned its nuclear program, which it eventually did. In 1992, under heavy American pressure, both Koreas signed a Joint Declaration of the Denuclearization of the Korean Peninsula. Since then, South Korea has kept its word, North Korea has not.[13]

There are now 28,500 American troops in South Korea, protected by an American nuclear umbrella and the powerful Seventh Fleet and backed by a mutual defense treaty between the two countries. In addition, the United States designated South Korea as "a major non-NATO ally" in 1987, another way of showing American support for South Korea. Still, in one conversation after another with senior South Korean officials and officers, I have sensed a measure of continuing concern out of all proportion to the obvious strength of the American commitment. One reason clearly is that North Korea, though an impoverished country, has developed nuclear weapons and long-range missiles, and its new leader, Kim Jong-un, has begun pushing for "more working satellites" and "carrier rockets of bigger capacity."[14]

Recently, I asked a South Korean general how he would define the "mutual defense treaty" between the two countries. He said that it was "fundamental, the very backbone of the alliance." The general was asked: Did the United States share this view? "Absolutely," he replied, as if he were persuading himself more than me. "If there is any threat, the U.S. will defend Korea. No question, we have a treaty." Is the threat today the same as it was in 1953, when the treaty was signed? "Absolutely," he repeated. "It was North Korea then, and it is still North Korea." The general said that South Korea alone has the capacity "to deter" North Korea, but to "destroy" North Korea, it would need the United States. "We have a very close alliance," the general stressed again and again. "When you asked for our help in Vietnam, we sent 320,000 troops, and 5,000 were killed. You needed our help in Iraq and Afghanistan, and we sent it. Wherever the U.S. goes, we go." He wanted me to understand his major point: that South Korea was a solid, reliable ally of the United States, and he expected the United States to be the same kind of ally to South Korea. They were lashed together by common interests, he seemed to be saying (and hoping), and so it would remain.

The underlying South Korean concern is understandable. It reflects not only current military realities and treaty obligations; it also reflects changes in global politics and American power. In 1953, the United States was the undisputed leader of a global anticommunist coalition. In 2013, the United States remains a global power, but one clearly intent on reducing its global obligations. President Barack Obama ended the American military involvement in Iraq, limited its military role in Libya, held back in Syria during its bloody, brutal civil war, and, clearly, has been heading toward the exits in Afghanistan. "We're gun-shy now," observed Brookings scholar Henry Aaron, "because of less than glorious experiences in Iraq and Afghanistan, also political polarization and economic difficulties—all of these things interact."[15] Still, though the United States is obviously gun-shy about its global commitments, there is a fairly widespread assumption among experts and pundits that if South Korea were attacked by North Korea, the United States would come to South Korea's defense. But for how long, and to what extent? That would, once again, depend on the decisions of one man: the president of the United States. It would be his call, and his alone.

Vietnam: A Commitment That Mushroomed,
Perished, and Is Now Reborn

It is, as of this writing, thirty-eight years since the end of the United States' military involvement in Vietnam. Both nations, the vanquished and the victor, are now involved in a surprising and serious courtship: a courtship that is already being described, on the U.S. side anyway, as a "commitment." From bitter enemies in war, they have now become, in the language of modern communiqués, "strong partners" in peace. Their common concern about the rising economic and military power of China has created a new dynamism in their expanding program of bilateral cooperation. They do not yet refer to themselves as "allies"—until Vietnam sheds its rigid communist form of government and improves its human rights record, that is not likely—but they are clearly moving in that direction. President Obama's appointments of former senators John Kerry and Chuck Hagel, both wounded Vietnam War veterans, to the jobs of secretaries of state and defense signal that the lessons of the Vietnam War, often referred to as the Vietnam syndrome, will now be front and center in U.S. deliberations about further American military commitments around the world. Kerry and Hagel are not afraid to use American power where and when appropriate, but they are both of the view that war must be a last resort and never a first option. It was one of the lessons they learned in Vietnam.

In 1995, twenty years after the war's end, the United States and Vietnam turned a new page and established formal diplomatic relations. In 2000, President Clinton visited Vietnam, where he received a warm and enthusiastic reception. It was his last foreign visit as president. Economic and political relations then blossomed considerably. In 2007, the United States and Vietnam signed a Trade and Investment Agreement, and Washington helped Vietnam gain admission to the World Trade Organization. In 2008, the two countries signed an Open Skies Agreement.[16] Bilateral trade has surpassed $15 billion and continues to grow impressively.[17] Even Starbucks has opened shops in Ho Chi-minh City.

Both nations, looking north toward a restless China, are strengthening their military ties as well, mindful perhaps of a famous quote ascribed to Napoleon. China, he is supposed to have said, is a "sleeping giant. Let her sleep; for when she wakes, she will shake the world."

At the moment, China may not yet be shaking the world, but it appears to be shaking the shipping lanes of the South China Sea, prompting a number of politicians and pundits in Washington to imagine the awakened giant as a global threat soon to be comparable to the Soviet Union during the cold war. Because Pentagon strategists prepare for every contingency, they are now also preparing for a war with China, laying out a "first island chain" of defense against possible Chinese aggression. Even popular novelists, such as Tom Clancy, have allowed their imaginations to envelop China, which they see as a mortal enemy of the United States. Clancy's latest best seller, *Threat Vector,* tells the story of a Chinese general, using the new technology of cyberwarfare, engaged in a cockeyed plot to attack American assets in the South China Sea, Hong Kong, and Taiwan. The Chinese lose, and the Americans win, of course, but not before both nations move to within inches of a thermonuclear exchange.

During the cold war, the United States surrounded the Soviet Union with defensive alliances. It now appears to be doing the same thing with China: setting up, or strengthening, a ring of defensive alliances with Japan, South Korea, Taiwan, the Philippines, and Vietnam. The United States denies any malevolent intent; and after the wars in Iraq and Afghanistan and the growing danger of another with Iran, the United States could benefit from a period of domestic nation-building, as Obama repeatedly reminds us. Therefore, it speaks often about a peaceful relationship with China, but there is no mistaking its new muscular policy in Asia and the Pacific. With a few of these Asian nations, such as the Philippines, Japan, and South Korea, the United States already has mutual defense treaties; with others, such as Vietnam, the United

States is moving rapidly to establish a "mutual defense partnership." An odd irony immediately becomes apparent. The United States is heavily indebted to China, and yet Washington has begun to act in Asia as if China is a strategic adversary and a threat to American interests.

Time and again, China warns Washington to mind its own business, insisting that the United States "respect China's sovereignty and territorial integrity." The United States, for its part, sees an important "national interest" in the South China Sea, where China claims exclusive rights to some areas more than a thousand miles from its shores. On the not-too-distant horizon, hazy and uncertain, like an etching in a Chinese scroll, a collision of American and Chinese interests seems to be forming, as the United States moves diplomatically and militarily to protect the "stability" of the region and to assert its "maritime rights" of free passage.[18] The Chinese cannot be indifferent to America's "new defense strategy," according to which the United States will over the next few years shift more than 50 percent of its air and naval power from Europe and the Middle East to Asia and the Pacific. Nor could they have been indifferent to Defense Secretary Leon Panetta's visit to Vietnam in June 2012.

The defense secretary stopped, quite deliberately, at the deep water naval base at Cam Ranh Bay, built by the United States in 1965, when President Lyndon Johnson began sending tens and then hundreds of thousands of American troops to Vietnam. Standing under a hot sun on the deck of a U.S. naval ship, Panetta spoke of "our bilateral defense relationship" with Vietnam as a fact of life—as if it had been carefully considered by the U.S. government, as if Congress and the public had been briefed, as if the media had done its legwork. Then, with General Phung Quang Thanh, a Vietnam War veteran and now defense minister, standing at his side, nodding in cautious approval, Panetta used a word that, in official U.S. jargon, carried heavy historical freight, especially in a Vietnam context. The United States, the defense secretary said, had "an enduring *commitment* to this important defense relationship" and to "advancing our defense cooperation."[19] "*Commitment*"—the same word, uttered time and again over the years by one president after another, sometimes with care and thought, often as encouragement to a fragile ally or as a warning to an enemy, real or imagined, always with the aim of sounding tough, determined, and committed to a policy option favorable to American interests. Was Panetta reading the words of a speechwriter? Was he adlibbing? Was he setting forth a new policy or merely articulating what he knew to be the president's evolving policy toward Vietnam? Was he stepping into a commitment that might oblige the United States to take military action at a time and place helpful to Vietnam but, possibly, harmful to the United States? In other words, had Panetta's "enduring commitment" to Vietnam been vetted?

When the United States began scanning the Asian horizon for potential allies against China, Vietnam came clearly into focus. It was an obvious candidate, given its long, tortured relationship with China, marked by suspicion, wars, and border conflicts—a rocky relationship known to every Vietnamese student but not apparently to American policymakers during the 1950s and '60s.

Even the Buddhist patriarch of Vietnam, Thich Quang Do, the 83-year-old victim of relentless government oppression, sided with his government's increasingly belligerent stance toward China. He told American ambassador David Shear during an unusual August 17, 2012, visit to his besieged monastery that "if you live next to a very powerful neighbor who spends its time double-crossing you, it is important to know who your friends are." According to the patriarch, who was a 2012 Nobel Peace Prize nominee, the United States was a friend of Vietnam, while China, by implication, was a "double-crossing" enemy. His fear was that Vietnam, unless it played its cards right, "could become a vassal of China as before."[20] Thich, who, under government order, has been a prisoner in his own monastery, finds himself ironically joining hands with his prison warden on the hot issue of "Chinese encroachment on Vietnamese waters and lands." On their conflicting claims in the South China Sea, Vietnam and China seem headed for a clash, and the United States has clearly been on Vietnam's side.

On December 11, 2012, during a week-long visit to Washington, Minister Wang Jiarui, who runs the International Department of the Central Committee of the Chinese Communist Party, struck the pose of an innocent observer of the rising tension in the South China Sea. He said at a luncheon that China sought only peace with its neighbors. If it were not for the fact that oil was discovered in the South China Sea more than thirty years ago, the minister asserted, no one would be challenging what he considered China's legal right to the riches of this now-contested body of water. Wang added that China has observed "military exercises" in the region, which "worry us a lot." Did he mean American military exercises? An aide smiled, shrugged, and said, "I think so."

One of the tragedies of American diplomacy in the twentieth century was that the United States was so hypnotized by the cold war that it failed to read the subtleties of Vietnamese culture and history or to appreciate the possibility of weaning Vietnam away from the communist world. In Europe, it had happened with Yugoslavia; in Asia, it might have happened with Vietnam. Given the costs of the war, it was certainly a policy option worth testing.

What is known at this writing is that the United States and Vietnam have been vigorously tightening their military ties. The United States recently lifted its ban on the sale of "non-lethal weapons" to Vietnam, and it is now on the edge of lifting the ban on the sale of "lethal weapons," which includes anything from rifles to tanks or warplanes—in the words of General Phung, "to purchase certain kinds of weapons for the potential modernization of our military."[21] In addition, the United States wants unimpeded access for its warships to Cam Ranh Bay and to all other naval bases in Vietnam, and the Vietnamese want to buy American technology to "repair" and "overhaul . . . weapons left from the war." This represents an upside-down change in Vietnam's strategy. During the war, Vietnam was totally dependent upon its communist allies, Russia and China, for its weapons of war—to be used at that time against the United States. Now it is becoming increasingly dependent on the United States for these same weapons. But, now, to be used against whom? To be used apparently, if necessary, against the Chinese, its traditional enemy for more than a thousand years. Many wars have been fought across their shifting, uneasy border. It is now one of the strange twists of modern history that Vietnam, once America's enemy but now its budding partner, has suddenly grown into a key piece of the "new defense strategy" for the "Asia-Pacific region." It is almost as though the Vietnam War was an unnecessary intrusion into the natural flow of Vietnamese history.

Israel: Is Commitment through Correspondence Enough?

Barack Obama's post-2008 election policy toward Israel was dramatized by big change, unsettling though not entirely unexpected: from George W. Bush's, which suggested unquestioned support of Israel, to Obama's, which seemed to raise doubts and highlight differences between the two countries.

Many Israelis regarded Obama with suspicion even before he became president. During a pre-election visit to Israel in 2008, Obama visited all the right places and said all the right things, from Israel's perspective, but his hosts still felt uncomfortable with this young African American presidential candidate whose middle name was Hussein. Obama seemed to admire Israel's grit, progress, and determination, and during his presidency he raised the level of American-Israeli security cooperation to new heights. But the feeling was that Israel never owned a place in his heart. It had been, for him, an acquired taste. He seemed to lack what many other Democratic politicians had at their finger tips—a ready sympathy for Jewish sensitivities and suffering. He understood

Israel with his head, not his heart, and his relations with Israel have been problematic ever since.

Shortly after his January 2009 inauguration, Obama unceremoniously upended Bush's 2004 promises about Israeli settlements, or "facts on the ground," sounding moral, righteous, and even-handed in the process, and he brushed aside Bush's policy on the Palestinian "right of return" but offered no alternative policy. Where Bush had been specific, Obama has been vague. Almost immediately, the Israelis had questions about the new president. In the springtime of his first administration, Obama kept a campaign promise and traveled to Cairo, where he delivered a warm, open-arms speech to his Muslim audience, promising a new day in American-Arab relations. Though in the neighborhood, he decided to bypass Jerusalem, an omission that instantly prompted Israelis to worry about a new American approach to their country. It was then that one recalled President Gerald Ford's controversial and quickly abandoned "reassessment" of U.S.-Israeli relations in 1975. Was Obama to launch another reassessment? Even when Obama announced that he would visit Israel in late March 2013, many Israelis, instead of preparing to roll out the red carpet, wondered why he was "meddling in Israeli politics" and whether he was capable of managing the delicate mess that the Arab Spring had produced in the Middle East.[22] But, these reservations notwithstanding, he would be received with the high honor he deserved as president of the United States.

Complicating matters still further, from the beginning Obama clearly did not like Prime Minister Benjamin Netanyahu, and Netanyahu did not like or trust Obama. From the prime minister's office came mischievous jokes about Obama's middle name—Hussein. And then, a few years later, when the question of Israeli borders came up for diplomatic deliberation, Obama explicitly cited the pre–June 1967 borders as the starting point for the Israeli-Palestinian negotiation rather than the 1949 armistice lines, which had been Bush's pledge in his 2004 letter of commitments to Sharon. "What was Obama up to?" was the question many Israelis asked.

In essence, Obama conveyed the impression, perhaps unintentionally, of injecting a deliberate distance between himself and Israel, a personal coolness that Israelis read as a step toward possible abandonment. That was Obama's nature, Israelis were assured. Nothing more. Israelis remained skeptical. Even though they were often reminded of Obama's generosity to Israel, his "iron-clad commitment" to its security, his diplomatic support at the UN, and finally his pledge that the United States would never allow Iran to become a nuclear power, they still have never felt comfortable with Obama. They were always quick to express their gratitude to the United States and their admiration of the American people, but, in the dark corners of their collective soul, they felt a disturbing uneasiness about the true extent of Obama's support for Israel—a feeling once again that, at the end of the day, when Israel faced what it considered an existential threat, it had only Israel to depend upon. Given the grim lessons of Jewish history, this can and should be understood.

U.S. Mideast expert and former negotiator Dennis Ross told me that "the Israelis appreciate the word [of a president] and would use it to call on the United States if they were in need, but they do not see it as a guarantee of an American commitment to Israeli security—the Johnson episode is a case in point here," a reference to the time in 1967 when President Johnson refused, for a number of good reasons, to live up to President Eisenhower's assurances in 1957 of American support for Israel's right to "free and innocent passage" through the Straits of Tiran.[23]

Perhaps more than any other issue, including the thorny question of Israeli settlements, Iran has come to symbolize the policy differences in the uneasy U.S.-Israeli relationship. Obama, time and again, has pledged that the United States would not permit Iran to develop nuclear weapons, and he has fully shared the secrets of American intelligence with Israeli defense officials. Nevertheless, on September 12, 2012, Netanyahu openly questioned Obama's policy on Iran, framing the differences between them in "moral" terms—something he had never done before. A comment the day before by Secretary of State Hillary Clinton might have been the reason for his angry eruption. Clinton had told a reporter that the United States would not set a "deadline" for Iran to comply with UN and U.S. demands that it stop the development of its nuclear program. Israel wanted a deadline, and more—it wanted military action, preferably by the United States, against the Iranian program, and it wanted such action now, not later. Because Netanyahu was convinced that Iran was intent on building a nuclear weapon, he had had enough of no-deadlines. "The world tells Israel," he said, with teasing sarcasm, "'wait, there's still time.' And I say, 'Wait for what? Wait until when?'" Then, pointedly, he added: "Those in the international community who refuse to put red lines before Iran don't have a moral right to place a red light before Israel."[24] Translation: *Obama, you are always urging us not to attack Iran, always saying you won't allow Iran to go nuclear, but you obviously don't have the guts to impose a deadline on Iran, to draw a red line and stop Iran from developing nuclear weapons. Basically, you're afraid.*

When Netanyahu officially informed Obama he was heading to New York for the annual UN General Assembly meeting in late September 2012, his way of requesting a private meeting with the president, and the White House made it clear that the president did not want to meet with Netanyahu, as he would routinely do during a prime minister's visit to the United States, the lid seemed to blow off the top of the Obama-Netanyahu relationship. Worsening the mood was a keen awareness on both sides that the president was in the midst of a strongly contested re-election campaign, and he did not need a public spat with an Israeli prime minister, which could seriously damage his prospects with Jewish voters in battleground states such as Florida and Ohio. Obama, hoping to contain the budding crisis, telephoned Netanyahu in Jerusalem. They spoke for over an hour. Obama reminded Netanyahu of his promise to the pro-Israel lobby, the American-Israel Public Affairs Committee (AIPAC), on March 12, 2012, that "all elements of American power will be used to stop" the Iranian nuclear program, including America's "military effort to be prepared for any contingency."[25] Both leaders then released a pablum-like statement saying they had a good talk and Netanyahu had not really asked for a meeting and therefore none was denied. All was well.[26]

Still, Netanyahu, in a *Meet the Press* interview on September 16, 2012, did not pull back from his earlier "red line" challenge to Obama, nor from his desire for a meeting with Obama; but he spoke in softer tones, clearly not wishing further to inflame his already strained relationship with the president.[27] When, a few days later, on September 28, 2012, he addressed the UN General Assembly, he seemed to hit two points: first, that Iran was still expanding its nuclear program and it had to be stopped; but, second, that there would not be any military action against Iran until the spring of 2013. "By next spring, at most next summer," Netanyahu said, "they will have finished the medium enrichment and moved on to the final stage. From there, it's only a few months, probably a few weeks, before they get enough enriched uranium for the first bomb."[28] By putting off military action until the spring or summer of 2013, he seemed to want to ease concerns in Washington (and the rest of the world) that Israel on its own would attack Iran before the U.S. presidential elections. One reason, perhaps, was that Netanyahu was planning a national election of his own in late January 2013, which everyone expected him to win. His campaign strategy was based, in part, on his insistence that he was tough enough to stand up to American pressure. At one point, he raised a few basic questions and then pointedly answered them. "When David Ben-Gurion declared the foundation of the state of Israel," he asked, "was it done with American approval? When

Levi Eshkol was forced to act in order to loosen the siege before 1967, was it done with American support?" There he was referring to the Israeli feeling of betrayal when President Johnson couldn't or wouldn't help Israel break the Egyptian "siege" at Sharm al-Sheikh. "If someone sits here as the prime minister of Israel and he can't take action on matters that are cardinal to the existence of this country, its future and its security [read the Iran nuclear program], and he is totally dependent on receiving approval from others [read Obama], then he is not worthy of leading." Then, sounding like Nixon during his Vietnam adventures, Netanyahu added, "I can make these decisions."[29]

Perhaps the complex American-Israeli relationship has now become so close that it resembles a family quarrel more than a diplomatic split. A number of U.S. ambassadors, surveying the global scene, told me that they considered Israel to be America's number one ally, supplanting the United Kingdom, which for decades had enjoyed the unparalleled rank of "special relationship" with the United States. But whether it be Israel or the United Kingdom judged to be the nation closest to the United States, Israel has in fact enjoyed a very special relationship with the United States, based more on a mutual appreciation of common values and presidential commitments than on mutual defense treaties or alliances. Though there are Americans, perhaps even including Obama, who feel the United States ought to loosen its ties to Israel for the sake of its broader interests in the Middle East, most Americans still overwhelmingly support Israel; and it's likely to remain that way for a long time.

On October 18, 2012, the *Washington Post* editorialized that it was time to "launch a badly needed 'reset' in U.S.-Israeli relations," primarily because the president and the prime minister "have made a mess of their personal relationship." The *Post* got it wrong. There might be a need for a "reset," but not because the two leaders did not get along, though that didn't help matters. The real problem was that these two closely allied nations based their relationship for too long on private presidential commitments. Now they need to institutionalize their relationship with a mutual defense treaty ratified by the Senate. J. William Fulbright, were he still a star maverick in the Senate, would probably say that it was about time. In this way, they would no longer have to rely on the word of a president, which, if changed by the next president, could quickly breed feelings of abandonment or betrayal. With a defense treaty, both sides would know in advance what to expect and what to do. There would be less likelihood of misunderstanding.

No doubt, the president who proposed a defense treaty with Israel would run into a political buzz saw, and the prime minister who accepted one would have to battle those in the Knesset who objected to an Israeli loss of "freedom of action." But if an Israeli prime minister like Ehud Barak could consider a defense treaty with the United States as the best way to sell a Palestinian agreement to the Israeli people, then an American president could also consider such a treaty as the best way to protect an Israel willing to risk a peace agreement with the Palestinians. A defense treaty would create rules of the road that would probably limit the freedom of action of both nations, especially Israel, but it was still a proposal worthy of the most serious consideration.

Let us suppose, for a moment, that Obama decides that in his second term, never having to run again, he can press for an Israeli-Palestinian peace agreement, a prize that has eluded previous administrations. No doubt, Israel would be called upon to make major concessions, which Israel would find objectionable. Differences would surface on the front pages of newspapers in both countries. Negotiations in the Middle East have often led to deadlocks and violence, but on this occasion Obama would defy his critics and, like Eisenhower in 1957, lean on Israel with warnings of aid cutoffs and worse. Many in Congress would oppose such pressure, and political storms would erupt up and down Pennsylvania Avenue. But the administration, this time determined to push for a deal, would keep pressing Israel and promising the Palestinians that peace would end their long struggle for statehood, and it was time for those long-delayed, gut-wrenching compromises. Concessions had to be made on borders, on Palestinian refugees, and, finally, on Jerusalem. Because from the beginning such a negotiation is by its very nature asymmetrical, Israel giving and the Palestinians getting, Israel might defiantly balk and battle the odds and resist the pressure and say no to an American-sponsored deal, arguing that the new turmoil in the Arab world makes major concessions by Israel impossible and irresponsible. But, at this point, if Israel had a defense treaty with the United States, guaranteeing its strength and security, easing its concerns about a possibly rocky future, Israel might agree to take the plunge and accept a deal. That would be an example of the supreme importance of a mutual defense treaty—to Israel and to the United States.

During the last presidential debate of the 2012 campaign on October 22, 2012, both candidates—President Obama and former Massachusetts governor Mitt Romney—carried presidential commitments to Israel to new, unprecedented heights. Moderator Bob Schieffer asked both candidates whether they would be "willing to declare that an attack on Israel is an attack on the United States." That was a question of consequence, deserving a careful, considered response. But with Jewish and evangelical voters dancing before their eyes, with the election only three weeks away, both candidates scrambled to sound totally, unquestionably committed to the proposition that, in the language of the NATO treaty, an attack on one (Israel) would be considered an attack on the other (the United States).

Obama: "Israel is a true friend. It is our greatest ally in the region. And if Israel is attacked, America will stand with Israel. I've made that clear throughout my presidency. . . . I will stand with Israel if they are attacked."

Romney: "I want to underscore the same point the president made, which is that if I'm president of the United States, when I'm president of the United States, we will stand with Israel. And if Israel is attacked, we have their back, not just diplomatically, not just culturally, but militarily. That's number one."[30]

They both went on to pledge as well that they would never allow Iran to become a nuclear power. In both cases, with Israel and with Iran, they pledged the United States to defend Israel, if Israel were attacked, and to deny Iran the capability of producing nuclear weapons. The pledges might well involve the United States in another war in the Middle East. In this way, a presidential commitment, even one made in the pressure cooker environment of a presidential campaign, would become the policy of the United States, understood as such by Israel, Iran, and other countries with interests in the Middle East. Would it not make sense for the United States and Israel to formalize these presidential commitments into a mutual defense treaty?

During the cold war, the United States considered a defense treaty with an ally to be the ultimate pledge of support in the global struggle against communism. Nations along the rim of the Soviet Union and China enjoyed the comfort and protection of American power based on their defense treaties with the United States. If they were threatened by communist expansion, they felt they could count on the United States.

Presidents used to go to Congress for resolutions of support, some so extensive they effectively (if not officially) were declarations of war. One was the Gulf of Tonkin resolution in August 1964, which Johnson used to up the ante in Vietnam until the United States was engaged in a major war. Now presidents can commit American forces to fight in a far-off field of battle, in an unconventional, asymmetrical struggle, without any formal approval from Congress or the American people. Of course, under the War Powers Resolution, presidents have to inform Congress within forty-eight hours after committing troops to battle. They also have the right to keep the troops engaged on the frontline for sixty or ninety days but are supposed to get the consent of Congress to keep them there longer. Presidents generally have kept Congress informed of war-time deployments, but Congress has never really pressed a president to comply to the full letter of the law. On matters of national security, the president trumps Congress almost every time.

These days, presidents have an all-volunteer military force, answerable increasingly only to them, and they exercise exceptional powers in all matters of war and peace. Career diplomat Negroponte believes that "presidential powers" have become "extraordinary"—"truer now than ever," he adds. Three other officials help—the secretary of state, the secretary of defense, and the national security adviser—but "everyone else is in a supporting cast."[31] The president's ability to use the Situation Room at the White House as a command center, hooking him up through modern technology to generals in the field, allowing him to follow and even, if necessary, second-guess operations in real time, concentrates all of his awesome powers in one room, under his command. Never before in American history has a president been able to exercise so much unchecked power in foreign policy and national security.

Such power, resting with one elected official, has been the essential ingredient in the always uneasy U.S.-Israeli relationship. The president makes the calls. It all rests with him: Will he honor past commitments to Israel, believing them to be in America's interests, or will he, for whatever reason, abandon them? Up to his point, this informal arrangement between the United States and Israel, pivoting around the president, has benefited both sides. But what about tomorrow?

The time has come to institutionalize the U.S.-Israeli relationship so that everything does not rest any longer on the decisions of one person. With a defense treaty, Israel could depend on an agreement ratified by the congressional representatives of the American people. If Israel at some point in the future reached a peace agreement with the Palestinians, it would know in advance that it had an American treaty obligation to help with its implementation. Without a defense treaty, there might well be occasions for miscalculation and misunderstanding that would lead only to confusion and conflict.

It is time for the United States and Israel to take the next step: a historic agreement for a defense treaty between two close allies.

NOTES

Introduction

1. Jack Kim, "North Korean Leader, in Rare Address, Seeks End to Confrontation with South," December 31, 2012 (http://uk.reuters.com/article/2013/01/01/uk-korea-north-idUKBRE90002020130101?feedType=RSS&feedName=topNews).

Chapter 1

1. Winston Churchill, "Sinews of Peace," March 5, 1946 (www.nationalchurchill museum.org/sinews-of-peace-iron-curtain-speech.html).

2. President Harry Truman, Address to a Joint Session of Congress, March 12, 1947 (www.trumanlibrary.org/whistlestop/study_collections/doctrine/large/documents/pdfs/5-9.pdf#zoom=100).

3. George C. Marshall, "The Marshall Plan speech at Harvard University," June 5, 1947 (www.oecd.org/general/themarshallplanspeechatharvarduniversity5june1947.htm).

4. Harry S Truman, "The President's News Conference," November 30, 1950, The American Presidency Project (www.presidency.ucsb.edu/ws/index.php?pid=13673&st=&st1=).

Chapter 2

1. Cordell Hull, *Memoirs,* vol. 2 (New York: Macmillan, 1948), p. 1597.

2. Robert J. McMahon, ed., *Major Problems in the History of the Vietnam War* (Washington: Heath and Company, 1995), p. 36.

3. David L. Anderson, ed., *Shadow on the White House* (University Press of Kansas, 1993), p. 24.

4. McMahon, *Major Problems in the History of the Vietnam War*, p. 38.

5. "Ho's Letter to President Truman in February 1946" (http://vietnamwar.lib.umb.edu/enemy/docs/Ho_letter_to_Truman_Feb_46.html).

6. Anderson, *Shadow on the White House*, p. 25.

7. McMahon, *Major Problems in the History of the Vietnam War*, p. 80.

8. Anderson, *Shadow on the White House*, pp. 26–27.

9. Ibid., p. 27.

10. McMahon, *Major Problems in the History of the Vietnam War*, p. 74.

11. "Department Of State Policy Statement On Indochina, September 27, 1948," in Gareth Porter, ed., *Vietnam: A History in Documents* (New York: New American Library, 1981); also available at http://vietnamwar.lib.umb.edu/origins/docs/State_Dept.html.

12. Stanley Karnow, *Vietnam: A History* (New York: Viking Press, 1983), p. 146–47.

13. Ibid., p. 172.

14. Ibid., p. 147.

15. James Chase, *Acheson: The Secretary of State Who Created the American World* (New York: Simon and Schuster, 1998), p. 167.

16. Ibid.

17. McMahon, *Major Problems in the History of the Vietnam War*, pp. 78–82.

18. Ibid., p. 84.

19. Ibid., p. 83.

20. Anderson, *Shadow on the White House*, p. 34.

21. Department of State, Foreign Relations of the United States, 1952–1954, vol. 12, pt. 1, East Asia and the Pacific (in two parts), Document 25, "Memorandum of Discussion among Acheson, Eden and others, May 25, 1952, pp. 96–97.

22. Department of State, Foreign Relations of the United States, 1952–1954, vol. 12, pt. 1, East Asia and the Pacific (in two parts), Document 15, "Memorandum for the President of Discussion at the 113th Meeting of the National Security Council Held on Wednesday," March 5, 1952, pp. 69–75.

Chapter 3

1. Eisenhower National Historic Site, "Who's Been Counting My Fish? The Quotable Quotes of Dwight D. Eisenhower," Letter to NATO Commander Gen. Al Gruenther, April 26, 1954 (www.nps.gov/features/eise/jrranger/quotes2.htm).

2. Stephen E. Ambrose, "The Wisdom of Non-Intervention," in Robert J. McMahon, ed., *Major Problems in the History of the Vietnam War* (Washington: Heath and Company, 1995), p. 135.

3. Harry S Truman, *Memoirs: Years of Trial and Hope* (Garden City: Hodder and Stoughton, 1956), p. 519.

4. Ambrose, "The Wisdom of Non-Intervention," p. 137.

5. Marvin Kalb and Elie Abel, *Roots of Involvement: The U.S. in Asia 1784–1971* (New York: W.W. Norton and Co., 1971), p. 74.

6. Ambrose, "The Wisdom of Non-Intervention," pp. 136–37.

7. Ibid., p. 144.

8. Kalb and Abel, *Roots of Involvement,* p. 74.

9. Ambrose, "The Wisdom of Non-Intervention," p. 140.

10. Stanley Karnow, *Vietnam: A History* (New York: Viking Press, 1983), p. 197.

11. Senator John Kennedy, "The Truth About Indochina," April 6, 1954, *American Experience: The Presidents: Primary Sources,* PBS (www.pbs.org/wgbh/americanexperience/features/primary-resources/jfk-indochina/).

12. *Washington Post,* April 22, 1954, p. 2.

13. Christopher Matthews, *Kennedy and Nixon* (New York: Simon and Schuster, 1996), p. 94.

14. "The President's News Conference," April 29, 1954, The American Presidency Project (www.presidency.ucsb.edu/ws/index.php?pid=10223&st=&st1=).

15. Rufus Phillips, *Why Vietnam Matters* (Naval Institute Press, 2008), Prologue.

16. "Eisenhower's Letter of Support to Ngo Dinh Diem, October 23, 1954," The Wars for Viet Nam, Vassar College (http://vietnam.vassar.edu/overview/doc5.html).

17. Ambrose, "The Wisdom of Non-Intervention," p. 140.

18. Dwight D. Eisenhower, "Address at the Gettysburg College Convocation: The Importance of Understanding," April 4, 1959, The American Presidency Project (www.presidency.ucsb.edu/ws/?pid=11698).

19. Matthews, *Kennedy and Nixon,* p. 94.

20. Kalb and Abel, *Roots of Involvement,* p. 144.

21. Ibid., p. 126.

Chapter 4

1. Arthur M. Schlesinger Jr., *A Thousand Days: John F. Kennedy in the White House* (Boston: Houghton Mifflin, 1965), p. 217.

2. Marvin Kalb and Elie Abel, *Roots of Involvement: The U.S. in Asia 1784–1971* (New York: W.W. Norton and Co., 1971), p. 107.

3. Dwight D. Eisenhower, *Waging Peace: The White House Years, 1956–1961* (New York: Doubleday, 1965), Appendix BB, pp. 712–16.

4. Kalb and Abel, *Roots of Involvement,* explained in detail in pp. 106–51.

5. Lawrence J. Bassett and Stephen E. Pelz, "The Failed Search for Victory," in Robert J. McMahon, ed., *Major Problems in the History of the Vietnam War* (Washington: Heath and Company, 1995), p. 180.

6. Ibid.

7. Ibid., p. 181.

8. Ibid.

9. Richard Reeves, *President Kennedy: Profile of Power* (New York: Simon and Schuster, 1994), p. 112.

10. Gordon M. Goldstein, *Lessons in Disaster: McGeorge Bundy and the Path to the War in Vietnam* (New York: Times Books, 2008), p. 235.

11. Stanley Karnow, *Vietnam: A History* (New York: Viking Press, 1983), p. 252.

12. Goldstein, *Lessons in Disaster,* p. 232.

13. Karnow, *Vietnam*, p. 253.

14. Kalb and Abel, *Roots of Involvement*, p. 118.

15. Dean Rusk and Robert McNamara, "Alternative Plan," November 11, 1961, in McMahon, *Major Problems in the History of the Vietnam War*, pp. 162–65.

16. John Kenneth Galbraith, *Letters to Kennedy* (Harvard University Press, 1998), p. 90.

17. Gary R. Hess, "Were There Viable Alternative Strategies?" in McMahon, *Major Problems in the History of the Vietnam War*, p. 273.

18. Goldstein, *Lessons in Disaster*, p 234.

19. Hess,"Were There Viable Alternative Strategies?" p. 271.

20. Colin Powell interview, November 13, 2008.

21. Galbraith, *Letters to Kennedy*, p. 99.

22. *Foreign Relations of the United States, 1961–1963, Volume II, Vietnam, 1962, Document 330*, "Report by the Senate Majority Leader (Mansfield)," December 18, 1962 (http://history.state.gov/historicaldocuments/frus1961-63v02/d330).

23. *Foreign Relations of the United States, 1961–1963, Volume III, Vietnam, January–August 1963, Document 19*, "Memorandum from the Director of the Bureau of Intelligence and Research (Hilsman) and Michael V. Forrestal of the National Security Council Staff to the President," January 25, 1963 (http://history.state.gov/historicaldocuments/frus1961-63v03/d19).

24. Karnow, *Vietnam*, p. 280.

25. Ibid., p. 281.

26. Ibid., p. 287.

27. *Foreign Relations of the United States, 1961–1963, Volume III, Vietnam, January–August 1963, Document 281*, "Telegram from the Department of State to the Embassy in Vietnam," August 24, 1963 (http://history.state.gov/historicaldocuments/frus1961-63v03/d281).

28. *Foreign Relations of the United States, 1961–1963, Volume IV, Vietnam, August–December 1963, Document 12*, "Telegram from the Embassy in Vietnam to the Department of State," August 29, 1963 (http://history.state.gov/historicaldocuments/frus1961-63v04/d12).

29. *Foreign Relations of the United States, 1961–1963, Volume IV, Vietnam, August–December 1963, Document 16*, "Telegram from the Department of State to the Embassy in Vietnam," August 29, 1963 (http://history.state.gov/historicaldocuments/frus1961-63v04/d16).

30. "Transcript of Broadcast With Walter Cronkite Inaugurating a CBS Television News Program," September 2, 1963, The American Presidency Project (www.presidency.ucsb.edu/ws/index.php?pid=9388&st=&st1=).

31. *Foreign Relations of the United States, 1961–1963, Volume IV, Vietnam, August–December 1963, Document 83*, "Memorandum of Conversation," September 10, 1963 (http://history.state.gov/historicaldocuments/frus1961-63v04/d83).

32. *Foreign Relations of the United States, 1961–1963, Volume IV, Vietnam, August–December 1963, Document 167*, "Memorandum from the Chairman of the Joint Chiefs of Staff (Taylor) and the Secretary of Defense (McNamara) to the President," October 2, 1963 (http://history.state.gov/historicaldocuments/frus1961-63v04/d167).

33. Karnow, *Vietnam*, p. 295.

34. Bundy cable to Lodge, in McMahon, *Major Problems in the History of the Vietnam War*, pp. 173–75.

35. Karnow, *Vietnam*, pp. 299–300.

36. *Foreign Relations of the United States, 1961–1963, Volume IV, Vietnam, August–December 1963, Document 249*, "Telegram from the President's Special Assistant for National Security Affairs (Bundy) to the Ambassador in Vietnam (Lodge)," October 30, 1963 (http://history.state.gov/historicaldocuments/frus1961-63v04/d249).

37. Karnow, *Vietnam*, p. 307.

38. Ibid., p. 310.

39. Schlesinger, *A Thousand Days*, p. 997.

40. Transcript of Memo, November 4, 1963, White House Tapes, Presidential Recordings Program, Miller Center of Public Affairs, University of Virginia.

41. Karnow, *Vietnam*, p. 311.

42. *Foreign Relations of the United States, 1961–1963, Volume IV, Vietnam, August–December 1963, Document 302*, Telegram from the Embassy in Vietnam to the Department of State, November 6, 1963 (http://history.state.gov/historicaldocuments/frus1961-63v04/d302).

Chapter 5

1. Tom Wicker, *JFK and LBJ: The Influence of Personality on Politics* (New York: William Morrow and Co., 1968), p. 205.

2. Robert Dallek, *Flawed Giant: Lyndon Johnson and His Times, 1963–1973* (Oxford University Press, 1998), p. 100.

3. Ronnie Dugger, *The Politician: The Life and Times of Lyndon Johnson, The Drive for Power—from the Frontier to Master of the Senate* (New York: W. W. Norton and Co., 1984), p. 220.

4. Dallek, *Flawed Giant*, p. 99.

5. David L. Anderson, ed., *Shadow on the White House* (University Press of Kansas, 1993), p. 1.

6. "Lyndon B. Johnson Explains Why Americans Fight in Vietnam," in Robert J. McMahon, ed., *Major Problems in the History of the Vietnam War* (Washington: Heath and Company, 1995), p. 211.

7. Kenneth O'Donnell, *LBJ and the Kennedys*, excerpt published in *Life* magazine, August 7, 1970.

8. *Foreign Relations of the United States, 1961–1963, Volume IV, Vietnam, August–December 1963, Document 374*, "Memorandum From the Secretary of Defense (McNamara) to President Johnson," December 21, 1963 (http://history.state.gov/historicaldocuments/frus1961-63v04/d374).

9. Doris Kearns, *Lyndon Johnson and the American Dream* (New York: Harper and Row, 1976), p. 251.

10. Dallek, *Flawed Giant*, p. 102.

11. Ibid.

12. David Halberstam, *The Best and the Brightest* (New York: Random House, 1972) pp. 641–46, 694–97, 716–18.

13. *Foreign Relations of the United States, 1964–1968, Volume I, Vietnam, 1964, Document 84*, "Memorandum from the Secretary of Defense (McNamara) to the President," March 16, 1964 (http://history.state.gov/historicaldocuments/frus1964-68v01/d84).

14. Lyndon Baines Johnson, *The Vantage Point: Perspectives on the Presidency 1963–1969* (New York: Holt, Rinehart and Winston, 1971), p. 116.

15. Robert J. Donovan, *Conflict and Crisis: The Presidency of Harry S Truman, 1945–1948* (New York: W. W. Norton and Co., 1977), p. 57.

16. The author interviewed Stockdale, Herrick, and others for an NBC News documentary he anchored called "Vietnam—Lessons of a Lost War," broadcast on April 27, 1985.

17. Johnson, *The Vantage Point*, p. 113.

18. How interesting that Johnson and Herrick used the same adjective to describe both a North Vietnamese boat commander and an American radar man! What was it about a stormy Gulf of Tonkin that made sailors so "overeager"?

19. Johnson, *The Vantage Point*, p. 117.

20. Ibid., p. 118.

21. Marvin Kalb and Elie Abel, *Roots of Involvement: The U.S. in Asia 1784–1971* (New York: W. W. Norton and Co., 1971), p. 173.

22. Robert McNamara, *In Retrospect: The Tragedies and Lessons of Vietnam* (New York: Times Books, 1995), p. 191.

23. Joseph A. Califano Jr., *The Triumph and Tragedy of Lyndon Johnson* (New York: Simon and Schuster, 1991), p. 172.

24. Johnson, *The Vantage Point*, pp. 147–52.

25. *Foreign Relations of the United States, 1964–1968, Volume II, Vietnam, January–June 1965, Document 42*," Memorandum from the President's Special Assistant for National Security Affairs (Bundy) to President Johnson," January 27, 1965 (http://history.state.gov/historicaldocuments/frus1964-68v02/d42).

26. Gordon M. Goldstein, *Lessons in Disaster: McGeorge Bundy and the Path to the War in Vietnam* (New York: Times Books, 2008), pp. 153–54.

27. Brian VanDeMark, *Into the Quagmire: Lyndon Johnson and the Escalation of the Vietnam War* (Oxford University Press, 1991), p. 178.

28. Lyndon B. Johnson, "Remarks to the National Rural Electric Cooperative Association," July 14, 1965, The American Presidency Project (www.presidency.ucsb.edu/ws/index.php?pid=27082&st=&st1=).

29. *Foreign Relations of the United States, 1964–1968, Volume III, Vietnam, June–December 1965, Document 85*, "Notes of Meeting," July 25, 1965 (http://history.state.gov/historicaldocuments/frus1964-68v03/d85).

30. Memorandum of July 1, 1965, in McMahon, *Major Problems in the History of the Vietnam War*, p. 217. Text also is at: *Foreign Relations of the United States, 1964–1968, Volume III, Vietnam, June–December 1965, Document 40*, "Paper by the Under Secretary of State (Ball)," undated (http://history.state.gov/historicaldocuments/frus1964-68v03/d40).

31. Michael R. Beschloss, *Reaching For Glory: Lyndon Johnson's Secret White House Tapes, 1964–1965*. Reprint (New York: Simon and Schuster, 2002), p. 390.

32. Ibid., p. 213.

33. Johnson, *The Vantage Point*, p. 232.

34. Jung Chang and Jon Halliday, *Mao: The Unknown Story* (New York: Alfred A. Knopf and Co., 2005), p. 565.

35. Johnson, *The Vantage Point*, p. 233.

36. *Time*, May 24, 1968, p. 17.

37. R. W. Apple Jr., "Casualties of US during Last Week the War's Highest," *New York Times*, January 20, 1968, p. 1.

38. *Foreign Relations of the United States, 1964–1968, Volume III, Vietnam, June–December 1965, Document 189*, "Draft Memorandum from Secretary of Defense McNamara to President Johnson," November 3, 1965 (http://history.state.gov/historicaldocuments/frus1964-68v03/d189).

39. Kalb, "Vietnam—Lessons of a Lost War." The text also is available at *Foreign Relations of the United States, 1964–1968, Volume III, Vietnam, June–December 1965, Document 235*, "Notes of Meeting," December 18, 1965 (http://history.state.gov/historicaldocuments/frus1964-68v03/d235).

40. McNamara, *In Retrospect*, p. 271.

41. Kalb, "Vietnam—Lessons of a Lost War."

42. Johnson, *The Vantage Point*, p. 262.

43. Ibid., p. 258.

44. Califano, *The Triumph and Tragedy of Lyndon Johnson*, p. 247.

45. Kalb, "Vietnam—Lessons of a Lost War."

46. Ibid.

47. Quoted in Califano, *The Triumph and Tragedy of Lyndon Johnson*, p. 248.

48. Johnson, *The Vantage Point*, p. 291.

49. Kalb and Abel, *Roots of Involvement*, p. 198.

50. *Newsweek*, November 19, 2007, p. 45.

51. Kalb and Abel, *Roots of Involvement*, pp. 199–200.

52. Kalb, "Vietnam—Lessons of a Lost War."

53. Stanley Karnow, *Vietnam: A History* (New York: Viking Press, 1983), p. 523.

54. Donovan, *Conflict and Crisis*, p. 135.

55. Kalb and Abel, *Roots of Involvement*, p. 205.

56. "The President's News Conference," February 2, 1968, The American Presidency Project (www.presidency.ucsb.edu/ws/index.php?pid=29149&st=&st1=).

57. Harry Summers, "Lessons: A Soldier's View," *Wilson Quarterly*, Summer 1983, p. 99.

58. I was one of the reporters, and I recorded Rusk's comments.

59. Kalb and Abel, *Roots of Involvement*, p. 211.

60. Ibid., p. 222.

61. Karnow, *Vietnam*, p. 479.

62. George C. Herring, "The Reluctant Warrior, Lyndon Johnson as Commander-in-Chief," in Anderson, *Shadow on the White House*, p. 95.

63. Ibid., p. 107.

64. Harry C. McPherson, *A Political Education: A Washington Memoir* (University of Texas Press, 1994).

65. "The Warnke Papers, Memorandum for Mr. Clifford," May 3, 1968, Lyndon B. Johnson Presidential Library, Box 9, document 96.

66. Johnson Presidential Library Audio Tapes.

Chapter 6

1. Robert McNamara, *In Retrospect: The Tragedies and Lessons of Vietnam* (New York: Times Books, 1995), p. 321.

2. Robert Dallek, *Nixon and Kissinger: Partners in Power* (New York: Harper-Collins, 2007), p. 126.

3. Henry Kissinger, *Diplomacy* (New York: Simon and Schuster, 1994), p. 676.

4. Dallek, *Nixon and Kissinger,* p. 126.

5. Walter Isaacson, *Kissinger: A Biography* (New York: Simon and Schuster, 1992), pp. 159–60.

6. Ibid., p. 160.

7. Ibid., p. 165.

8. Henry Kissinger, *White House Years* (Boston: Little, Brown and Co, 1979), p. 262.

9. Richard Reeves, *President Nixon: Alone in the White House* (New York: Simon and Schuster, 2001), p. 36.

10. William Safire, *Safire's Political Dictionary* (Oxford University Press, 2008), pp. 646–47.

11. Reeves, *President Nixon,* p. 34.

12. Dallek, *Nixon and Kissinger,* p. 106.

13. Reeves, *President Nixon,* p. 53.

14. Ibid., p. 54.

15. Richard Nixon, "Address to the Nation on Vietnam," May 14, 1969, The American Presidency Project (www.presidency.ucsb.edu/ws/index.php?pid=2047&st=&st1=).

16. Reeves, *President Nixon,* p. 80.

17. Melvin Laird interview, October 21, 2008.

18. Walter Isaacson, "Vietnam and the Nixon-Kissinger World Order," in Robert J. McMahon, ed., *Major Problems in the History of the Vietnam War* (Washington: Heath and Company, 1995), p. 462.

19. Isaacson, "Vietnam and the Nixon-Kissinger World Order," p. 238.

20. Reeves, *President Nixon,* p. 141.

21. Full text in McMahon, *Major Problems in the History of the Vietnam War,* pp. 432–37, and Richard Nixon, "Address to the Nation on the War in Vietnam," November 3, 1969, American Presidency Project (www.presidency.ucsb.edu/ws/index.php?pid=2303&st=&st1=).

22. Reeves, *President Nixon,* p. 196.

23. Richard Nixon, "Address to the Nation on the Situation in Southeast Asia," April 30, 1970, The American Presidency Project (www.presidency.ucsb.edu/ws/index.php?pid=2490&st=&st1=).

24. Reeves, *President Nixon,* pp. 202–03.

25. Ibid., pp. 200–01.

26. Dallek, *Nixon and Kissinger,* p. 202.

27. Kissinger, *White House Years,* p. 511.

28. Ibid., p. 513.

29. Ibid., pp. 275–76.

30. Laird interview, October 21, 2008.

31. David Fulgham and others, *South Vietnam on Trial: Mid-1970 to 1972* (Boston: Boston Publishing Company, 1984), p. 72.

32. Kissinger, *White House Years,* p. 1008.

33. Bernard C. Nalty, *The War Against Trucks: Aerial Interdiction in Southern Laos, 1968–1972* (Air Force History and Museums Program, 2005), p. 271.

34. Earl H. Tilford, *Setup: What the Air Force Did in Vietnam and Why* (Maxwell AFB, Ala.: Air University Press, 1991), p. 203.

35. Richard Nixon, "Address to the Nation on the Situation in Southeast Asia," April 7, 1971, The American Presidency Project (www.presidency.ucsb.edu/ws/index.php?pid=2972&st=&st1=).

36. Phillip Davidson, *Vietnam at War, 1946–1975* (New York: Presidio Press, 1987), p. 699.

Chapter 7

1. Walter Isaacson, *Kissinger: A Biography* (New York: Simon and Schuster, 1992), p. 336.

2. Robert Dallek, *Nixon and Kissinger: Partners in Power* (New York: Harper-Collins, 2007), p. 289.

3. Ibid., p. 293.

4. Ibid., p. 292.

5. Richard Smyser interview, October 29, 2008.

6. Dallek, *Nixon and Kissinger,* pp. 302–03.

7. Henry Kissinger, *White House Years* (Boston: Little, Brown and Co, 1979), p. 1017.

8. Ibid., p. 977.

9. Richard Reeves, *President Nixon: Alone in the White House* (New York: Simon and Schuster, 2001), p. 333.

10. Kissinger, *White House Years,* p. 1028.

11. Ibid., p. 1036.

12. Reeves, *President Nixon,* pp. 439–40.

13. Ibid., p. 1098.

14. Dallek, *Nixon and Kissinger,* p. 372.

15. Reeves, *President Nixon,* p. 469.

16. Scott Shane, "Indexed Trove of Kissinger Phone Transcripts Is Completed," *New York Times,* December 24, 2008, p. A14.

17. Kissinger, *White House Years,* p. 1161.

18. Frederick Z. Brown interview, October 28, 2008.

19. Richard M. Nixon, *RN: The Memoirs of Richard Nixon* (New York: Simon and Schuster, 1990), pp. 593–94.

20. Dallek, *Nixon and Kissinger,* p. 384.

21. Richard Nixon, "Address to the Nation on the Situation in Southeast Asia," May 8, 1972, The American Presidency Project (www.presidency.ucsb.edu/ws/index.php?pid=3404).

22. *Foreign Relations of the United States, 1969–1976, Volume VIII, Vietnam, January–October 1972, Document 139,* "Memorandum From President Nixon to the President's Assistant for National Security Affairs (Kissinger)," May 9, 1972 (http://history.state.gov/historicaldocuments/frus1969-76v08/d139).

23. Nixon, *RN: The Memoirs of Richard Nixon,* p. 609.

24. Dallek, *Nixon and Kissinger,* pp. 389–90.

25. *Foreign Relations of the United States, 1969–1976, Volume XIV, Soviet Union, October 1971–May 1972, Document 271,* "Memorandum of Conversation," May 24, 1972 (http://history.state.gov/historicaldocuments/frus1969-76v14/d271).

26. Marvin Kalb and Bernard Kalb, *Kissinger* (Boston: Little, Brown and Co., 1974), pp. 327–28.

27. Richard Nixon, "Address to a Joint Session of the Congress on Return from Austria, the Soviet Union, Iran, and Poland," June 1, 1972,The American Presidency Project (www.presidency.ucsb.edu/ws/index.php?pid=3450&st=Nixon&st1=).

28. *Foreign Relations of the United States, 1969–1976, Volume XV, Soviet Union, June 1972–August 1974, Document 16,* "Memorandum of Conversation," July 20, 1972 (http://static.history.state.gov/frus/frus1969-76v15/pdf/frus1969-76v15.pdf).

29. Reeves, *President Nixon,* p. 522.

30. Kissinger's report to Nixon on the negotiations is at *Foreign Relations of the United States, 1969–1976, Volume VIII, Vietnam, January–October 1972, Document 263,* "Memorandum from the President's Assistant for National Security Affairs (Kissinger) to President Nixon," September 19, 1972 (http://history.state.gov/historicaldocuments/frus1969-76v08/d263).

31. *Foreign Relations of the United States, 1969–1976, Volume IX, Vietnam, October 1972–January 1973, Document 9,* Editorial Note based on October 12, 1972, conversation between President Nixon and Henry Kissinger (http://history.state.gov/historicaldocuments/frus1969-76v09/d9).

32. "Letter from President Nixon to President Thieu," October 16, 1972, The Nixon Library (http://www.nixonlibrary.gov/exhibits/decbomb/documents/rn-thieu-10-16-72.pdf).

33. Kissinger, *White House Years,* p. 1379.

34. Ibid., p. 1375.

35. De Borchgrave explained his role in a long email to me sent at 5:30 p.m. on December 22, 2008.

36. Ambassador Bunker recounted the meeting in a backchannel message to Alexander Haig, at *Foreign Relations of the United States, 1969–1976, Volume IX, Vietnam, October 1972–January 1973, Document 42,* "Backchannel Message from the Ambassador to Vietnam (Bunker) to the President's Deputy Assistant

for National Security Affairs (Haig)," October 22, 1972 (http://history.state.gov/historicaldocuments/frus1969-76v09/d42).

37. Ambassador Bunker recounted the meeting in a backchannel message to Alexander Haig at *Foreign Relations of the United States, 1969–1976, Volume IX, Vietnam, October 1972–January 1973, Document 49,* "Backchannel Message from the Ambassador to Vietnam (Bunker) to the President's Deputy Assistant for National Security Affairs (Haig)," October 22, 1972 (http://history.state.gov/historicaldocuments/frus1969-76v09/d49).

38. Kalb and Kalb, *Kissinger,* p. 374.

39. "Hanoi Says U.S. Backs Off After an Accord in Paris," *New York Times,* October 26, 1972, p. 1.

40. Kissinger, *White House Years,* p. 1398.

41. *Foreign Relations of the United States, 1969-1976, Volume IX, Vietnam, October 1972–January 1973, Document 73* (undated), Editorial Note (http://history.state.gov/historicaldocuments/frus1969-76v09/d73).

42. *Foreign Relations of the United States, 1969–1976, Volume IX, Vietnam, October 1972–January 1973, Document 79,* "Letter from President Nixon to South Vietnamese President Thieu," October 29, 1972 (http://history.state.gov/historicaldocuments/frus1969-76v09/d79).

Chapter 8

1. Henry Kissinger, *White House Years* (Boston: Little, Brown and Co., 1979), p. 1417.

2. "Memorandum for the President from Henry A. Kissinger (by cable)," November 23, 1972, The Nixon Library (www.nixonlibrary.gov/exhibits/decbomb/documents/hakto-11-23-72.pdf).

3. Kissinger, *White House Years,* p. 1419.

4. "Memcon: President Nixon meets with Special Advisor to President Thieu Nguyen Phu Duc," November 29, 1972, The Nixon Library (www.nixonlibrary.gov/exhibits/decbomb/documents/memcon-11-29-72.pdf).

5. "Cable: Henry A. Kissinger to President Nixon," December 4, 1972, The Nixon Library (www.nixonlibrary.gov/exhibits/decbomb/documents/hakto-12-4-72-628.pdf).

6. "Cable: Henry A. Kissinger to President Nixon," December 6, 1972, The Nixon Library (www.nixonlibrary.gov/exhibits/decbomb/documents/hakto-12-6-72.pdf).

7. Ibid., p. 1434.

8. "Cable: Henry A. Kissinger to President Nixon," December 7, 1972, The Nixon Library (www.nixonlibrary.gov/exhibits/decbomb/documents/hakto-12-7-72.pdf).

9. *Foreign Relations of the United States, 1969–1976, Volume IX, Vietnam, October 1972–January 1973, Document 151,* "Message from the President's Assistant for National Security Affairs (Kissinger) to President Nixon," December 8, 1972 (http://history.state.gov/historicaldocuments/frus1969-76v09/d151).

10. *Foreign Relations of the United States, 1969–1976, Volume IX, Vietnam, October 1972–January 1973, Document 156,* "Message From the President's Assistant

for National Security Affairs (Kissinger) to the President's Deputy Assistant for National Security Affairs (Haig), December 11, 1972 (http://history.state.gov/historicaldocuments/frus1969-76v09/d156).

11. Robert Dallek, *Nixon and Kissinger: Partners in Power* (New York: HarperCollins, 2007), p. 443.

12. Kissinger, *White House Years,* p. 1445.

13. Richard Reeves, *President Nixon: Alone in the White House* (New York: Simon and Schuster, 2001), p. 552.

14. Kissinger, *White House Years,* p. 1449.

15. *Foreign Relations of the United States, 1969–1976, Volume IX, Vietnam, October 1972–January 1973, Document 187,* "Transcript of a Telephone Conversation between President Nixon and the President's Assistant for National Security Affairs (Kissinger)," December 17, 1972 (http://history.state.gov/historicaldocuments/frus1969-76v09/d187).

16. Ibid.

17. *Foreign Relations of the United States, 1969-1976, Volume IX, Vietnam, October 1972–January 1973, Document 189,* "Letter from President Nixon to South Vietnamese President Thieu," December 17, 1972 (http://history.state.gov/historicaldocuments/frus1969-76v09/d189).

18. *Foreign Relations of the United States, 1969–1976, Volume IX, Vietnam, October 1972–January 1973, Document 206,* "Backchannel Message from the President's Deputy Assistant for National Security Affairs (Haig) to the President's Assistant for National Security Affairs (Kissinger)," December 20, 1972 (http://history.state.gov/historicaldocuments/frus1969-76v09/d206).

19. National Intelligence Council, *Estimative Products on Vietnam: 1948–1975* (Government Printing Office, 2005), p. xxxiv.

20. Kissinger, *White House Years,* p. 1462.

21. "Cable: Henry A. Kissinger to President Nixon," January 9, 1973, The Nixon Library (www.nixonlibrary.gov/exhibits/decbomb/documents/hakto-1-9-73.pdf).

22. Kissinger, *White House Years,* pp. 1468–69.

23. *Foreign Relations of the United States, 1969–1976, Volume IX, Vietnam, October 1972–January 1973, Document 278,* "Letter from President Nixon to South Vietnamese President Thieu," January 14, 1973 (http://history.state.gov/historicaldocuments/frus1969-76v09/d278#fn1).

24. "Letter: President Nixon to President Thieu," January 17 1973, The Nixon Library (www.nixonlibrary.gov/exhibits/decbomb/documents/rn-thieu-1-17-73.pdf).

25. Thieu's letter to Nixon is at *Foreign Relations of the United States, 1969–1976, Volume IX, Vietnam, October 1972–January 1973, Document 310,* "Backchannel Message from the Vice Chief of Staff of the Army (Haig) to the President's Assistant for National Security Affairs (Kissinger)," January 20, 1973 (http://history.state.gov/historicaldocuments/frus1969-76v09/d310).

26. Reeves, *President Nixon,* pp. 562–63.

27. *The New York Times, The Complete Front Pages: 1851–2008* (New York: Black Dog and Leventhal Publishers, 2008), p. 336.

28. World History Center, "Vietnam War Statistics" (http://history-world.org/vietnam_war_statistics.htm).

29. Henry Kissinger, *Years of Upheaval* (Boston: Little, Brown and Co., 1982), p. 302.

30. Ibid., p. 318.

31. Ibid., p. 986.

32. National Intelligence Council, *Estimative Products on Vietnam,* pp. 598–99, 622–23.

Chapter 9

1. Peter Grose, *Israel in the Mind of America* (New York: Knopf, 1984), p. 316.

2. "Letter from President Ford to Prime Minister Rabin," September 1, 1975, Jewish Virtual Library (www.jewishvirtuallibrary.org/jsource/Peace/ford_rabin_letter.html).

3. Yehuda Avner, *The Prime Ministers: An Intimate Narrative of Israeli Leadership* (New Milford, Conn.: Toby Press, 2010), p. 298. Avner, an Israeli diplomat, worked for a succession of Israeli prime ministers, including Rabin and Begin, and his book is based largely on notes he took during many important meetings.

4. Ibid., p. 299.

5. Dennis Ross interview, June 11, 2012.

6. Robert Satloff, "The Monitor, Merrimac, and Middle East," ForeignPolicy.com, January 31, 2012 (www.washingtoninstitute.org/policy-analysis/view/the-monitor-merrimac-and-middle-east).

7. Martin Indyk interview, July 6, 2012.

8. "The Sinai Campaign: Statement to the Knesset by Prime Minister Ben-Gurion, 5 March 1957," Israeli Ministry of Foreign Affairs (www.mfa.gov.il/MFA/Foreign+Relations/Israels+Foreign+Relations+since+1947/1947-1974/29+Statement +to+the+Knesset+by+Prime+Minister+Ben-.htm).

9. Michael B. Oren, *Six Days of War: June 1967 and the Making of the Modern Middle East* (New York: Random House, 2002), p. 86.

10. Michael Oren interview, July 23, 2012.

11. David Ignatius, "Reviving Eisenhower's Doctrine," *Washington Post,* January 27, 2013, p. A15.

12. Peter L. Hahn, *Caught in the Middle East: US Policy toward the Arab-Israeli Conflict, 1945–1961* (University of North Carolina Press, 2006), p. 212.

13. Ibid. p. 214.

14. Dwight D. Eisenhower, "Radio and Television Address to the American People on the Situation in the Middle East," February 20, 1957, The American Presidency Project (www.presidency.ucsb.edu/ws/index.php?pid=10980&st=&st1=_).

15. Hahn, *Caught in the Middle East,* p. 214.

16. Ibid., p. 215.

17. *Foreign Relations of the United States, 1955–1957, Volume XVII, Arab-Israeli Dispute, 1957, Document 204,* "Telegram From the Embassy in Israel to the Department of State," March 8, 1957 (http://history.state.gov/historicaldocuments/frus1955-57v17/d204).

18. Oren, *Six Days of War,* p. 77.

19. Oren interview.

20. Oren, *Six Days of War,* p. 102.

21. Ibid., pp. 114–15.

22. Ibid., pp. 115–16.

23. Joseph A. Califano Jr., *The Triumph and Tragedy of Lyndon Johnson* (New York: Simon and Schuster, 1991), p. 205.

24. Samuel Lewis interview, June 15, 2012.

25. Richard Reeves, *President Kennedy: Profile of Power* (New York: Simon and Schuster, 1994), pp. 32–33.

26. See Martin Kramer, "No Democratic President Has Ever Strong-armed Israel," *Sandbox* (blog), October 30, 2012.

27. Seth Anziska, "A Preventable Massacre," *New York Times*, September 17, 2012 (www.nytimes.com/2012/09/17/opinion/).

28. Dan Ephron, "Bibi in a Box: Netanyahu Loses Support on Bombing Iran," *Newsweek*, September 24, 2012 (www.thedailybeast.com/newsweek/2012/09/23/bibi-in-a-box-netanyahu-loses-support-on-bombing-iran.html_).

29. Senator J. W. Fulbright, "OLd Myths and New Realities," August 24, 1970, University of Arkansas Libaries Digital Collection (http://scipio.uark.edu/cdm4/item_viewer.php?CISOROOT=/Fulbright&CISOPTR=55&CISOBOX=1&REC=1).

30. J. William Fulbright, "Getting Tough with Israel," *Washington Monthly*, February 1975, p. 24.

31. Bruce Riedel, "Camp David: The U.S.-Israeli Bargain," July 15, 2002, *The Best of Bitterlemons*, edited by Yossi Alpher, Ghassan Khatib, and Charmaine Seitz (2007), p. 240 (www.bitterlemons-books.org/books/bitterlemons.pdf).

32. Ibid.

33. "Exchange of Letters Between PM Sharon and President Bush," April 14, 2004, Israeli Ministry of Foreign Affairs (www.mfa.gov.il/MFA/Peace+Process/Reference+Documents/Exchange+of+letters+Sharon-Bush+14-Apr-2004.htm).

34. Bret Stephens, "The Truth About Gaza," *Wall Street Journal*, November 30, 2012.

Chapter 10

1. John Negroponte interview, June 28, 2012.

2. "Mutual Defense Treaty between the United States and the Republic of the Philippines; August 30, 1951, Yale University Law School (http://avalon.law.yale.edu/20th_century/phil001.asp).

3. Ministry of Foreign Affairs of Japan, "Treaty of Mutual Cooperation and Security between Japan and the United States of America," January 1960 (www.mofa.go.jp/region/n-america/us/q&a/ref/1.html).

4. Jean-Marc F. Blanchard, "The U.S. Role in the Sino-Japanese Dispute over the Diaoyu (Senkaku) Islands, 1945–1971," *China Quarterly* 161 (March 2000): 95.

5. Ibid., pp. 96–97.

6. Jane Perlez, "China Criticizes Clinton's Remarks about Dispute with Japan over Islands," *New York Times*, January 20, 2013.

7. Ibid.

8. U.S. Department of State, Daily Press Briefing, September 23, 1996, University of Illinois at Chicago, University Library (http://dosfan.lib.uic.edu/ERC/briefing/daily_briefings/1996/9609/960923db.html).

9. Richard C. Bush interview, June 25, 2012.

10. Michael O'Hanlon interview, June 29, 2012.

11. Barton Bernstein, "Dubious Venture," *Inquiry,* June 1982, p. 44.

12. Don Oberdorfer, *The Two Koreas* (Reading, Mass.: Addison-Wesley, 1997), p. 10.

13. Richard C. Bush, "The US Policy of Extended Deterrence in East Asia: History, Current Views and Implications," Brookings Arms Control Series Paper 5 (February 2011), p. 4.

14. "North Korean Leader Calls for More Powerful Rockets," VOA News, December 22, 2012 (www.voanews.com/content/north-korean-leader-calls-for-more-powerful-rockets/1570384.html).

15. Henry Aaron interview, June 29, 2012.

16. "The United States and Vietnam: Expanding Relations Fact Sheet," Embassy of the United States, Hanoi, Vietnam (http://vietnam.usembassy.gov/relationsfactsheet.html).

17. Jay Solomon, "Clinton Presses Vietnam on Human Rights," *Wall Street Journal,* July 22, 2010, p. 1.

18. "US Is Right to Assail China on Its South China Sea Claims," The Post's View by Editorial Board, *Washington Post,* August 16, 2012, p. A12.

19. "Joint Press Briefing with Secretary Panetta and Vietnamese Minister of Defense Gen. Phung Quang Thanh from Hanoi, Vietnam," U.S. Department of Defense, Office of the Assistant Secretary of Defense (Public Affairs), June 4, 2012 (www.defense.gov/transcripts/transcript.aspx?transcriptid=5052).

20. "US Ambassador David Shear Visits Detained Buddhist Patriarch Thich Quang Do—Police in Danang Beat UBCV Monks and Followers," Quême, Action for Democracy in Vietnam, August 20, 2012 (www.queme.net/eng/news_detail.php?numb=1894).

21. "Joint Press Briefing with Secretary Panetta and Vietnamese Minister of Defense Gen. Phung Quang Thanh," June 4, 2012.

22. Uri Dromi, "Israel Abuzz: Guess Who's Coming to Visit?" *Miami Herald,* February 7, 2013 (www.miamiherald.com/2013/02/07/3222570/israel-abuzz-guess-whos-coming.html).

23. Dennis Ross interview, June 7, 2012.

24. Jeffrey Heller, "Has No Right to Block Israel in Iran—Netanyahu," *Chicago Tribune,* September 11, 2012 (http://articles.chicagotribune.com/2012-09-11/news/sns-rt-israel-irannetanyahu-update-3l5e8kb9dc-20120911_1_world-powers-nuclear-programme-iran).

25. Barack Obama, "Remarks by the President at AIPAC Policy Conference," March 12, 2012, The White House (www.whitehouse.gov/the-press-office/2012/03/04/remarks-president-aipac-policy-conference-0).

26. "Readout of the President's Call with Israeli Prime Minister Netanyahu," September 11, 2012, The White House (www.whitehouse.gov/the-press-office/2012/09/11/readout-president-s-call-israeli-prime-minister-netanyahu).

27. "PM's Netanyahu's Interview on NBC," Prime Minister's Office, September 15, 2012 (www.pmo.gov.il/English/MediaCenter/Interviews/Pages/interviewNBC150912.aspx).

28. "PM Netanyahu's Speech to the United Nations General Assembly in New York," Prime Minister's Office, September 27, 2012 (www.pmo.gov.il/English/MediaCenter/Speeches/Pages/speechUN270912.aspx).

29. Jodi Rudoren, "Netanyahu Says He'd Go It Alone on Striking Iran," *New York Times,* November 5, 2012.

30. "October 22, 2012, Debate Transcript," Commission on Presidential Debates (www.debates.org/index.php?page=october-22-2012-the-third-obama-romney-presidential-debate).

31. Negroponte interview, June 28, 2012.

INDEX

Aaron, Henry, 232

Abrams, Creighton: and Cambodian invasion, 122; and Ho Chi-minh trails, U.S. effort to sever, 132, 133, 134; on Vietnamization, 131, 132, 133; and Vietnam strategy, 114; on Vietnam War, possibility of winning, 107; and withdrawal from Vietnam, 114

Acheson, Dean: on Indochina policy, 33–34, 36, 37, 40; on Indochina War, 31; and Korean War, 13–14, 18, 20, 22, 23

Afghanistan War, 114, 232

African Americans, urban protests of 1960s, 97–98

Agnew, Spiro: attacks on media, 120–22; and Vietnam peace talks, 179, 182

"Agreement on Ending the War and Restoring Peace in Vietnam." *See* Vietnam War peace agreement

Algeria, Khrushchev on, 57

Alliances, anti-communist. *See* mutual defense treaties

Alsop, Stewart, 124

American system, demand for quick foreign policy results in, 64

Anti-colonialism, communist characterizations of insurgencies as, 57, 60

ANZUS, and U.S. anti-communism efforts, 47, 226–27

Appeasement of Nazis in World War II: as lesson to Johnson, 77, 78; as lesson to Kennedy administration, 57–58; as lesson to Truman, 14

Arab Spring, and Middle East diplomacy, 237

Arab states: stirring of anti-Israeli hatred by, 209–10; U.S.-Israel defense treaty and, 7

Arafat, Yasser, 219–21

Arms control agreement with Soviet Union, 139, 140, 142, 159, 161

ARVN (Army of the Republic of Viet Nam). *See* South Vietnamese Army

Associated Press, 21, 66, 133

Attlee, Clement, 22

Baghdad Pact (CENTO), and U.S. anti-communism efforts, 47

Ball, George: and Diem coup, 69; on Gulf of Tonkin incident, 85; and Johnson administration Vietnam policy debate, 89, 90, 92, 98; and Ngo Dinh Diem coup, 69; on South Vietnam commitment, 64

DISCARD